MOMENT OF TRUTH

MOMENT OF TRUTH

How to Think About Alberta's Future

Edited by
Jack M. Mintz, Ted Morton and Tom Flanagan

sh.
SUTHERLAND
HOUSE

Sutherland House
416 Moore Ave., Suite 205
Toronto, ON M4G 1C9

First edition, September 2020

If you are interested in inviting one of our authors to a live event or
media appearance, please contact publicity@sutherlandhousebooks.com
and visit our website at sutherlandhousebooks.com for more
information about our authors and their schedules.

Manufactured in Canada
Cover designed and book composed by Lena Yang

Library and Archives Canada Cataloguing in Publication
Title: Moment of truth : how to think about Alberta's future / editors, Jack M.
Mintz, Ted Morton & Tom Flanagan.
Other titles: Moment of truth (Toronto, Ont.)
Names: Mintz, Jack M., editor. | Morton, F. L. (Frederick Lee), 1949- editor. |
Flanagan, Thomas, 1944- editor.
Description: Includes bibliographical references.
Identifiers: Canadiana 20200293893 | ISBN 9781989555361 (softcover)
Subjects: LCSH: Secession—Alberta—Forecasting. | LCSH: Alberta—Politics and
government—Forecasting. | LCSH: Alberta—Economic conditions—Forecasting.
Classification: LCC FC3676 .M66 2020 | DDC 971.23—dc23

ISBN 978-1-989555-36-1

Contents

Preface

THE CONTRIBUTORS TO THIS BOOK deal with the problems of both Alberta and the West in Canada. By the West we mean the prairie provinces plus the interior of British Columbia. While the West and Alberta have much in common, each province has distinct issues and makes its own decisions. In this preface, I speak about both because I am an Albertan and a westerner at the same time.

I know the authors well, and they are all independent thinkers in the classical liberal tradition. They are not the type to be carried away by the latest intellectual trend and are often the first to say when the emperor has no clothes. For them, society should shape its future based not on fads or popular whims but on principles derived from objective facts and reason. Still, their tenacious preference for hard realities cannot hide their passion. They are emotional about our society and have dedicated much of their careers to public policy and, in some cases, public life. They have sacrificed material gain in their pursuit of ideas that matter. Their personalities and their values shine through their contributions to this book.

The contributors are people who care at a human level about issues important to society. They know that who we are as a culture, a people, and society, is not the facts and statistics, but rather the stories we tell ourselves. Across this broad country, it turns out the stories we tell ourselves about what it means to be Canadian are different, and they depend greatly on when Canada started for us. Canada is not a common date or time; it varies from place to place. Our First Nations would be the first to tell you that.

First Nations see Canada from time immemorial. Quebec sees Canada beginning in the time of Champlain. The Atlantic Provinces had a second origin as English colonies after their first French foundation. Canada only starts for Ontarians with the loyalist migration and the early days of the town of York. British Columbia has its own origins starting with Captain

Cooke, and Canada comes later. For Albertans the country really begins with railways and settlements. It should be no surprise that we tell ourselves unique stories about what it means to be Canadian.

Quebec and Alberta are on the opposite ends of Canadian history and the differences are accentuated by language. But the differences between even Alberta and Ontario are profound. We each know our own stories well and can fall into a trap of assuming they are the only right ones. Yet our stories across this country, based on different histories, are all valid even when they are contradictory. It just means our histories create cultures across Canada that are in some ways distinct and often exceptional.

By way of example, many commentators have noted the culture of the American West is in some ways more similar to the Western Canada than to the rest of Canada. This makes sense based on the timing of our histories. Some of my great-great-grandparents came to Alberta from America as part of their migration west starting in Scituate, Massachusetts, in 1630. The border was open. For an American moving west, Alberta was likely less of a culture shock than for many Europeans and Asians who came at the same time. And my family's experience is not unusual. The American progressive migration, American oilman migration, the gold rushes, all set the stage for distinctly different attitudes to the United States in the West.

Ours is a recent story and one of the newer places in the world. Our first permanent settlement was 1788 in Fort Chipewyan. This was a Northwest Company corporate post. European settlement didn't start in a meaningful way until the railroad arrived in Calgary in 1883. Our post-European set-tlement history is so recent it literally came from my great-grandmother's lips to my ears. This newness means that more than other areas of Canada, Alberta's culture is a state of mind. It is an emerging attitude that you can be here for six generations and still not understand, or you can be here for six months and completely get it.

Even today, more people are from away, than from here. This means we have little shared history. Plus, we are remote. We were one of the last places in the world to be settled because we are a far-away place at the edge of the world. It takes a certain type of culture to ensure there even is a future to share, when you choose to clear a homestead connected to the world only by a long thin ribbon of railroad.

Our short history and newness mean that the West's shared values and culture are based more on a shared future than a shared past. A shared culture based on a shared future is welcoming of all who want to share that future. It is more naturally a meritocracy, measured by who can best contribute to a better future. This begat the rugged individualism and celebration of risk-takers, wildcatters, and entrepreneurs that Alberta is known for. However, with little foundation or laurels to rest on, and help very far away, it also necessitated a culture of cooperation and collective effort. It was Western Canada that introduced social credit, socialized medicine, and suffrage for women. In these provinces you will still find large credit unions and co-op grocery stores.

Alberta's story is one of difficult trials and great contributions to Canada. Alberta's entrepreneurialism and financial strengths are matched by political and social leadership. Prairie socialists were trailblazers for a better Canada. Even more than conservatives, prairie socialists tended to be "cash and carry" and not in favour of debt on their personal or government balance sheets. Western women were the ones to challenge the status quo to be declared persons, convincing the British House of Lords to overrule a hidebound eastern Canadian judicial decision ruling that they were not. Western conservatives and prairie socialists often disagree on methods, but we share a culture of looking forward to a common and better future.

Because settlement was so recent, we also are highly likely to have a personal connection to the land, where our family recently came from. It also means we have the closest connections with First Nations who also heard their pre-European histories from their ancestors' lips. Our dealings with First Nations are recent dealings, and just like family members who know each other the most, we squabble more. But no one in the country has closer or more successful economic ties with First Nations than westerners.

We are progressives in the sense that a better future means progress for people. We imagine this distinct Albertan and Western approach to life is shared and understood by other Canadians. We assume the rest of Canada is just excited about our stories about a shared future as we are. It has been the times in Alberta's history when we most needed the rest of the country that this assumption is belied.

Albertans are mystified when this happens. Thinking it is a lack of knowledge, we spend great effort on communicating statistics and facts on our contribution to the country and our current needs. The fundamental problem is they already understand our contributions. It is we who do not understand them. The question we should ask is: does Canada really want to contribute to and share our future? You can stop here and go right to Chapter One if you are not interested in my opinion on this question. However, I was given licence to give my point of view and here it is. The rest of the country has generations of history and largely shared values based on shared pasts. The other provinces are as much about protecting their patrimony as building it. The former, Rupert's Land, including most of Alberta, Saskatchewan, and Manitoba, is part of their patrimony. We only ceased to be a territory in 1905 and were only grudgingly given nominal control over our resources in 1930, less than one hundred years ago. According to these sensibilities, our land is their land, our wealth their wealth.

I think Westerners need to understand that for some people whose history starts well before 1867, we are upstarts. Our resources were only given to us out of their largesse, and we should be thankful. These older Canadians who came before us have a colonial mindset. It is this attitude that dominates the Laurentian Elite's thinking when it comes to "their" former territories. And our attitudes are fed by resentments and slights felt by colonials of all ages.

Part of the history I heard from my great-grandparents lips was the struggle of becoming a province, the Crow rate, the March on Ottawa, and the refusal of Ottawa to help us during the Great Depression. The other part of the history I heard from my grandparents is that hacking a life out of the wilderness was not easy. It was pioneers and, those who have come since with the Alberta state of mind, who built the West. We have suffered from over-taxation with under-representation for most of our history and it has never been truer than today. My own personal experience with the National

Energy Policy through to today's blockade on Alberta and its pipelines, can be included in this history.

As when Americans presented their list of resentments to King George, and Quebec presented its resentments to Canada in the Quiet Revolution, I believe Alberta's long list of resentments is underestimated by the rest of Canada. The resentments fester in the West even though our culture by its nature looks to the future and does not habitually dwell on the past.

Ottawa is a reflection of the majority of Canadians and their cultural values; a mélange of the majority's national stories, if you like. Ottawa does not tell Atlantic Canada, Ontario, or even Quebec (since the Quiet Revolution) who they are, or what their way of life should be. My ancestors did not come here at the turn of the twentieth-century to be told how to live their lives, or how to make a living either. They did not come to hack a life out of the wilderness because Canada at the turn of the twentieth-century was a great power with amazing social programs. Canada was struggling and offered nothing more, and nothing less, than a chance for people willing to take exceptional risks, suffer great hardships, work unendingly, and accept the results, fair or not.

I stand on the shoulders of those everyday giants. I think we all do. Those giants gave us an exceptional and distinct culture as well as shared values and they never looked back. They gave us a future open to all who want to contribute to it. We have an obligation to pass that future on to the next generations. We are again at one of those moments where we need Canada. We need it to show it cares about a shared future. We need Canada to fulfill its constitutional obligations to allow free movement of goods across the country. We need Ottawa to stand up to unfair trade practices, in particular by China, Russia, and OPEC, but also to interference by partly foreign-funded environmental nongovernmental organizations (ENGOS's) and the United Nations. We need to know Canada wants to share the future with us and not just share in the benefits of our resourcefulness and hard work. Disturbingly, what we hear now is how Albertans' way of life and some of our core ways to make a living are not contributing to Canada, but rather are a problem to be fixed.

Places as similar as Norway and Sweden, Ireland and England, the Czech Republic and Slovakia found that preservation of their shared culture and values required full political autonomy. These countries work in close economic and federated unions today while preserving control over their own futures. At minimum, we need the autonomy and respect for provincial rights a true federation promises. We need more Alberta and less Ottawa.

Under any scenario of more autonomy, I cannot see Western Canada losing things like our rights gained over a thousand-year history of fighting for liberty and responsible government, our common law, or, more recently our hard fought constitutional relationships with First Nations. I do not see why an autonomous Alberta or Western Canada would need to or want to lose those rights if we lose Ottawa (who arguably hurts not helps in this regard).

People say we could end up land locked. The people who say this do not have the courage or fortitude of my great-great-grandparents, because so are the Swiss, so are the Slovaks and many other countries. Being enclaved within a Canada that literally blockades our future is much worse than being landlocked with access to international treaties such as the Law of the Sea Convention. Our recent history has shown us this very clearly.

There is no reason why Alberta could not gain autonomy like the Irish, Norwegians, Slovaks, and others. As one of the world's largest and most responsible energy producers, economic cooperation with our cousins in Canada, or the United States, or both, would likely be mutually beneficial. With more oil and gas and fewer people, we could become the Norway of North America and be the most prosperous people in the world, in control of our own future, culture, and values.

The authors of this book explore the actual balance of give and take between the West and the rest of Canada. If you are willing to read carefully, you will find value in their thoughts. It will help you make up your mind. Does the rest of Canada genuinely wish to share a future with the West—a future that is cooperative; a future of progressivism that will work for all Canadians and demonstratively improve all our futures; a future of joint prosperity? Or, as I have suggested, is it time for Alberta and Western Canada to find the courage of our founders to take greater control of our own future. With that courage we can create a new relationship with Canada and North America. Albertans can together create the stories we will tell ourselves going forward and become a beacon to all North America and the world.

Are we little westerners or big westerners?
Preston Manning

Introduction

O N DECEMBER 18, 1901, an historic political debate took place in Indian Head, Saskatchewan. It was between Rodman Roblin, premier of the original province of Manitoba, when it was only one third the size it is today, and F.W.G. Haultain, premier of the vast North-West Territories, when they stretched from the American border to the Arctic Ocean and from the Ontario border to the Rocky Mountains.

What brought these two western leaders together, along with hundreds of other Westerners who had come by sleigh and horseback on a cold winter night to hear them, was an anticipated threat to the future of the West, posed, you guessed it, by the proposed actions of the distant federal government in Ottawa headed by Wilfred Laurier, a Liberal Quebec-based Prime Minister.

F.W.G. Haultain's vision of the future for the original North-West Territories was for them to transition, as their population and economic power increased, into one big province with the size and political power to balance the influence of Quebec and Ontario within confederation.

What Laurier and the federal Liberals wanted was to forestall any such development by carving the great northwest into three provinces and two territories and to retain federal control of their natural resources, a result which, in Haultain's words, would permanently render the great northwest as an "unwilling, inferior, and imperfect" member of confederation.

While Haultain vigorously opposed this carving up of the old North-West Territories, Roblin supported it, in part because he would be premier of at least one of those smaller jurisdictions.

Haultain would come to label those in the West who supported this federal dissection of the region "little westerners." Those who supported his position of developing the northwest into one large and united coalition with control of its natural resources and a capacity to counterbalance the influence of Quebec and Ontario within confederation, he called "big westerners."

Haultain proposed calling this one big northwest Buffalo. It was to be a big Buffalo, not a little buffalo grazing only in Alberta or Saskatchewan. It was to get its strength and power from westerners moving collectively as a herd, not as a lone single-province buffalo like Manitoba. And it was to head, as buffalo instinctively do, directly into the storms and headwinds blowing from the east to emerge stronger and intact once the storms subsided, not turn tail and run from those storms as frightened cattle are prone to do.

Haultain won the debate that night at Indian Head but unfortunately for the West, it was Laurier's position, with the support of little westerners, that prevailed. Haultain's prediction of the West being constitutionally placed in an "unwilling, inferior, and imperfect" position has regrettably come true.

Decision-making time

In many respects, what has motivated this chapter and what occasioned the recent establishment of the Fair Deal Panel by Alberta Premier Jason Kenney is the inherent unfairness and inequality of the West's position within confederation, a situation made even more unfair and intolerable by the ill-considered actions of yet another Liberal Quebec-based Prime Minister.

What westerners ultimately need to decide is this: is the best response to that unfairness and inequality to carve out of Canada and the great northwest a smaller but separate country?

Or is the best response to clearly define what would constitute a genuine Fair Deal, not just for Alberta but for all Canadians who share our values and perspectives on what this country should be?

This second approach would involve building a large informal coalition of all those interests who largely share our Fair Deal demands, not just in Alberta but throughout the northwest, including Manitoba, Saskatchewan, Alberta, most of B.C., the present day Northwest Territories, and the Yukon. It would require us to energize and use that great coalition to press our Fair Deal demands upon the federal government and the rest of Canada as they have never been pressed before, and to persist until they are met.

In other words, as the great northwest, comprising 48 per cent of the land mass of the entire country and already holding one third of Canada's population, inexorably grows in population and economic and political clout in the twenty-first century, will it apply its weight and influence collectively and persistently to bring about fundamental changes in the terms and conditions of confederation, amounting to a virtual re-confederation in which the northwest and all those who share our values and perspectives can at long last feel truly at home?

That is the decision we invariably have to make. Do we pursue the little western path of yet another division of the northwest, this time via secession? Or do we pursue the big western path aimed at nothing less than fairness for ourselves and for all Canadians through a re-confederation?

I will return to this decision in a moment. But first, to assist us in making it, let me review three things.

First, the major points on which most westerners, little and big, are agreed. After all, we have a lot in common and agree on much, regardless of our differing positions on whether to secede or re-confederate.

Second, the major questions which little Westerners still need to answer, and answer substantially, if they wish their fellow citizens to consider separation as a viable option.

Third, the major questions which big westerners still need to answer, if they wish their fellow citizens to consider re-confederation as a real and achievable possibility.

Here are the major points on which most Westerners are agreed. Public meetings to discuss the current state of the West and the Western economy, as well as public opinion polls, confirm that the vast majority of western

Canadians feel that our people and our region are treated unfairly within confederation, consistently and systematically.

Our people are frustrated, angry, and have every right to demand a Fair Deal, and to consider every possible option for securing a better and more equitable future for ourselves and for our children. On that, surely the vast majority of us are agreed.

Examples of this unfair treatment abound and include:

- The failure of the federal government to recognize the economic, political, and cultural distinctiveness of the great northwest
- The inequitable distribution and administration of equalization, federal transfer payments, and federal-provincial programs
- The political vetoing of Energy East and Northern Gateway pipelines, lack of support for the Obama-rejected Keystone XL pipeline, and the interminable delays in proceeding with the Trans Mountain pipeline expansion and the Coastal GasLink
- The continued failure of the federal government to provide and maintain unobstructed transportation corridors from the interior of the country to the Atlantic, Pacific, and Arctic
- The inadequate representation of the electors and interests of Western Canada in the House of Commons, the Senate, and the federal civil service
- The unresponsiveness, and outright opposition of the federal government, to repeated requests and demands from Western Canadians that these clearly identified inequities be redressed.

These are the major points—instances and examples of unfair treatment—on which we are for the most part agreed.

Questions little westerners need to answer

Little westerners have responded to these inequities by proposing that a small, separate, independent country be carved out of the northwest.

Presentations to the public, to the Fair Deal Panel in Alberta, and to the provincial governments of Alberta and Saskatchewan by those advocating secession, have played a useful role in expressing the anger and frustration of westerners concerning our current situation within the federation and in articulating its root causes.

But for the secession option to be taken seriously by a majority of westerners, or to be the subject of a referendum as some have proposed, there are a host of fundamental questions which have yet to be answered substantively by those advocating it.

For instance, have those advocating the secession of Alberta carefully examined previous secession attempts by others, in particular Quebec? And have they ascertained the reasons why these previous secession attempts have all failed, and why a similar attempt by Alberta would not also fail for the same reasons?

The first major attempt at secession by the Province of Quebec in 1980 was backed by a multi-billion dollar provincial government, most of the Quebec public service unions, the French language media, and an organized political party with a large membership and a charismatic leader, a much stronger support base than that which currently exists for the secession of any western province.

And yet, in the 1980 referendum on Quebec secession after a prolonged and expensive campaign, only 40 per cent of the Quebec electorate could be persuaded to support the secessionist option and the referendum failed by a substantial margin. Post-referendum analysis revealed that one of the basic mistakes made by the pro-secession forces, one which western separatists seem determined to repeat, was to continually "preach to the near converted" and to do so in increasingly strident tones in order to maintain their support. As a result, the secession campaign increasingly frightened and alienated the unsure and undecided, precisely the segment of the electorate whose support is essential to winning a public referendum in a polarized political environment.

To date, no evidence has been presented to the public or the Fair Deal Panel that those advocating the secession of a western province have thoroughly studied these previous unsuccessful attempts or learned any lessons from them.

In addition, those advocating secession by Alberta and Saskatchewan have not yet articulated what they believe to be the clear question and clear majority required for any secession referendum to be recognized as legitimate and lawful by the federal government and the rest of Canada under the Clarity Act, legislation originally proposed and supported by Western Canadians.

Here's another question for aspiring secessionists. Where is the draft constitution for the seceding region, one that would provide its potential citizens with a form of government and fundamental rights superior to those provided by the current Canadian constitution, imperfect as it is?

If Albertans and other Westerners are to be invited to create and become citizens of a new, independent country, surely they have a right to know in advance what kind of country that will be. In particular, what will be the form of its government and the status of their rights and responsibilities as citizens?

It is highly unlikely that any of us as westerners, angry and frustrated as we may be, will be willing to "buy a pig in a poke," even if that pig is dressed in western garb. In any referendum on the secession option, we will rightfully be entitled to see, in advance, the draft constitution of the new country we are being asked to create and join. So where is it, this draft Constitution of the new country?

To date no such draft, or anything remotely resembling one, has been presented to the public or the Fair Deal Panel by those advocating secession.

Another question: how will becoming a separate, landlocked country increase rather than decrease the prospects of getting unobstructed transportation corridors and pipelines to tidewater, east, west, or north?

The future economic prosperity of Alberta and Saskatchewan is absolutely dependent on our landlocked provinces securing unobstructed transportation corridors to tidewater so as to be able to freely move our goods and resources to international markets.

As is well known, in the absence of expanded east-west pipeline capacity, Alberta and Saskatchewan are captives of the American market and obliged to sell our petroleum resources at severely discounted prices. The absence of such unobstructed transportation corridors is therefore one of the principal causes of western alienation, prompting consideration of the secessionist option.

But this being the case, our people will rightfully ask: won't being a separate, landlocked country further decrease rather than increase the prospects of getting unobstructed east-west transportation corridors including pipelines to tidewater? And won't becoming a de facto fifty-first state further increase rather than reduce our dependency on the U.S., and even further reduce the capacity of Canada's petroleum-producing provinces to influence national energy and transportation policy in our favour?

Substantive and satisfactory answers to these questions are a necessity if the secession option is to be seriously considered as anything more than political bluster. But to date no such answers have been persuasively presented. We have no answers sufficient to dispel the cloud of uncertainty that the prospect of secession will invariably raise in capital markets and among the general public when these questions are raised.

Other substantive questions which arise with respect to the secession option include these:

- If Alberta were to secede and become an independent country, what currency would it adopt: the Canadian dollar, the American dollar, the Buffalo chip, or something else?
- To what extent could such a country claim to be truly independent if it were still subject to monetary policy set by a central bank and government in Ottawa or Washington, D.C.?
- What principles and strategies would the government of a seceded province adopt to resolve the unresolved claims of Indigenous Albertans who might wish to remain within Canada?

The list of substantive questions such as these, raised by the secession proposal, is long and challenging. Perhaps well-researched, substantive, and satisfactory answers to these questions do exist. But to date these have not been adequately presented to the general public and certainly not to Alberta's Fair Deal Panel. Until they are, much more work remains to be done before the little western position of secession can be considered a viable alternative or made the subject of a legally binding referendum.

Questions big westerners need to answer

Over the past few years, much work has been done by western based think tanks, advocacy groups, political parties, and provincial governments to propose remedies to the inequities to which the Western provinces are subjected within confederation. This has also been the task of the Fair Deal Panel and the consultative process established by Premier Kenney in November 2019.

One of the objectives of all this work has been to determine the principal components of that Fair Deal big westerners and their allies want to relentlessly press upon the federal government and the Rest of Canada. What are they?

That question may be answered on two levels.

First, at the national, collaborative level (requiring support from other governments), the intent would be to vigorously and persistently press for:

- Recognition by the federal government and the rest of Canada of the economic, political, and cultural distinctiveness of Alberta and the northwest.
- Federal policies recognizing and treating the natural resource sectors as foundational and absolutely essential to the wellbeing of the Canadian economy.
- The reform of equalization, including removing restrictions on the Fiscal Stabilization Fund which prevent Alberta from receiving the $2.4 billion equalization rebate it is entitled to, now that its economy has suffered a major reversal.
- Federally legislated rights of way for unobstructed transportation corridors to the Atlantic, Pacific, and Arctic to move inland natural resources to tidewater and world markets.
- A prohibition, via a federal provincial agreement or a constitutional amendment, of federal spending, taxing, legislating, or treaty-making in areas of provincial jurisdiction (such as natural resources development and conservation), or joint jurisdiction (such as the environment) unless the consent of the affected province(s) is secured.

- Challenging federal overreach in areas of provincial or joint jurisdiction and collaborating with other provinces and industry to advance market-based approaches to environmental protection, including the reduction of greenhouse gas emissions.
- Constitutional amendments and/or federal-provincial agreements and compatible federal legislation to reform equalization and the administration of federal transfers, to entrench property rights, to eliminate interprovincial barriers to trade via a Domestic Free Trade Agreement and to establish fair representation of the northwest in the Canadian House of Commons, the Senate, and the federal civil service.

Second, at the provincial level, there are additional measures for securing a Fair Deal for Alberta which the province (and other provinces) could pursue unilaterally. These might include:[i]

- Holding province-wide referenda to secure public approval for the Alberta government to withdraw from the Canada Pension Plan to create an Alberta Pension Plan;[ii] end its current agreement with the RCMP and establish an Alberta provincial police force;[iii] and seek the removal of the principle of equalization (Section 36) from the constitution.
- Strengthening law and order, and respect for the rule of law, by creating the Alberta Police Force, appointing an Alberta Chief Firearms Officer, and possibly creating an Alberta Parole Board to take over responsibility for provincial inmates from the Parole Board of Canada.
- Demanding reforms to the employment insurance program to make it fair to Alberta workers who continue to subsidize unemployed beneficiaries in other parts of the country.
- Withdrawing, with full compensation, from federal-provincial programs for services better operated by the province, and resisting further federal intrusions into health and social service programming.
- Strengthening Alberta's presence in Ottawa and securing a seat at the table when the federal government negotiates and implements international agreements affecting Alberta's interests.
- Continuing to diversify Alberta's economy while aggressively seeking additional international markets for Alberta's exports.

These big western initiatives and proposals for achieving a Fair Deal for our provinces and the Western region within confederation are at present far more substantive and more thoroughly researched than the secession proposal offered by little westerners. But little westerners and other disillusioned citizens may rightfully pose a second set of question to big westerners which also deserve substantive answers. For instance, how do big westerners propose to promote and advance this Fair Deal agenda so as to be more successful than the previous attempts of the Reform Party and Stephen Harper Conservative government?

Little westerners allege that "the West wants in" endeavor of the 1980s and 1990s was a failure and that the Harper government, despite its western roots, failed to substantially improve the West's position within the federation. So why should westerners believe that this Fair Deal initiative now proposed by big westerners will succeed where these previous efforts allegedly did not?

These questions and assertions deserve substantive responses so let us take them one at a time.

"The west wants in" initiative

In accusing the federal government and the rest of Canada of treating the West unfairly, it is important that westerners not treat each other unfairly. And surely it is unfair and inaccurate to suggest that the Reform effort achieved nothing. It played a crucial role in defeating the Laurentian-inspired Charlottetown Accord which would have made the West's position even worse. Its anti-deficit crusade led to the balancing of the federal budget in 1998, a top concern of western Canadians at the time. It secured the appointment of the first and only democratically selected senators, all from the West. And it laid the foundations for a minority and then a majority government with strong western roots and representation.

But the two most important results of the Reform movement, the two results most relevant to advancing a Fair Deal for the West today, the two most important lessons taught by the Reform experience and completely overlooked by the secessionists who say that movement was a failure, are these:

- First, the Reform experience proved that just five westerners meeting in a boardroom in Calgary and using the tools that democracy gives us all could start a process that resulted in the formation of a national majority government.[iv] To put it more bluntly, it's possible to secure a pro-western federal government from a western political base. And if it has been done successfully before, it can be done again
- Second, the Reform experience proved that the key strategy to achieve that result—a west-friendly national government—is consistent, ever-expanding coalition building.

Reform itself was a loose coalition of disillusioned Progressive Conservatives, a few disillusioned Liberals, and a plethora of disillusioned citizens who had no previous partisan allegiances at all. And then to increase its ability to push its agenda within the federation what did Reform do? It formed a loose coalition with the Ralph Klein conservatives in Alberta, the Gary Filmon conservatives in Manitoba, and the Mike Harris conservatives in Ontario to create a bigger coalition, the Canadian Alliance.

And then to further expand that coalition to the point where it could become the government of Canada, what did Stephen Harper and Peter McKay do? They formed yet another coalition between the Canadian Alliance and what was left of the old federal Progressive Conservative Party to create the present day Conservative Party of Canada: coalition building, coalition building, and more coalition building, principally initiated and guided by westerners, until the last of those coalitions formed a minority federal government in 2006 and a majority federal government in 2011.

If that western-based initiative with coalition-building as its principle *modus operandi* was able in essence to take control of the government of Canada fifteen years ago, are not such takeovers going to be even more feasible in the years ahead as the northwest inexorably grows in population, economic clout, and political sophistication?

Why then settle for the uncertain creation of a small new country when, by big western coalition-building, pro- western forces can again take control of the government of a huge, established one?

The accomplishments of the Harper government

There is still one more accusatory question that the little western secessionists can put to the big westerners, and it is this: supposing that fairness advocating, pro-western, pro-resource development, pro-free enterprise forces can once again form the government of Canada by coalition building, what's the guarantee that such a government will actually implement the West's Fair Deal agenda? Did not the Harper government, rooted in the West, fail to substantially improve the West's position within the federation? Why should westerners believe that some future federal government, even if it is constructed by westerners, will do any better?

Again, we are debating among westerners who share much in common so let's start by being fair. Surely the Conservative government of Stephen Harper was better for the West than a Liberal government under Michael Ignatieff. And if you ask the Harper folk what they did to advance the interests of westerners, especially Alberta, they will list the following:

- Six additional seats for Alberta in the House of Commons under the Fair Representation Act
- Equal per-capita health funding under the Canadian Health Transfer, resulting in billions more for health care in Alberta[v]
- Privatization of the Canadian Wheat Board, taking the Western grain industry away from Ottawa bureaucrats and giving it back to western farmers
- Abolition of the federal gun registry and resisting the Montreal/Toronto agenda on guns over successive years
- Addressed the "fiscal imbalance" with provinces with a 2007 budget that increased provincial transfers by a total of $39 billion
- Introduction of a responsible resource development initiative in the 2012 budget, designed to streamline environmental reviews, reduce duplication, and allowing provinces like Alberta to conduct their own

project reviews. Had the Harper government remained in office in 2015, this would have meant that all projects delayed or cancelled by Justin Trudeau would have been approved and underway now, including Northern Gateway and Energy East[vi]

- Consistent efforts internationally, in public meetings and in private meetings with other leaders, to advocate for Alberta's interests and push back on misinformation about the oil-and-gas industries[vii]
- Pursuit of an aggressive free trade agenda (trade deals with forty-three countries across the world, up from five when Harper took office), and the opening up of global markets for western agriculture and energy. (It should also be noted that both the EU-Canada free trade agreement and the Pacific Partnership Agreement were initiated by the Harper government, although concluded by the Trudeau government.)

The Harperites may also point out, diplomatically, I'm sure, that during the Harper government's years in office, it was not exactly bombarded with specific demands to "do more" for the West. If it had been, Harper has said he would have responded positively.

All of this raises troubling questions: having acquired a federal government sympathetic to western interests and concerns, did westerners (including western provincial governments) simply assume that their specific interests and their position within confederation would automatically be advanced? And if that was the assumption and it actually led to a slackening of western demands, whose fault was that? It can't all be laid on the Harper government.

If after reflecting on these arguments, little westerners still maintain that these measures pursued by the Harper government, good as far as they went, were still not enough to get a truly Fair Deal for the West, then there is yet another option besides jumping immediately to secession as the only alternative. Rather than abandon the federal government of Canada as an instrument to advance western interests, draw up a more substantive and aggressive list of what some future government with a strong western base should do when it again gets the opportunity as it surely will.

Getting Action on the Fair Deal demands

If pushing for a fairer deal, not just for Alberta but for the northwest and all Canadians who desire genuine fairness and equality in all of our constitutional arrangements and national government policies, is the ultimate objective, there is still one more big question which big westerners are obligated to answer, and answer substantively.

Is threatening secession, as the little westerners propose, not the best and most certain way to get action from the federal government and the rest of Canada? And, if so, how do big westerners propose to get action from the federal government and the rest of Canada on those Fair Deal demands?

What all of us want is not more talk, not more writing, not more tweeting on this subject, but *action* to achieve a genuinely Fair Deal for the West.

So here are six major instrumentalities and strategies that big westerners propose to force action from the federal government and the rest of Canada on a Fair Deal for the West and re-confederation. These are focused particularly on getting a Fair Deal for Alberta, but can be expanded to secure a Fairer Deal for all within confederation.

1. Use province-wide referenda to demonstrate widespread public demand for all or some of the Fair Deal demands.

Properly worded and managed referenda can be used to give hundreds of thousands of people the opportunity to vigorously express themselves on the fairness issue, to give the public a chance to decide between several options for resolving it, and to show massive public support for particular planks of the Fair Deal platform.

Premier Kenney has already indicated that he favors a referendum to ascertain the magnitude of public support for equalization reform, i.e., the removal of the Section 36 reference to the principle of equalization from the constitution and its replacement with an equitable administrative arrangement.

And he has indicated a willingness to give Albertans a chance, via a referendum, to say whether or not they would favor Alberta withdrawing from its contract with the RCMP to establish a provincial police force, and from the Canada Pension Plan to establish an Alberta pension plan.

Referenda or citizens initiatives could also be used to rally and express massive public support for other Fair Deal initiatives such as the creation of federally legislated, unobstructed rights of way for transportation corridors to the Atlantic, Pacific, and Arctic, and the creation of an elected, equal, and effective Senate.

The concept here is that province-wide referenda and referenda campaigns be used to provide channels for grassroots political energy to actively express itself in favor of, or in opposition to, proposed actions to secure a Fair Deal.

2. Encourage Alberta's representatives in the House of Commons to introduce motions, resolutions, and draft bills calling for federal support of those Fair Deal recommendations accepted by the Alberta government and approved by the Alberta Legislature.

Alberta's thirty-four representatives in the House of Commons are more than an advocacy group that can only speechify or issue manifestos in favor of a Fair Deal for the province. They are also legislators who can introduce motions, resolutions, and draft bills in support of Fair Deal demands.

So what are some of those legislative initiatives which could be taken by Alberta's federal MPs in support of Fair Deal proposals? Here are some suggestions:

- An Equalization Transparency resolution or bill[viii] requiring the publication of contributions and receipts from and to each province via equalization, federal transfers, and joint federal-provincial programs, accompanied by measures to remedy any obvious inequities
- A motion or draft bill removing the current restrictions on the Fiscal Stabilization Fund and re-funding a $2.4 billion equalization rebate to Alberta
- A draft bill establishing federally-legislated rights of way for unobstructed transportation corridors to the Atlantic, Pacific, and Arctic oceans, exercising the right of the federal government to provide

"works to the advantage of Canada" as authorized by s. 92. ss. 10 (a) and (c) of the constitution

- Draft amendments to the Criminal Code making any obstruction of the movement of people, goods, and resources via these corridors a criminal offence, and making those responsible for any such obstructionism financially liable for costs and damages caused to third parties
- A draft bill, the Economic Impact Assessment Act, or amendments to the existing Bill C-69, requiring the federal government to provide a detailed economic impact assessment of every major environmental protection measure it proposes or adopts, including its carbon tax legislation and the Paris Accord.
- A National Unity Motion calling on the federal government to offer the provinces a federal-provincial agreement whereby the federal government is prohibited from spending, taxing, legislating, or treaty-making in areas of provincial jurisdiction and joint jurisdiction, unless it secures the consent of the province(s) affected
- A draft constitutional amendment along the same lines
- A draft Domestic Free Trade Agreement (an extension of the New West Partnership Agreement) with a call for the federal government to bring it to a federal-provincial conference, negotiate its acceptance, and implement its provisions
- A motion calling for an immediate Justice Department investigation into the increase in rural crime, especially on the prairies, accompanied by recommendations for its redress
- A motion shortening the time requirements for opting out of provincial contracts with the RCMP, the CPP, and other federal-provincial programs
- A resolution calling for the federal Parliament to recognize the cultural, economic, and political distinctiveness of the Canadian northwest, the inequitable position it currently occupies within confederation, and the need for remedial action
- Draft amendments to the Alberta Act [1905, 4-5 Edw. VII, c. 3 (Can.)] to more fully provide a provincial constitution for the province of Alberta.

As opposition members in the House of Commons, Alberta's MPs do not currently have the research or drafting resources to produce such motions, resolutions, and draft bills. But these resources can and should be provided by the Alberta government, perhaps through its expanded Ottawa office, as an important component of its Fair Deal initiative.

Of course, the current Liberal/socialist coalition in the House of Commons is likely to vote down any and all such legislative initiatives. But raising, explaining, and promoting such legislative initiatives will help draw national attention to, and support for, Alberta's case for fairness. And if the next federal election were to produce a change of government, those draft bills could well become law, vastly improving the position of Alberta and the entire northwest within confederation.

3. Develop an informal coalition of likeminded provincial governments to vigorously press for two important measures.

The first of these would be a constitutional amendment prohibiting the federal government from spending, taxing, legislating, or treaty-making in areas of provincial jurisdiction or joint jurisdiction unless it first secures the consent of the province(s) affected.

Virtually every provincial government should be in favor of such a constitutional amendment, but if securing it proves to be too difficult and time consuming, the same objective should be rigorously pursued via a federal-provincial agreement.

Second, a Domestic Free Trade Agreement to remove internal barriers to trade, including the removal of barriers to the free movement of natural resources across provincial boundaries.

This initiative could begin as an effort to expand the 2010 New West Partnership Trade Agreement between the Western provinces to include other provinces.

4. Build and operationalize additional "action coalitions" among interest groups, individuals, and donors in support of particular Fair Deal demands.

The push to achieve a genuine Fair Deal for Alberta and the great northwest should not be confined to the efforts of governments. That's not the Western way.

Environmental extremists and anti-resource sector activists have created non-governmental action coalitions comprised of dozens of like-minded organizations, hundreds of donors donating millions of dollars, and thousands of members capable of commanding media attention, public support, the attention of politicians, and the acquiescence of governments to their demands.

But where, then, are the action coalitions to press for the major Fair Deal demands with equal vigor and persistence?

Where is the TransCanada Corridor Coalition, comprised of dozens of organizations, hundreds of donors, and thousands of members, pressing relentlessly for federally legislated, unobstructed rights of way from the interior to the Atlantic, Pacific, and Arctic?

Where is the National Unity Coalition, comprised of dozens of organizations, hundreds of donors, and thousands of Canadian citizens, that believes federal spending, taxing, legislating, and treaty-making in areas of provincial jurisdiction or joint jurisdiction without the consent of the affected provinces is the principal source of national disunity in our time?

Where is the National Unity Coalition, composed of people like you and me and all the organizations we are connected with, demanding a federal-provincial agreement or constitutional amendment prohibiting such unilateral interventions in the future.

Where is the Natural Resource Sectors Coalition, comprised of dozens of organizations, hundreds of donors, and thousands of members employed by or invested in the resource sectors, pressing relentlessly for public policies that recognize and nurture the natural resource sectors—energy, agriculture, forestry, mining, and fisheries—as foundational to the strength and progress of the national economy?

5. Pursue "Fair Deal Plus"

While the government of Alberta, hopefully joined by the governments of the other Western provinces and the northern territories, should do everything in its power to secure a Fair Deal from the federal government and the rest of Canada as discussed above, there are other measures that it can and must take to improve the economic and political prospects of the province and the northwest regardless of the response of the federal government and the rest of Canada. These efforts might be called "Fair Deal Plus."

Without fully elaborating on these measures here, that list of Fair Deal Plus measures could include:

- The continued support of Alberta's resource sectors and pipelines to get Alberta energy resources to tidewater.
- Identifying and prohibiting interference by foreign-financed interest groups in Alberta's domestic affairs.
- The long overdue diversification of Alberta's provincial economy.
- The expanded and focused application of science and technology to Alberta's greatest challenges.
- The export of the technologies and regulatory provisions for reducing greenhouse gas emissions which make Alberta a genuine, although unacknowledged, leader in this regard, to other petroleum producing regions of the globe.
- An Alberta job-sharing initiative.
- A "buy Alberta" initiative.

6. Hold and implement the recommendations of a series of re-confederation conferences culminating in a Fair Deal for the West and Canada.

In 1867, the pre-confederation conferences were initiated by the colonies, Upper and Lower Canada, which the Atlantic colonies then joined, not by any central government because no such government existed.

In the 1970s, the constitutional conferences that led to the imperfect Constitution Act of 1982 were initiated and dominated by Pierre Elliott Trudeau and the federal government. In the 1980s and 1890s, it was again the federal government under Prime Minister Brian Mulroney that took the lead in organizing the Meech Lake and Charlottetown Constitutional Accords (both of which failed). This time, let the provinces desiring a new and fairer position within confederation again take the lead as the colonies once did from 1864 to 1867.

Let these conferences be organized and attended initially by representatives of British Columbia, Alberta, Saskatchewan, Manitoba, the NWT, and the Yukon with later expansion to include the other provinces and the federal government. And let the initial agenda include:

- Drafting a northwest Charter clearly defining the identity, values and rights of the great northwest region of Canada
- Identifying the challenges and opportunities which securing peace, order, and good government in the twenty-first century will entail
- Redrafting the constitution of Canada to remove the inequities which currently restrict the aspirations and future development of the northwest region.

Let that re-drafted constitution of Canada, the re-confederation plan, then be presented to the provinces of central and Atlantic Canada, the territory of Nunavut, and the federal government, urging its consideration and adoption if it is desired that the northwest be fairly treated and remain an integral part of the Canadian federation.

The Bigger the Better

The most important thing to keep in mind with respect to securing action on all these Fair Deal proposals, especially in pursuing them through the creation and activities of action coalitions, is "the bigger the better".

It's one thing when the energy-producing sector crusades for policies that recognize its importance and facilitate rather than suppress its development. But it's quite another thing and much more persuasive politically when its efforts are linked with and supported by the energy manufacturing sector, the energy service sector, and the energy knowledge sector.

It's one thing for the energy sector by itself to crusade for policies that recognize its importance and facilitate rather than suppress its development. But it's quite another thing and much more persuasive politically when representatives of all the resource sectors—energy, agriculture, forestry, mining, and fisheries—sing from the same song sheet in terms of recognition and policies that nurture rather than retard their development.

It's one thing when one or two Western provinces demand a Fair Deal for themselves and their people. But it would be quite another thing if an action coalition of the entire northwest, including Alberta, Saskatchewan, Manitoba, northwest Ontario, the NWT, the Yukon and most of B.C., were to demand better terms and conditions for themselves and their people within confederation.

Now we are talking about shared demands coming not just from 4.5 million Albertans inhabiting 7 per cent of the land mass of the country, but Fair Deal demands coming from eleven million inhabitants of the great northwest occupying 48 per cent of the land mass of Canada, demands that no federal government could ignore or resist without committing political suicide.

Now we are talking about much more than "tinkering" with confederation. We are proposing nothing less than re-confederation on more fair and equitable terms for the twenty-first century.

Conclusion

And so, after this long review of our current situation and the options, we return to the basic question: do we pursue the little western path of yet another division of the northwest, this time via secession? Or do we pursue the big western path aimed at a Fair Deal for us and for all through big-thinking, big-public-referenda, big-coalitions, and re-confederation?

In clearly defining and relentlessly pressing the federal government and the rest of Canada for positive responses to the Fair Deal demands, I would again invoke the spirit and vision of F.W.G. Haultain, appealing to us to act as big westerners not little westerners and to emulate the buffalo.

Like the buffalo, let us head directly into and face up to the storms of inequity and unfairness to which we are presently subject, rather than turning tail and running away from them as frightened cattle are wont to do.

Like the buffalo, let us take full advantage of the strength and security of the herd by remaining closer together and moving collectively rather than allowing the storms of adversity and unfairness to drive us apart.

In other words, let us resist the temptation of one province going it alone or hastily carving out a small portion of the great northwest into a separate, land locked country. Instead, let us press on together with renewed vigour and cunning to secure a Fair Deal for our entire region and all our people and to emerge through the re-confederation effort into the lush and sunny pastures of a new and better homeland for ourselves and all Canadians.

Just as the Western sedimentary basin, the oil sands, the valleys and rivers of the Rocky Mountains, the bounteous sunshine and the warm chinook winds of the great northwest contain vast amounts of physical energy, there are also enormous deposits of political energy among its inhabitants—populist energy, people energy—which in times past the West has successfully harnessed to the attainment of noble political ends.

Let us once again harness that energy, this time to get a better deal, a Fair Deal, a twenty-first-century deal, not just for ourselves and our children but for all Canadians.

I am for a Fair Deal through big-thinking, big-referenda, big-coalition-building, and re-confederation. What about you?

The status quo must go
Ted Morton

Introduction

THREE DECADES ago, Albertans helped to create a new federal political party under the demand, "The West Wants In." As noted in the last chapter, the creation of the Reform Party was the most recent episode in Alberta's century-long struggle to improve its position within confederation. So it's time to ask: did we succeed? Are we better off today than we were thirty years ago? The results are not encouraging. In the eight different policy areas reviewed in this study, Alberta has lost ground. On the whole, we are more vulnerable to confiscatory and destructive federal policies today than we were in the 1980s. The political strategies of my generation of Albertans have not worked, and will not work, to improve Alberta's position within confederation. Does this mean "The west wants out"? Not necessarily. But the status quo must go. It's time for a new plan.

From provincial equality to the Quebec veto

The years 1980-81 were pivotal in Alberta's relationship with Ottawa. Pierre Elliott Trudeau and the Liberal Party had just won a majority government with the promise of "constitutional renewal" and defeating the Quebec separatist movement. This culminated in the Constitution Act, 1982, which in addition to the Charter of Rights, gave Canada its first entrenched constitutional amending formula.

To rally Quebec support for remaining in Canada, Trudeau had sought to constitutionalize what had been an unwritten constitutional convention: that there could be no constitutional changes without the support of both Quebec and Ontario. These "veto powers" for Quebec and Ontario can be traced to their economic and demographic dominance at confederation in 1867, but they had never before been written into law. As early as 1971, Trudeau had attempted to give these vetoes a legal status in the Victoria Charter, but failed. His 1980 re-election gave him a second opportunity.

Alberta Premier Peter Lougheed strongly objected to constitutionalizing any special vetoes for Quebec or Ontario. He argued that they would entrench forever the second-class status of all the Western provinces. Whatever historical logic these vetoes might have had, Lougheed asserted they were inconsistent with the significant economic contributions now made by the Western provinces. Led by Lougheed, the Western premiers made it clear to Trudeau that they would never accept such second-class status. Rather, they demanded a "new constitutional order which would match the new economic order."[i] This meant an amending formula that recognized the equality of the provinces.[ii] The result is what is now the Section 38 amending formula: approval by Parliament plus at least seven of the ten provinces with at least 50 percent of Canada's population. This meant no more unilateral vetoes for Quebec (or Ontario).

This was a huge victory for Western Canada, both symbolically and practically. It brought the British North America Act, 1867 more into line with the economic and demographic realities of late twentieth-century Canada. But it did not even survive to see the twenty-first century. In 1996, after almost losing (by less than one percent) the second Quebec secession referendum, the Liberal federal government of Jean Chrétien was desperate to appease separatist sentiment in Quebec. To do this, his government restored Quebec's unilateral veto power with a piece of legislation called the *Regional Veto Act*. This act divides Canada into five regional blocks and states that the federal cabinet will refuse to introduce any constitutional amendments unless it has first been approved by Quebec, Ontario, British Columbia, and at least two of the Atlantic provinces with 50 percent of the region's population, and at least two of the Prairie provinces with 50 percent of the region's population.

The math is convoluted and confusing, but the bottom line is simple: Ottawa will in effect "loan" its veto to Quebec. If a proposed constitutional amendment has the support of seven (or more) of the other provinces, the Section 38 amending formula, but is opposed by Quebec, the government will not support it.

This new "arrangement" is extremely problematic. How can a constitutional rule be amended by an ordinary statute? Legally speaking, of course, it cannot. That is the whole point of any constitutional rule. (And the Supreme Court said as much in its 2014 **Senate Reform** ruling. See below.) But 1996 was twenty-four years ago, and the Regional Veto Act is still on the books. And until a majority government has the courage to repeal it, it more or less guarantees constitutional gridlock. Among other things, it virtually ensures that there will be no formal amendments to bring in an elected and more equal Senate. The work of an entire generation of Western Canadian leaders will have been for naught.

Losing control over our natural resources

Another of Lougheed's historic achievements was a constitutional amendment, section 92A of the **Constitution Act, 1982**, designed to ensure that Alberta would never again see a federal government implement anything like Pierre Trudeau's disastrous National Energy Program (NEP). Section 92A explicitly affirms each province's exclusive jurisdiction over the "exploration, development, conservation and management of non-renewable natural resources." Again, this was a non-negotiable demand of Lougheed and the other Western premiers. Trudeau would never have received their consent to the new Charter of Rights without it.

But once again, Alberta and the West now face the prospect of an important constitutional victory being reversed by another Liberal government led by yet another Prime Minister Trudeau. The cumulative effects of the Trudeau climate change policies, the recently enacted Bills C-69 and C-48, and the federally-imposed carbon tax, will leave section 92(A) and the Alberta economy in tatters.

C-69 further complicates the regulatory and legal hurdles that have already prevented the building of any new export pipelines and destroyed investor confidence. C-48 prohibits any new Canadian-based oil tanker traffic off the northern coast of British Columbia. This will effectively landlock any future expansion of oil in Alberta, Saskatchewan, and the Northwest Territories. Any new oil production will have to be transported by rail tanker cars, which are more expensive, more dangerous, and produce more CO_2 emissions than pipelines. Canadian oil will be sold at a steep discount to American refineries on the Gulf Coast, where much of it will be subsequently exported and sold at higher international prices. For U.S. refineries, it's a sweet deal: buy cheap, sell high. And of course, there will be no net reduction in global CO_2 emissions.

If this were not bad enough, tankers carrying oil from Alaska will continue to navigate down the coast of northern British Columbia on their way to the seventeen refineries in the San Francisco and Los Angeles areas. Similarly, tankers carrying oil from Saudi Arabia and Nigeria will continue to come down the St. Lawrence River to deliver their oil to refineries in Montreal.

As for the carbon tax, it will make it more expensive to live in and do business in Alberta. The result will be what economists call "carbon leakage." New capital investment will be directed to less expensive jurisdictions in the U.S. and elsewhere, with no appreciable reduction in CO_2 emissions, supposedly the whole purpose of the tax.

This is precisely why the carbon tax is also unconstitutional. It is a transparent attempt by the Liberal government to do indirectly what section 92A prohibits it from doing directly. Ottawa does have broad constitutional powers to levy taxes. But the carbon tax is not a true tax. Taxes are defined by their purpose: to raise money for government programs. But Trudeau proposes to give back all the carbon tax revenues. The real purpose of the carbon tax, as everyone knows, is to regulate CO_2 emissions. In Alberta's case, this means primarily from the development and management of our non-renewable natural resources—coal, oil and gas. That is, exactly what 92A declares to be the "exclusive jurisdiction" of each province.

The Saskatchewan, Ontario, and Alberta governments have all used their reference powers to challenge the constitutionality of the Trudeau carbon tax. Both the Saskatchewan (by a vote of 3-2) and Ontario (by a vote of 4-1) Courts of Appeal upheld its validity, but with dissenting opinions in each. Most recently, these dissenting opinions became a majority in the Alberta Court of Appeal, which ruled 4-1 that the carbon tax is an unconstitutional "Trojan horse" designed to usurp exclusive provincial jurisdiction over the development of non-renewable natural resources. The Alberta majority explicitly referenced the 1982 negotiations by Alberta and Saskatchewan, stating that their purpose was precisely to protect against this type of federal co-opting of provincial resource development. These conflicting lower court decisions are now on appeal to the Supreme Court of Canada for resolution.

For reasons outlined below, the prospects of the Supreme Court ruling against Ottawa are dim. As explained in Tom Flanagan's chapter, this risks becoming another instance in which the gains Alberta won through constitutional negotiation and reform have subsequently been erased by Supreme Court decisions that either ignore the clear meaning intended by the framers, systematically favour Central Canadian interests, or both.

Aboriginal veto over resource development

A final Lougheed achievement was his insistence on limiting the scope of section 35 to "existing Aboriginal rights." He successfully demanded the insertion of the adjective "existing" to prevent it from becoming a "blank cheque" for judicial policy-making. The Supreme Court subsequently ignored the framers' intent and invented the "duty to consult," words found nowhere in the constitution. This means that pipeline policy in Canada is now made mainly by judges. The result has been a decade of gridlock and the flight of foreign capital out of Western Canada's energy sector.

The original wording of section 35 of the Constitution Act, 1982 declared that, "The Aboriginal and treaty rights of the Aboriginal peoples of Canada are hereby recognized and affirmed." The meaning of this sentence was so unclear and broad that it was immediately opposed by Lougheed and the premiers of other resource-based provinces.[iii] They forced Trudeau to insert the adjective "existing" at the front of the section. Without this concession, there would have been no section 35.

The restrictive intent of this new wording was crystal clear. In the words of Canada's leading constitutional authority, Peter Hogg, the final wording "would 'freeze' native rights in their condition on April 17, 1982."[iv] Section 35 only protected and affirmed Aboriginal rights that already existed before 1982. It did not create new rights or invite to the courts to begin "discovering" new Aboriginal rights.

The Western premiers had won, and Aboriginal groups understood this. The National Indian Brotherhood (NIB) declared April 17, the day Queen Elizabeth came to Canada to proclaim the new Constitution Act, "a day of mourning. The NIB leader, George Manuel, warned that any Indigenous peoples participating in this ceremony would be guilty of "treasonous" conduct.[v]

This "original understanding" did not even last a decade. In its 1990 **Sparrow** decision, the Supreme Court ignored the "framers' intent" and re-instituted Aboriginal fishing rights on the Fraser River that had been extinguished well before 1982. A decade later, in the **Haida Nation** case, the Supreme Court extended the Sparrow precedent to create "the duty to consult and to accommodate." Where did this duty come from? The court declared that it is required by "the honour of the Crown," another judge-created concept.[vi] Who decides what this duty to consult actually means and whether it has been met? The judges, of course.

In the ensuing fifteen years, the courts did nothing to clarify what this "duty to consult" entails. Each case was different. Different courts gave different interpretations, often to similar sets of facts. Each time a pipeline company thought they had done what was required, the judges expanded the test: good, but not good enough.

Both the Harper and Trudeau governments could have corrected this legal confusion by enacting legislation that provided guidelines and a "check list" of actions needed to meet the "duty to consult." But for political reasons, neither did. With an eye toward the 2015 federal election, abdicating policy responsibility to the courts seemed the safest political option. As it turned out, climate-change voters helped the Liberals win their majority government in 2015, and they wanted to keep this support for the 2019 election. So they were content to let the legal confusion and ensuing gridlock continue.

If Peter Lougheed could see what the courts have done with section 35, he would roll over in his grave. His achievement, limiting section 35 to "existing" Aboriginal rights, has been undermined by two decades of judicial misinterpretation. Section 35 has become a "blank cheque" for judicial policy-making, enabling the "lawfare" strategy of Aboriginal militants and their climate change allies. The result has been no new export pipelines for over a decade and the exodus of foreign capital out of Western Canada's energy sector.

The campaign to landlock Alberta oil and gas

This legal uncertainty and policy vacuum has resulted in endless litigation, delays and associated costs, which are just what the anti-pipeline movement wants. They are waging "lawfare" and understand how the "death by delay" strategy works. For companies trying to build new pipelines, time is money. At a certain point, they abandon the project as no longer economically feasible. The Aboriginal and environmental groups bringing these legal challenges have never wanted better, safer pipelines. They want no pipelines. And so far, that's what they've got.

After ten years of litigation and over a billion dollars, Enbridge abandoned its Northern Gateway project in 2015. After five years and a billion dollars of expenses, TransCanada abandoned its Energy East pipeline in 2017. Kinder-Morgan announced its plans to expand its Trans-Mountain pipeline (TMX) in 2013. TMX was not a new pipeline, but simply an expansion of the existing line, so a minimal new footprint along its route. But after five years of concerted opposition and litigation, Kinder-Morgan was ready to walk away. To rescue it, the Trudeau government paid $4.5 billion to buy the project in 2018. Four months later, the Federal Court of

Appeal ordered the government to stop all work on the TMX expansion, again because the duty to consult was not adequately fulfilled.

This resulted in another year and half on additional consultation and an increase in the TMX budget from $7.4 billion to $12.6 billion. Finally, in February 2020, a new Federal Court of Appeal decision ruled that the government's duty to consult had finally been met and gave the green light to resume construction.

Equally important, the court stated explicitly that the "duty to consult" does not create an Aboriginal veto over such projects. "The law is clear: that no such veto exists."[vii] Aboriginal and climate change activists denounced this decision as wrong, and appealed it to the Supreme Court. But the Supreme Court refused to accept their appeal. For the first time in over decade, it appeared not just that TMX might be completed, but that there might be legal clarity for future projects.

Unfortunately for Alberta, this will not happen if the Trudeau government adopts the United Nations Declaration on the Rights of Indigenous Peoples (UNDRIP), which it has pledged to do. UNDRIP declares that a government must obtain "free, prior and informed consent" from Indigenous groups before adopting any policies or projects that "may affect them" or any territories they have "traditionally owned, occupied or used." Adopting this language into Canadian law would reverse the recent Federal Court ruling and give Indigenous militants and their climate change allies a virtual veto over all future pipelines and other major infrastructure projects. The Liberal minister responsible, Carolyn Bennett, has admitted as much: "We are now a full supporter of the declaration, without qualification… By adopting and implementing the declaration, we are excited that we are breathing life into Section 35 and recognizing it as a full box of rights for Indigenous Peoples in Canada."[viii]

The campaign to block the construction of new export pipelines has not been waged just by militant Aboriginals and climate-change activists. Some provincial governments have also joined this effort. In 1980, it would have been unthinkable that a provincial government could unilaterally block the construction of an oil or gas pipeline that crossed from one province to another. The regulation of interprovincial commerce has been an exclusive power of the federal government since 1867, and the well-established doctrine of "paramountcy" ensures that federal pipeline policies prevail in any conflicts with otherwise valid provincial laws. Yet this is precisely what has happened not once but twice in the past several years.

In British Columbia, the minority NDP government elected in 2017 promised to "use every tool in the toolbox" to block the expansion of Kinder-Morgen's TransMountain Pipeline (TMX). And for three years, they succeeded. As the new owners of TMX, it would have been reasonable for the Trudeau government to take action to end this obstruction, either through overriding legislation or by cutting off discretionary funds to B.C. until they cooperated. But the Trudeau government did neither. With the 2019 election on the horizon—and their seventeen seats in B.C. up for grabs—the Liberals did nothing to pressure the minority NDP government for its unconstitutional behaviour. Finally, in February 2020, the Supreme Court declared the B.C. obstruction unconstitutional. But in terms of investor confidence (see below), the damage had been done.

Similarly, Quebec effectively killed TransCanada Pipeline's proposed Energy East project with an assist from the Trudeau government. Energy East would have carried 1.1 million barrels of oil a day from Alberta and Saskatchewan to refineries in Eastern Canada and an export marine terminal in St. John, New Brunswick. Given the federal government's exclusive jurisdiction, Quebec's opposition was legally irrelevant. But politically, it was very relevant.

In the 2015 election, Justin Trudeau's Liberals had won forty seats in Quebec, and keeping these seats was critical to winning another majority government in the upcoming 2019 election. So when the National Energy Board (NEB) retroactively added an additional test—indirect "downstream CO_2 emissions"—half-way through the approval process for Energy East, it seemed like more than a coincidence. This was a policy promise made by the Trudeau Liberals in the 2015 Federal election.

For TransCanada, the additional test was the last straw. Having already spent a billion dollars and being frustrated by delays caused by the Quebec government, they abandoned the entire project. Then-Montreal mayor Denis Coderre publicly celebrated the demise of Energy East.[ix] Ottawa's official response was that changing "market conditions" had caused the cancellation. Writing in the *Globe and Mail*, Professor Donald Savoie had a different explanation:

> Politics, not market conditions, killed the Energy East pipeline.... Atlantic Canadians have learned that when Ottawa speaks about national unity, it speaks, in reality, to Quebec's place in the federation and that national unity are code words for the economic interests of Ontario and Quebec.[x]

The politics that killed Energy East and delayed other new export pipelines do not stop at the border. The campaign to land-lock Western Canadian oil has been well-financed by a coalition of U.S. foundations and climate change activists. Working with their Canadian counterparts, they have helped to fund and organize non-stop legal challenges that have blocked or delayed new pipelines.[xi]

In 2008, the Rockefeller Brothers Fund organized a meeting of a network of leading U.S. and Canadian non-governmental organizations (NGOs) to launch what they called "The Tar Sands Campaign." The top priority of this campaign was to "stop/limit pipelines and refinery expansion." It was to be a "coordinated campaign" with an annual budget of $7 million provided by the Rockefeller Brothers Fund and the Hewlett Foundation. American NGO participants included the Sierra Club, Green Peace, Indigenous Environmental Network, World Wildlife Fund, Natural Resources Defense Council. Canadian participants included Forest Ethics and the Pembina Institute.

Their objective is hardly a secret. Bill McKibbon is the founder of 350. org, one of the largest and best-funded climate change NGOs in the U.S. In a 2017 interview with CBC's Power and Politics, he was asked: "What common ground might you be able to find with the Alberta government?" His answer was blunt:

At this point, a common ground can't be found.... The only thing we can do is keep as much carbon in the ground as possible.... Canada, a rich country, needs to keep that carbon safely underground.[xii]

This position is echoed by McKibbon's Canadian allies, such as David Suzuki. In 2017, Suzuki, whose foundation has received substantial U.S. funding over the years,[xiii] told an Alberta audience:

I'm sorry Alberta, but we have to keep that fuel in the ground.... The tar sands have to be shut down.... No more infrastructure getting that stuff out—that means rails, pipelines, shipping. There's no point in investing in infrastructure when they're all going to be shut down.

Since 2008, the campaign to land-lock Western Canadian oil and gas has expanded greatly. The recent campaign to block Coastal Gas Link (#shutdowncanada) was supported by a number of Canadian NGOs that were receiving funding from U.S. foundations. These included Dogwood B.C. ($490,467); Sierra Club of B.C. ($641,048); West Coast Environmental Law ($2,678,460); Western Canada Wilderness Committee ($32,500); LeadNow ($59,041); Stand.Earth ($316,795). These funds are used to pay NGO staff, cover the costs of litigation, and organize public protests.[xiv]

LeadNow has gone further and tried to influence the outcome of the last two federal elections. In 2015, it ran a voter identification campaign to identify which parties had the best chance to beat Conservative incumbents in twenty-nine swing ridings. Their recommended candidates, Liberal, NDP and Green, defeated the Conservative incumbents in twenty-four of these ridings.[xv] This helped the Trudeau Liberals achieve and pass the 170 MP threshold required for a majority government by seventeen seats. In 2019 it ran a similar campaign focused just on metro-Vancouver.[xvi]

This type of foreign interference in domestic Canadian politics and elections is unprecedented, but the Trudeau Liberals have turned a blind-eye to this out of electoral self-interest. It has contributed both directly and

indirectly to their election victories in 2015 and 2019. It also explains why the
their anti-pipeline policies have catered to the climate change constituencies
in Ontario, Quebec and the lower mainland in British Columbia.

For Alberta, the results have been an economic disaster. There has been
a $100 billion dollar exodus of capital investment from the oil and gas sec-
tor since 2015. In the early 2000s, foreign capital investment poured into
Alberta. Conoco-Phillips, Marathon, Apache, and Chevron all made major
new investments in their existing operations. New investors included Shell
from the United Kingdom; Total from France; Statoil from Norway; BP and
Centrica from England, and a host of smaller companies from Korea, China,
and Japan. Today they are almost all gone. Half of the exodus of capital
since 2015—$50 billion—has been foreign money. Add the equity sell-off
of Canadian oil and gas companies, and the loss soars past $100 billion.

Capital Flight from Western Canada

Seller	Buyer	Price
Statoil [Norway]	CNRL	$7.25 billion
Total [France]	Suncor	$310 million
Shell [Anglo-Dutch]	CNRL	$17.7 billion
Marathon [US]	CNRL	$1.25 billion
Conoco-Phillips [US]	Cenovus	$10.6 billion
Apache [US]	Cardinal	$330 million
Centrica PLC [UK]	Maple Felix	$722 million
Chevron[US]	Parkland	$1.1 billion

This economic collapse has been driven by policy, not oil prices. South of
the border, business was booming in oil and gas producing states like Texas
and North Dakota. From 2014 to 2019, capital expenditure in Canada's
energy sector declined from $80 billion to $35 billion. In the U.S., capital
expenditure grew by 38 percent. (See Ogle, chapter 9). While Alberta used
to rank near the top in terms of energy sector competitiveness, it recently

ranked sixteenth in a survey of twenty North American states and provinces. The problem: regulatory uncertainty, lack of pipeline access, and taxes. Lack of access to global markets and global prices has driven the discount on Canadian oil exports to new highs, costing producers $30 billion a year—yet another reason for investors to leave Western Canada.

This explains why even Canadian energy companies are bailing out of Canada. TransCanada Pipeline has purged "Canada" from its new name—TC Energy—and is re-allocating its investments to Texas and Mexico. After losing $1 billion on Energy East, it paid $10.2 (U.S.) billion to acquire Columbia Pipeline Group, an American gas pipeline system. EnCana, which began as Alberta Energy Company and grew to the highest-valued Canadian-owned energy company in the world, has changed its name to Oventa and slinked away to Denver. Canadian-owned service companies, those that have survived, have done so by moving more of their operations to the states.

In summary, the campaign to landlock Western Canadian oil and gas is succeeding. A decade and half of pipeline politics has destroyed investor confidence and driven out capital investment. Again, this economic collapse has been driven primarily by policies, not price. Some policies are direct, such as the Liberals' climate change policies enacted since 2015. Others are indirect but equally devastating: the Liberals' abdication of responsibility of pipeline policy to the courts; their passive response to obstruction of pipelines by B.C. and Quebec; and their continued toleration of unprecedented foreign interference in Canadian policy and politics.

For Trudeau and the Liberal party, this has helped them win elections in 2015 and 2019. But it has put Alberta into an economic death spiral. Twenty years ago, everyone wanted to be in Alberta. Today, nobody does, not even our own companies.

The erosion of provincial rights under the Charter

Nobody understood the centralist/federal bias of the Supreme Court of Canada better than Peter Lougheed. After becoming Premier in 1971,

Lougheed witnessed how Pierre Trudeau disregarded established conventions to appoint a well-known advocate of broader federal powers, Bora Laskin, as chief justice in 1973. Subsequently, the Laskin-led court struck down a series of provincial statutes dealing with the development of oil and potash, areas of law previously thought to be well within provincial jurisdiction.[xvii]

So, in 1980, when Prime Minister Trudeau insisted that the proposed new Charter of Rights and Freedoms would apply to provincial as well as federal laws, Lougheed said no. (The 1969 Canadian Bill of Rights applied only to federal laws.) He rallied support from other premiers who shared his suspicion that the Supreme Court would use the Charter to second-guess policy decisions that had historically been the sole responsibility of each province. Together, the "Gang of Eight" premiers forced Trudeau to accept the Section 33 notwithstanding power in return for their support for his Charter of Rights.[xviii] Simply put, if the Supreme Court strikes down a provincial law as a violation of the Charter, Section 33 allows a provincial government to re-instate the law by adding a clause that it shall still be in effect "notwithstanding" the Court's ruling.

Lougheed explained why he had included a notwithstanding power in in the 1972 Alberta Bill of Rights. Judges are not infallible, and the notwithstanding power serves as a check on judicial misinterpretation of rights. It also ensures that elected governments, not unaccountable judges, have the final say with respect to public policies. At the time, it was hailed as a sensible compromise between the British model of parliamentary supremacy and the American practice of judicial supremacy. From Lougheed's perspective, it was also a constitutional guarantee that Albertans would continue to be governed by accountable governments in Edmonton and not unelected judges in Ottawa.

Forty years later, the notwithstanding power is in disrepute and disuse. The national media cited its extensive use by the Quebec government during the 1980s to stigmatize it as a way that governments can violate Canadians' rights. It is no longer seen as a prudent check on judicial fallibility. And, as Lougheed feared, the adoption of the Charter has opened the floodgates to a wave of judicial policy-making unprecedented in Canada's history.

In the years leading up to the adoption of the Charter of Rights, the Supreme Court of Canada was accurately described as "the quiet court in the unquiet country."[xix] Forty years later, the court was given the dubious distinction of being named "Policy Maker of the Year" by the Macdonald-Laurier Institute.[xx] In the preceding twelve months, the court had blocked five major policy reforms that the Harper-led Conservative Party had promised in its electoral platforms.[xxi] The court's Charter impact on provincial legislation has been even greater.[xxii] Canada's experience is consistent with what has happened in other federal states. Final national courts of appeal tend to "serve upper class and nationalizing interests rather than dominant local interests and thus [are] more satisfactory to persons trying to break through the web of local interests."[xxiii] Translation: they overrule provincial policies that central Canadian elites don't like.

Ottawa augmented the centralizing impact of the Charter by creating the Court Challenges Program (CCP). The CCP pays the legal costs of individuals and groups challenging laws they believe violate their Charter rights. Almost all cases funded by the CCP have been Charter challenges to provincial laws.[xxiv] In equality rights litigation, most of the groups that have received funding have been partisans of the identity politics of the progressive left. This explains why Stephen Harper's Conservative government cancelled the CCP and Justin Trudeau's Liberal government restored it.[xxv]

This federal funding of interest-group litigation against recalcitrant provincial governments allows Ottawa to do indirectly what it lacks the jurisdiction to achieve directly, except through the now discredited federal powers of reservation and disallowance.[xxvi] Indeed, one of the great ironies of contemporary Canadian history is that just when it became politically unacceptable for the federal government to use its legal power to disallow provincial laws, it was able to achieve the same results by moving this policy veto from cabinet to the Supreme Court and dressing it up as a legal issue.

Until more premiers have the courage of their convictions and are willing use Section 33, the very principles that Alberta fought so hard to protect in 1981—regional diversity, provincial rights and "responsible government"— will continue to be eroded.

Bilingualism: Ideology of the New Class

When Pierre Trudeau introduced official bilingualism in the civil service, it was sold as a language proficiency test. In practice, it has meant much more. As Pierre Trudeau's biographer Richard Gwyn observed in 1981, "Bilingualism in truth was nothing less than a social revolution.... [but] no one in authority in Ottawa in the late 1960s... let on that massive change was about to happen."[xxvii] Gwyn understood that bilingualism was not just about language, but an ideology and a new mission statement for the federal government.

Its immediate effect has been to benefit the sixteen percent of Canadians who are bilingual, two-thirds of them francophones and nearly all from central Canada.[xxviii]

Indeed, Canada has the most centralized civil service of all the English-speaking democracies. Over forty percent live in or near Ottawa. Forty-five years ago, before official bilingualism, it was only about 25 percent.[xxix]

Geography is only half the story. Official bilingualism has enhanced the influence of small and unrepresentative demographic groups of Canadians: Francophones, Anglophones who chose to remain in Quebec (a small minority), and the more educated, upper-middle-classes of Ontario. Not coincidentally, each of these groups is shrinking as a proportion of Canada's increasingly diverse and increasingly western population. As Peter Brimelow observed, this "accentuates its isolation and its distinct tendency to believe, like the Prussian army, that it is the supreme repository of national values." In the endless government hallways of Ottawa-Gatineau, "unilinguals are second-class citizens."[xxx]

The larger the government becomes, the more influential the governmental elites become. This trend is found in all modern welfare states. As the state grows, so too does the permanent bureaucracy. This "new class" is powerful because it has what elected politicians don't have: job security and policy expertise. This is the new "permanent government" that is eroding democratic accountability in all contemporary welfare states. Predictably, "it invents policies that advantage itself and its clients."[xxxi]

Since the adoption of official bilingualism, the size and scope of the federal government has expanded from a budget of $15 billion in 1970 to over $355 billion today.[xxxii] Over this same time period, the size the civil service has increased 50 per cent, from just under 200,000 in 1970 to 290,000 today. Almost half, or 43 per cent, are designated as bilingual.[xxxiii] At the senior levels, this figure is higher, but not available to the public.

Bilingualism is about more than just proficiency in French and geography. It entrenches the belief that a central priority of the federal government is to pre-empt the separatist threat by making Quebeckers "feel wanted." Civil servants who survive the government's multi-year bilingualism training program emerge with this deeply entrenched belief.

This means that the bureaucracy's advice to cabinet ministers as well as administrative decisions are made through an ideological lens that prioritizes national unity, and national unity is understood as keeping Quebeckers happy. The concerns of Western Canada (and Atlantic Canada) are decidedly secondary. As Donald Savoie observes: "The votes for winning power in Ottawa are in Ontario and Quebec, the senior bureaucracy straddles the Ontario-Quebec border, and the national media speak from these two provinces."[xxxiv] In other words, official bilingualism was never just about language. It was, and is, about the ideology of Quebec-centric national unity and its promotion by a powerful and permanent bureaucracy.

Equalization and Transfers: then and now

Since 1961, the net dollar value of federal transfers out of Alberta has been $630 billion. Over the same time period, the net dollar value of federal transfers into Quebec was a positive gain of $497 billion (see Mansell, chapter 6). Except for Pierre Trudeau's 1980 National Energy Policy (NEP), this disparity was annoying but tolerable for most Albertans. (The NEP, the single largest transfer in Canadian history, resulted in a net transfer of $70 billion out of Alberta, mostly to Quebec and Ontario.) Over these five decades, thanks to the development of the oil and gas industries, Alberta evolved from one of Canada's poorest provinces to by far the wealthiest. Its population increased from less than one million to over four million. Except for the

1980s, its government not only had balanced budgets, but also saved over $16 billion from energy royalties in the Heritage Savings Trust Fund. In this environment, the federal government's enthusiasm for spreading Alberta's wealth around to other provinces, particularly Quebec, was largely tolerable.

All this changed in the past decade. Since 2010, the average net outflow from Alberta to Ottawa has been $20 billion *a year*. This computes to $21,600 annually for a family of four. In this same time frame, oil and gas prices dropped significantly, and Alberta ran up ten deficit budgets under both PC and NDP governments. By 2019, Alberta's total debt was projected to hit $90 billion. And this was before the 2020 catastrophe of the Covid-19 pandemic and the Saudi-Russian oil price war, which may turn the Alberta government's projected deficit for 2020 from $6.8 billion to $20 billion.

Meanwhile, Quebec has continued to see its share of equalization dollars increase from less than $3 billion a year in the early 1980s to over $13 billion a year today, or 66 cents of every equalization dollar Ottawa sends out. In 2019, while Alberta ran an $8.7 billion deficit, Quebec posted a $4-billion budget surplus. Quebec's surplus was made possible by the $13 billion in federally-mandated equalization payments, much of it from Alberta. The obvious unfairness of this treatment prompted Thomas Courchene, one of Canada's leading authorities on fiscal federalism, to write a study entitled "Fiscal Fairness: How Equalization failed Alberta in its time of need," declaring that this double-standard "left many Canadians dumbfounded."[xxxv]

Quebec's 2019 payment was a turning point. In a twenty-four-hour period, Quebec Premier Francois Legault declared, "There is no social acceptability for a pipeline that would pass through Quebec territory." The very next day, Finance Minister Bill Morneau announced a $1.4 billion equalization increase over Quebec's 2018 payment.[xxxvi] The timing of Quebec's equalization boost did not seem like a coincidence. The next election was only eleven months away, and the Liberals needed to win their forty seats in Quebec to keep their majority government. The Liberals' $1.4 billion boost to Quebec's equalization cheque looked a lot like a political bribe. It also followed the cancellation of proposed Energy East pipeline, largely because of opposition from Quebec.

Without new oil pipeline access to global markets and global prices, how were Alberta and Saskatchewan expected to continue to carry their disproportionate share of equalization payments? It seemed like Quebec was killing the goose that lays the golden eggs, and then getting rewarded for it. The message seemed to be: we are happy to take your dirty money, but not your dirty oil.[xxxvii]

How are we to understand this double standard? Conrad Black has bluntly called it "vote-buying by trying to move resources to people and not the other way around."[xxxviii] A more diplomatic but still succinct explanation is provided by the most recent, full-length book on equalization: "[E]xecutive discretion has remained the defining principle for governing equalization in Canada. As a result, equalization is never far away from partisan politics."[xxxix]

> Equalization has most likely helped federalists in Quebec make the case against independence.... The economic arguments in favour of Quebec remaining part of Canada have often featured reference, sometimes explicit and other times implicit, to the equalization program as important to the financing of the province's social programs.[xl]

This should hardly be a surprise. For the post-war generation, the "Quebec issue" has been explicit or implicit in almost every federal election and policy dispute. From supply management (dairy, eggs and chickens) to official bilingualism to Meech/Charlottetown ("the Quebec round") to aerospace (Bombardier) and now climate change, appeasing Quebec has always been the fourth dimension of federal politics. With respect to equalization, the price keeps going up, especially for Albertans.

The Rise and Fall of Senate Reform

In the 1980s, Preston Manning helped to form and then lead the new Reform Party. Senate reform was one of their key policy pillars. It embodied the Reform battle-cry, "The West wants in!" A "Triple E" Senate (Equal,

Elected and Effective) was intended to end the under-representation of Western Canadian interests by giving each province an equal number of senators. This would give the four Western provinces 40 per cent of the seats in a reformed Senate.[xli] Currently, each of the Western provinces has six senators, while Ontario and Quebec each have twenty-four.

Initially progress came quickly. In 1987, Alberta held Canada's first ever senatorial advisory election. The Reform Party candidate, Stan Waters, won and was appointed to the Senate by Prime Minister Brian Mulroney in 1990, another Canadian first. That same year the Mulroney government included Senate reform as part of its package of constitutional reforms known as the Charlottetown Accord. After Charlottetown failed, Alberta held another Senate election in 1998, won by Reform Party candidates Bert Brown and myself. But Liberal Prime Minister Jean Chrétien, still reeling from almost losing Quebec's 1995 separation referendum, had no interest in making concessions to Alberta. When an Alberta Senate seat opened just weeks before the scheduled 1998 election, Chrétien tried to pre-empt the election by appointing Doug Roche. Subsequently Chretien ignored the results of the election and appointed two more Liberals to the Senate from Alberta.

In 2004, Brown ran again in Alberta's third senate election, and this time was appointed to the Senate in 2007 by the newly elected Conservative Prime Minister Stephen Harper. Harper began his political career as a Reform Party MP from Alberta and strongly supported Senate reform. He subsequently appointed three more winners of Alberta Senate elections: Betty Unger in 2012; and Doug Black and Scott Tannis in 2013.

Harper also attempted to give the Senate reform movement a more formal legal foundation. He referred to the Supreme Court the questions of whether the government of Canada could pass legislation with regards to advisory or consultative elections (such as Alberta's), term limits, and abolition. Harper's proposed legislation would neither force provinces to hold Senate elections, nor would it require prime ministers to appoint the winners of such elections. It would have simply created a formal process for provinces and prime ministers that chose to use it. But even this modest reform was too much for the Supreme Court.

The court ruled that any legal changes to the selection of senators such as consultative elections could only be done through a formal constitutional amendment requiring the unanimous consent of all ten provinces. This is a virtual impossibility. No Quebec government would ever agree, even if the nine other provinces did. Why would Quebec consent to a constitutional reform that would alter a status quo that systematically privileges and promotes its interests? The Supreme Court's decision effectively killed any prospects for either reforming or abolishing the Senate. Rather than facilitating the reform of an institution that has ceased to serve any political purpose (other than patronage), the court's ruling unnecessarily condemns Canadians to endure this dysfunctional second chamber for at least another generation.[xlii]

Twenty-four years ago, the upstart Reform Party had become the official opposition in the House of Commons. Fourteen years ago, a new prime minister from Alberta began appointing the winners of Alberta's Senate elections. Reform's flagship policy of a Triple E Senate seemed within reach. Today, it is only a distant memory.

Conclusion

In the eight policy areas reviewed above, Alberta is worse off today than we were in 1980. Despite the considerable efforts of such exceptional leaders as Peter Lougheed, Preston Manning, Ralph Klein, Stephen Harper and others, we are now more vulnerable to predatory fiscal policies from Ottawa than we were thirty years ago. The strategies pursued by my generation of political leaders and activists have not improved Alberta's position within confederation. There now is no reason to expect they ever will. It would be a disservice to the next generation to encourage them to pursue the same strategies that we have. Fool me once, shame on you. Fool me twice, shame on me.

If Quebec was treated as Alberta has been treated, it would have separated long ago. And if Albertans had the opportunity to re-negotiate the terms of our relationship with Canada, we would never consent to the status quo. This does not mean Alberta (or Western Canada) should secede from Canada. But it does mean making the rest of Canada understand that for Alberta and, really, all of Western Canada, the status quo is unacceptable. There is a lot of room for constitutional reforms between these two extremes, room to strike a new balance, a fair balance, for Alberta and Western Canada.

This will require bolder, more effective strategies. In politics, the beneficiaries of the status quo never willingly give up their advantages. Change requires push. And it will be up to the next generation of Alberta leaders to force the rest of Canada to see that such reforms are preferable to the alternative. On this note, it is worth recalling a similar warning by a scholar from the other end of Canada:[xliii]

> We need to rethink Canada's institutional arrangements so that we have a two-way mirror that reflects the economic interests of Western and Atlantic Canada, not just Quebec and Ontario.... The Atlantic region does not have the political or economic clout to do something about extending the national unity debate beyond Quebec's interest. The same does not apply, however, for Western Canada, and policymakers in Ottawa should take note before it is too late.

Voters in Ontario and Quebec must be brought to understand Peter Lougheed's oft repeated challenge: A strong Alberta makes for a strong Canada.

Alberta and the myth of Sisyphus
Tom Flanagan

Introduction

I N GREEK mythology, Sisyphus was a legendary king with a knack for cheating death. When he was killed by lesser gods or heroes, he would find ways to escape from Hades. Zeus finally grew tired of his games and sentenced him to roll a rock uphill for all eternity. Just as Sisyphus would reach the top of the hill, the rock would roll down and he would have to start over.

The fate of Sisyphus is an apt metaphor for the position of Alberta in Canada. Ever since confederation, Albertans, and before them residents of the North-West Territories, have made use of many political strategies while attempting to vindicate their rights to land and resources. This chapter looks at some of these strategies in detail, picking out the highlights from a century and a half of conflict. I treat these strategies separately for clarity of explanation, but in reality they have always been used in combination.

Two types of strategies are grounded in conventional politics: (1) attempts to establish constitutional protection for western public lands and natural resources; (2) attempts to gain leverage through the system of political parties and Members of Parliament. These two approaches are part and parcel of Canadian politics and are recorded in detail in standard works of Canadian history and political science. Less conventional strategies include: (3) using provincial referendums to demand constitutional change; (4) threatening to pull out of pan-Canadian programs, making them more beneficial for Alberta while reducing Alberta's subsidy to the rest of Canada; and (5) reducing or cutting off oil shipments. The latter two involve some degree of coercion by imposing costs on the rest of Canada. Political strategies based on threats of harm are distasteful, but they will have to be considered if all conventional attempts at securing Alberta's natural resources continue to be rebuffed. Moreover, Canadian energy policies supported by voting majorities have repeatedly imposed much larger costs on Albertans in terms of income losses, unemployment and bankruptcies than anything Alberta can impose upon Canada, so Albertans needn't feel guilty about playing tit for tat.

Historical sketch

Alberta's Sisyphean destiny began with the purchase by Canada of Rupert's Land in 1869.[i] Canada paid the Hudson's Bay Company £300,000 pounds sterling ($1.5 million U.S. in 1869 values). It was a bargain by any standard. In 1867, the United States had paid Russia $7.2 million for Alaska, a territory smaller and less valuable than Rupert's Land. But Canada had only a tenth of the population of the United States, so Canadians had to carry a greater proportional burden, and they were determined to get their money's worth.

The plan was to admit Rupert's Land to confederation as a territory, to be administered for the "purposes of the Dominion,"[ii] which meant constructing railways *a mari usque ad mare* and filling up the land with settlers. But the plan hit a snag almost immediately because Canada had not stopped to consider that there was a civilized community already present in the Red River Colony. It included a small white element descended from the Selkirk Settlers, plus missionaries, merchants, and adventurers from Ontario, Quebec, and the United States. Far more numerous, however, were the mixed-race Métis, or half-breeds as they were then known, both English- and French-speaking. Although descended in part from Indians, these mixed-race people had largely adopted the practices of western civilization.

They went on long buffalo hunts, but they also farmed and built homes on private property. They were familiar with money, contracts, and loans. There were several churches and schools at Red River. Literacy was not universal, but those who could not read and write could get help from those who could. Red River was a world apart from the Indian tribes of the West and north who still followed their traditional migratory life of hunting, fishing, and trapping.

When Canada did not consult Red River about purchasing Rupert's Land, the young firebrand Louis Riel set up a provisional government and demanded negotiations. The Canadian position was weak because there was no military presence in Red River and American annexation was a concern. Riel's most prominent demand was entry of Rupert's Land into confederation as a province with control over public lands and natural resources, as enjoyed by the four founding provinces. That would have turned over the vast territory of Rupert's Land to the political control of 10,000 people living at Red River, which from the Canadian point of view would have meant the loss of the £300,000 purchase price and the associated dream of a transcontinental nation.

In the event, Riel sent delegates to Ottawa and a compromise was reached. The "postage stamp province" of Manitoba was created, but even that tiny entity would not have ownership of its public lands and natural resources. The rest of Rupert's Land would be a territory under federal control. To sweeten the deal, the Manitoba Act provided for 1.4 million acres of land in Manitoba that the federal government would distribute to "the children of the half-breed heads of families."[iii]

The consequences of this compromise have bedeviled the politics of Western Canada ever since. Without control of public lands and natural resources, Manitoba and the North-West Territories were largely dependent on Canadian subsidies for revenue. Political relations were poisoned by the endless demands from the West for "better terms." Such demands were staunchly opposed by the old provinces, who had paid for Rupert's Land and wanted to get their money's worth.

Louis Riel entered the picture again in 1884, when he sent a petition to the federal cabinet asking *inter alia* that the North-West Territories be reorganized as a province with control of natural resources.[iv] When the cabinet granted some of the requests but stayed completely away from provincial status and other far-reaching demands, Riel's radical side took over and he ended up declaring a provisional government and independence from Canada. Ottawa crushed the rebellion with military force, marking the failure of separatism as a political tactic.

In the following years the leading politician in the Western territories, Frederick Haultain, kept up a peaceful agitation for better financial treatment as well as provincial status. The latter was finally granted in 1905 to the two provinces of Alberta and Saskatchewan, not to the one big province of Buffalo that Haultain had wanted to create, but Ottawa retained ownership of public lands and natural resources. The federal government still wanted to control immigration and to be able to make land grants to finance construction of railways. Thus the two new provinces, like Manitoba, remained heavily dependent on federal subsidies.

It took another twenty-five years for the ownership of natural resources to be transferred to the three prairie provinces. After a seemingly endless round of first ministers meetings, ministerial negotiations, parliamentary debates, court cases, and three royal commissions, the transfer was finally completed in 1930 with legislative approval of the Natural Resources Transfer Agreements negotiated with the provinces. As always, the sticking point had been money. The Western provinces wanted compensation for the alienation of their public lands since 1870, plus continuation of subsidies, while the other provinces balked at the cost. The intricate financial issues were finally sorted out by a series of three royal commissions headed by Justice W.F.A. Turgeon of the Saskatchewan Court of Appeal.[v]

Apart from money, an episode about schools illustrated the second-class status of Alberta compared to Quebec. After Prime Minister Mackenzie King and Alberta Premier Brownlee had negotiated a settlement in 1925, King added a new rider to the agreement when it was introduced in the House of Commons. At the behest of Justice Minister Ernest Lapointe, who said it was necessary to appease Catholic voters in Quebec, King unilaterally added a clause specifying that schools land funds had to be used to support separate schools, under s. 17 of the Alberta Act. When Brownlee demurred at what he saw as an intrusion into provincial jurisdiction, King referred the matter to the Supreme Court of Canada. When he won there, he appealed to the Judicial Committee of the Privy Council, which refused to hear the case on grounds that it was the wrong appellant. Caught between Quebec and Alberta, King was playing for time until compromise wording could be arrived at, which eventually took place in 1929. Alberta was required to administer school lands and funds "in accordance with the laws of the Province, but in keeping with the letter and spirit of the constitution."[vi] The episode could be considered comic except that it delayed the transfer of natural resources by about three years, a tribute to the influence of Quebec over the newer provinces.

As a matter of constitutional law, Alberta, Saskatchewan, and Manitoba were finally on an equal footing with the other Canadian provinces with respect to public lands and natural resources, but old beliefs die hard. Federal politicians, supported by public opinion in central Canada, continued to think they could dispose of the resources of the Western provinces in ways they would never have attempted elsewhere. This became obvious for Alberta when, after the Yom Kippur War of 1973, OPEC drove up the international price of oil. For more than a decade, Ottawa reacted with a series of price controls, export taxes, and expropriations, all designed to keep the price of oil lower for consumers—i.e., voters—in the eastern provinces; siphon off a much greater share of the economic rents for the federal government; and prevent Alberta from becoming too rich. As federal Energy Minister Marc Lalonde later said, the motive was "to transfer wealth from Alberta to central Canada."[vii] That series of ad hoc measures was formalized in the National Energy Program announced after the Liberals were re-elected in 1980. Alberta fought these measures with every weapon at its disposal, even reducing the volume of oil shipments to the rest of Canada in 1981. Later that year, a truce was reached, with a pricing regime to split the economic rents among Ottawa, Alberta, and the industry.

Alberta and the industry were not happy at the way Ottawa had appropriated so much revenue from oil and gas, but it seemed to be the best agreement that could be obtained at the time. Then the election of the Progressive Conservatives in 1984 led to the repeal of the National Energy Program in its entirety in 1986. It had in any case become unaffordable for Ottawa because of falling international prices, which meant that imported oil had to be subsidized by Canada. The whole NEP had been premised on high and rising prices, so it became a loser for Ottawa when international prices fell.

It seemed for a generation that Alberta had vindicated its control over its natural resources, but the rock of Sisyphus rolled down again in the 2010s. As detailed in other chapters, Alberta's oil has been blockaded through a combination of actions taken in the name of climate-change environmentalism by the federal government; by other provinces, especially British Columbia and Quebec; and by some (not all) First Nations. This second National Energy Program is different from the first; it seeks not to transfer Alberta's wealth to other governments but to reduce Alberta's use of its hydrocarbon resources to generate wealth, even if it also reduces incomes and wealth in other provinces. But it is similar in that it was calculated to appeal to voters in Ontario and Quebec for whom climate change was a priority issue. And it worked. It's not a coincidence that in 2015 Justin Trudeau was the first Liberal leader to win a majority of seats from Quebec since his father did in 1980.

The long-term strategy of the climate alarmists is to cap the size of Alberta's oil industry by preventing the construction of new pipelines, then gradually euthanize the industry as alternative sources of energy become available. The link with the past is that, despite constitutional guarantees, federal politicians as well as those in other provinces still see western resources as subservient to "the purposes of the Dominion." They feel free to dispose of these resources in ways that they would never attempt for a natural resource such as hydroelectricity in Quebec.

Having looked briefly at the history, let us now turn to the strategies that Albertans have used in the past and may use in the future in attempting to protect their natural resources.

The Constitutional Mirage

Louis Riel pursued constitutional change by sending emissaries in 1870 to negotiate the terms by which Rupert's Land would enter confederation. The result was the Manitoba Act, 1870, which was given constitutional status by British legislation the following year.[viii] The victory was real but meagre: provincial status for an under-sized Manitoba without control of public lands and natural resources. Riel tried to address some defects of that arrangement in a new petition of rights in 1884, but that did not go anywhere. Ottawa was not interested in a new deal, and Riel by that time was so caught up in his own religious psychodrama that he could not effectively pursue conventional politics.[ix]

The three prairie provinces received their public lands and natural resources in 1930 through the Natural Resources Transfer Agreements, which became part of the constitution of Canada. That did not yield much wealth in the short run because of the Great Depression, but it did become a source of wealth for Alberta after World War II, with the discovery of a major oil field at Leduc in 1947. It took about a generation for Alberta's new wealth to become a target of political spoliation by voting majorities in eastern Canada, culminating in the National Energy Program of 1980.

Among many responses, Alberta Premier Peter Lougheed essayed a form of political jujitsu, trying to divert Pierre Trudeau's campaign for constitutional change, which originally had nothing to do with natural resources, for Alberta's own purposes. Lougheed would not sign on to Trudeau's package of amendments, including the Canadian Charter of Rights and Freedoms, until it included two measures designed to protect Alberta's jurisdiction over its natural resources.

First was insertion of the word "existing" in section 35(1) of the Constitution Act, 1982: "The existing aboriginal and treaty rights of the aboriginal peoples of Canada are hereby recognized and affirmed." "Aboriginal rights" at the time were a black box whose contents were largely unknown. By insertion of the word "existing," Lougheed hoped to curb the future discretion of judges to discover or invent hitherto unknown aboriginal rights that might affect Alberta's control of public lands and natural resources. In fact, however, the word "existing" has not limited the ingenuity of the courts. Since 1982, judges, led by the Supreme Court of Canada, have simply ignored the clear framers' intent.

The most fateful development for Alberta's resources was the creation of the "duty to consult and accommodate" in the Haida Nation and Mikisew Cree cases, based on s. 35 Aboriginal rights interpreted according to the nebulous doctrine of the "honour of the Crown." Neither of these two concepts is in the text of section 35 of the Constitution Act, 1982. After these decisions, all natural resource development projects had to be negotiated with nearby First Nations. The requirement is particularly onerous for long corridor projects, such as pipelines, which may cross the "traditional territories" of dozens of First Nations. The Supreme Court has repeatedly said that the right to be consulted is not a veto power, but in practice the distinction is often moot, because protracted consultations accompanied by court challenges can impose delays that amount to a veto.[x]

First Nations in British Columbia won a decision in the Federal Court of Canada that there had been inadequate consultation for the Northern Gateway pipeline, even though the National Energy Board and the federal cabinet had already approved it. The resulting delays allowed the political climate to shift with election in 2015 of a Liberal government, which proceeded to kill the whole project by forbidding tankers to load more than 12,500 metric tons of crude oil or bitumen off the northern coast of British Columbia.[xi] The Trans Mountain Expansion (TMX) of an existing pipeline to Vancouver was also delayed by legal challenges over aboriginal consultation to the point where its owner, Kinder Morgan, announced that it was going to abandon the project. The Trudeau government, which in this one case was favourable to construction, had to buy the pipeline from Kinder Morgan for $4.5 billion. (TMX may actually be built because the prime minister has repeatedly declared his intention to see it through, and the Federal Court of Appeal handed down a favourable decision about Indigenous consultation on February 4, 2020.)[xii]

These maneuvers, combined with legal problems in the United States over

Keystone XL (TransCanada) and Line 3 (Enbridge), which Canada's federal government did nothing to protest, have created a severe blockage of Alberta's petroleum exports, particularly to markets outside the United States. For several years now, Alberta's capacity to produce oil has exceeded its ability to export it from the province by pipeline and rail. The result has been deeply discounted prices for producers—to over $40 (U.S.) below the American price in fall 2018. Prices began to recover only when Alberta imposed a rationing scheme to curtail production. Predictably, investors have stampeded for the exits, and many of those who are left are facing bankruptcy if export capacity is not enlarged. This is precisely what climate alarmists have hoped to achieve ever since the Rockefeller Foundation kicked off its so-called anti-tar sands campaign in 2008.[xiii] By funneling money and legal advice to First Nations who oppose development, environmentalists have frustrated the constitutional victory that Alberta appeared to have won in 1982.

Lougheed's other victory in 1982 was insertion of s. 50 into the Constitution Act, 1982, to confirm provincial control over the "exploration for" and "development, conservation, and management of" non-renewable natural resources. This was reinforced the same year by Alberta's victory in the Supreme Court of Canada, which held that the federal government could not levy a direct tax on natural gas because s. 125 of the Constitution Act, 1867 prohibits one level of government from taxing the property of another level of government.[xiv]

Notably, this victory was won through use of the provincial government's ability to refer cases to the Alberta Court of Appeal, which gives the province an expedited means to fight constitutional battles in the courts. Alberta is now using the reference procedure to fight the federal carbon tax (discussed below). However, it has used the reference procedure sparingly over the years, and very rarely in the field of natural resources. All the judges of the Alberta Court of Appeal and the Supreme Court of Canada are appointed by the federal cabinet, so a sympathetic reception for Alberta's concerns is far from assured. Nonetheless, the reference procedure has occasionally been a useful weapon for Alberta in its ongoing struggles with the federal government.

The decision in the natural gas tax case, however, had an escape clause because it only nullified taxes levied for the purpose of raising revenue, which the court thought applied to this instance. Taxes for regulatory purposes would be permissible. This escape clause has now become highly topical because of the carbon tax introduced by the Trudeau government. Alberta and other provinces have challenged the constitutionality of the legislation through reference cases. The Saskatchewan Court of Appeal has upheld the carbon tax on grounds that it is a regulatory instrument based on the Peace, Order, and Good Government wording of the Constitution Act, 1867.[xv] The Alberta Court of Appeal, on the other hand, struck down the tax as an overreach of federal power into areas of provincial jurisdiction.[xvi] The Supreme Court of Canada will have to decide the issue, and many constitutional law experts predict the Court will upheld the tax. If so, a constitutional victory gained by Alberta will once again prove to be not as robust as originally thought.

Alberta may have nominal control of natural resources within its own boundaries, but the federal government still has jurisdiction over interprovincial trade and commerce including transportation, navigable waters, and the environment, which now includes climate change, although no one was thinking of that in 1982. Also, the federal government, which has jurisdiction over "Indians, and lands reserved for Indians," has given the courts a free hand to evolve the doctrine of consultation and accommodation. This has allowed a small number of activist First Nations, financially supported by environmental organizations both Canadian and American, to block the Northern Gateway pipeline and delay the Trans Mountain Expansion to the point where it was no longer viable as a private-sector project.

Constitutional change appears to offer certainty because the provisions of the constitution are beyond the reach of ordinary legislation or judicial decision. But the lesson of Canadian history, as far as Western resources are concerned, is that political pressure can always find a way to get around the constitution. Courts can explain rights away, and Parliament can circumvent ownership rights if it cannot go straight through them. Thus, 150 years after Louis Riel started the struggle for Western provinces to control their own public lands and natural resources, Alberta finds its resources blockaded. The great constitutional victories of 1930 and 1982 each lasted for a generation or two until outside forces succeeded in frustrating them. Constitutional amendments may be necessary, but they are obviously not sufficient to protect Alberta's resources from outside control.

Party games

Governments and voters in the West have often resorted to electoral politics in an attempt to defend their interests. Voters in Quebec did this for generations, massively supporting the Liberal Party in almost every election from 1896 through 1980, becoming in effect the keystone of Liberal power. Louis Riel probably had something similar in mind, though on a much smaller scale, when he got elected to Parliament as a Conservative from Manitoba in 1873. However, Sir John A. Macdonald wasn't interested in having such a controversial supporter and allowed the Commons to take away Riel's seat and exile him from Canada for five years.

Ever since John Diefenbaker's leadership, western voters have massively supported the Conservative Party and its successors, and sometimes received benefits for their resource economy when the Conservatives were in power. Most notably, Kim Cambell cancelled the National Energy Program, privatized Petro-Canada, and moved the National Energy Board to Calgary. Stephen Harper tried to promote pipeline construction but was voted out of office in 2015 before the job was done, leaving Northern Gateway to be cancelled by the Liberals and TMX to be harassed by a coalition of environmentalists, First Nations, and the NDP government of British Columbia.

Loyally supporting one of the traditional parties can bring benefits, particularly if that support was crucial in winning power, as western support was for Mulroney in 1984 and 1988, and in Harper's victories in 2006, 2008, and 2011. The west, however, is likely to be left on the outside looking in when that party loses power, as always happens sooner or later.

Western provincial leaders have sometimes tried to intervene in federal politics, attempting to elect a government that will be more sympathetic to western desires. The most straightforward intervention is to support one of the existing parties. Frederick Haultain pursued this course in the election of

1905, when he openly supported Robert Borden's Conservatives and opposed Wilfrid Laurier's Liberals.[xvii] Haultain had previously maintained a non-partisan posture in the politics of the North-West, but he had lost patience with Laurier's delays in giving provincial status to the Western territories.

In the event, however, the Liberals won the election, leaving Haultain to reap the whirlwind he had sown. Laurier granted provincial status to the two smaller provinces of Alberta and Saskatchewan, not the one big province of Buffalo that Haultain had desired. Moreover, Ottawa retained federal control of public lands and natural resources in the Western provinces. And, to gild the lily, Laurier set up the Liberals in a preferred position in the politics of the new provinces, appointing Liberal Lieutenant-Governors and choosing Saskatoon and Edmonton for the capital cities, away from the Conservative-leaning Canadian Pacific Railway, whose main line ran through Regina and Calgary. Haultain, who was by far the preeminent figure in western politics, was frozen out and had to wait until after Robert Borden's election in 1911 to be appointed a judge. The outcome of elections is unpredictable and intervention is not without risks. As Ralph Waldo Emerson is supposed to have said, "When you strike at the king, you must kill him."

Alberta Premier Jason Kenney emulated Haultain in the federal election of 2019, supporting Andrew Scheer's Conservatives and vociferously opposing Justin Trudeau's Liberals. Trudeau may have been wounded but he was not killed, and he emerged with a minority government. There have been no obvious reprisals against Kenney or Alberta yet, but maybe refusing to act on Alberta's requests is sufficient reprisal for him.

Another option is to challenge the traditional parties by creating a new western party. There have been three major cases of this in western history: the Progressives, Social Credit, and Reform:

- The Progressives appeared on the federal scene in the election of 1921, in which they won enough seats to become the official opposition, although they subsequently declined to play that role. Throughout the 1920s, the Progressives won enough seats to hold the balance of power between the Liberals and the Conservatives, but their lack of internal discipline impeded them from using their parliamentary votes in a consistently strategic way. Obtaining provincial control over public lands and natural resources was one of many policies in their platform. After that goal was achieved, the Progressives disintegrated, with their supporters fanning out among the traditional parties and two new parties: Social Credit and the Co-operative Commonwealth Federation (CCF)

- Social Credit became a federal party in 1935 as an offshoot of William Aberhart's provincial Social Credit League, which won power in Alberta that year. As a federal party, it remained mostly based in Alberta, in spite of a short-lived merger with William Herridge's New Democracy Party in 1940, and an uneasy alliance with Réal Caouette's Crédit Social in the 1960s. It was a symptom of western, especially Albertan, unease with Canada's traditional parties, but it did not play a major role in the struggle over natural resources that is the theme of this chapter. Social Credit seats were of some importance in the three minority governments of the 1960s, but that did not lead to any great policy victories for the party

- Preston Manning's Reform Party of Canada was founded in 1987 and won fifty-two seats in the federal election of 1993. Reaction against the National Energy Program provided much of the energy for its founding. The Triple-E Senate (equal, elected, and effective) was supposed to provide a barrier against future raids on western resources. Manning envisioned a new national party with its base in the West, but it could never overcome the limitations of its western origin. In an attempt at achieving true national reach, it morphed into the short-lived Canadian Alliance in 2000, which merged with the remnants of the Progressive Conservatives in 2003 to form the Conservative Party of Canada (CPC). Under the leadership of Stephen Harper, the CPC formed the government of Canada from 2006 to 2015. In one sense, it fulfilled Manning's vision of a new national party with its base in the West, but in the course of becoming national, it had to shed most of its distinctive policies. Harper did try hard to reform the Senate while he was in power, but he was frustrated first by the absence of a majority in the House of Commons and then by a Supreme Court decision requiring provincial consent to create an elected Senate.[xviii]

This summary of electoral history is admittedly brief, but justifies several conclusions about the West, party politics, and natural resources.

- The treatment of the West by the rest of Canada, particularly appropriation of western resource wealth, has created a long-lasting suspicion of the traditional parties, and this suspicion has repeatedly made it possible for political entrepreneurs to found major new parties based in the West

- Such new parties can win enough seats in the West, or at least in Alberta as Social Credit did, to play at times a significant role in the House of Commons, creating situations of minority government. The Western party has sometimes held the balance of power or even become the official opposition. However, no western party has ever been able to exploit such a position in the Commons to gain major concessions for the West. The closest thing to a major achievement by a western party was the transfer of public lands and natural resources in 1930. But by then the Progressives had been in Ottawa for nine years. The long delay was caused mainly by inability to get agreement from the founding provinces about financial compensation

- There are not enough seats in the West, even including British Columbia, for a western party to form a government. Thus western parties must seek allies from elsewhere in Canada, even to the point of merging with a traditional party. But after the merger, western MPs become only one element within a larger party, a situation not greatly different from, say, Brian Mulroney's Conservative government 1984-93

- The west has to face the inexorable arithmetic of Canada's population statistics. In the 2016 census, the West, including British Columbia, had a little over 31 per cent of Canada's population and slightly under 31 per cent of the seats in the House of Commons. In a contest of "the West against the rest," the West will always lose. Donald Savoie has summarized the situation succinctly: "The votes for winning power in Ottawa are in Ontario and Quebec, the senior bureaucracy straddles the Ontario-Quebec border, and the national media speak from these two provinces."[xix]

Creation of a western party may shake up the system temporarily, but ultimately, as long as the West is part of Canada, it must find allies, either within or across parties, to vindicate its interests in Parliament.

An interesting variation on the new-party strategy is furnished by the new Wexit Alberta party, which was granted official status by Elections Canada in January 2020. Wexit hopes to run candidates in every riding in the four Western provinces in the next federal election. According to leader Peter Downing, "With the expected seats we're going to win in Alberta, British Columbia, Saskatchewan and Manitoba, the Conservative Party of Canada will never govern again."[xx] The aim seems to be to make conditions worse for Alberta by guaranteeing that the Liberals will stay in power in Ottawa, thereby increasing separatist sentiment and helping to elect a Wexit provincial government, which will be committed to secession from Canada. Wexit may seem like a fringe player now, but the same could be said of Reform at the time of its founding. If the federal government imposes further burdens on Alberta's resource economy, that could drive votes to Wexit in future elections.

The unelected Senate should also be mentioned. As Savoie points out elsewhere in this volume, the Canadian Senate, unlike the upper house in other federal systems, has rarely been a protector of provincial interests, even though a reading of the constitution makes this appear to be one of its functions. But Justin Trudeau's Senate reforms, which included disbanding his government caucus in the Senate and appointing independent senators recommended by an advisory body, have made the Senate more autonomous, and this may sometimes work to the advantage of western resource interests. In 2019, for example, Conservative senators under western leadership managed to block passage of a private member's bill that would have introduced the UNDRIP principle of "free, prior and informed consent," essentially a veto by First Nations, into the approval of resource development.[xxi] They were able to talk the bill to death because time allocation does not apply to private member's bills in the Senate.

Realistically, however, prospects for using the Senate are limited. In the same session, Alberta and Saskatchewan lobbied strenuously in the Senate against Bills C-48 and C-69, which respectively closed the coast of northern British Columbia to oil tanker traffic and revamped the whole approval process for resource projects to the extent that it is often called "The No New Pipelines Act." Western intervention in the Senate hearings produced a lot of publicity and some minor amendments,[xxii] but the legislative juggernaut could not be stopped because time allocation could be invoked on government bills. Going forward, the West may win occasional small victories in the reformed Senate but will probably not be able to block anything that the government really cares about.

Referendums and separation

The only serious attempt at separation in the West occurred in the spring of 1885, when Louis Riel formed a provisional government at Batoche, took up arms, and tried to rouse other Métis and Indian communities to join his cause. The Canadian government put down the rebellion by force of arms and executed Riel for high treason. But these dramatic events have little relevance to the contemporary scene. Riel saw himself as the divinely inspired "Prophet of the New World," and his rebellion was as much religious as political. It started with his singular declaration, "Rome est tombée (Rome has fallen)."[xxiii] He did not represent a provincial or territorial government, only a self-selected group of dissidents.

Separatism has been a topic of conversation in Alberta ever since I moved here in 1968. Discussion was particularly intense after 1973, when the federal government started levying an export tax on oil revenues, until the end of the National Energy Program in 1986, and it has flared up again with the blockade of Alberta's oil exports and Justin Trudeau's second National Energy Program. Over a dozen separatist political parties have come and gone in Alberta and elsewhere in the West, but separatism was always a fringe phenomenon.[xxiv] Only one separatist was ever elected to the Alberta Legislature, and major political leaders such as Peter Lougheed, Ralph Klein,

Preston Manning, Stephen Harper, Rachel Notley, and Jason Kenney have all rejected it, arguing that necessary reforms can be achieved within confederation. Having said that, it is also probably true that public discussion of separatism has lent urgency to Alberta's demands and contributed to the occasional successes achieved by Lougheed and others.

In contrast to the West, there has been a powerful separatist movement in Quebec since the 1960s, which has won important concessions from Canada using two provincial referendums as threats. Prime Ministers Trudeau, Mulroney, and Chrétien were all led to make high-profile promises to meet the demands of Quebec political leaders. Although two attempts at mega-constitutional change, Meech Lake and Charlottetown, failed, Quebec has received the substance of its original Meech Lake demands through a combination of federal legislation and inter-governmental agreements.

Two developments have made it harder for Alberta to pursue a similar strategy. In the 1998 Secession Reference, the Supreme Court of Canada held that the rest of Canada would have to negotiate in response to a provincial referendum vote on secession where there was a clear question and a clear majority. A province would not have a unilateral right to secede without an amendment to the constitution of Canada, but it would have the right to be heard.[xxv] Parliament tried to narrow this further with the Clarity Act (2000),[xxvi] specifying that the House of Commons would have to determine whether the referendum question was clear before negotiations could take place. The question would have to be yes or no on separation, with no bells and whistles about alternate arrangements or further negotiations. The questions in both Quebec sovereignty referendums, it will be recalled, were ambiguous and would have not have passed the tests laid down in the Clarity Act. Both were designed as much to extract concessions as to lead to sovereignty.

Because of these developments, it is harder now to use provincial referendums as a political strategy, but perhaps not impossible. The Supreme Court wrote in s. 69 of the Secession Reference:

> The Constitution Act, 1982 gives expression to this principle [democratic discussion], by conferring a right to initiate

constitutional change on each participant in confederation. In our view, the existence of this right imposes a corresponding duty on the participants in confederation to engage in constitutional discussions in order to acknowledge and address democratic expressions of a desire for change in other provinces. This duty is inherent in the democratic principle which is a fundamental predicate of our system of governance.

The court was speaking of all provinces here, not just of Quebec. The words suggest that a provincial referendum could be used to articulate Alberta's demand for constitutional change with respect to, say, equalization. The case for challenging the equalization program via a referendum was initially proposed by Ted Morton in 2017, and immediately adopted by the two main candidates then running for the leadership of Alberta's new United Conservative Party, Brian Jean and Jason Kenney.[xxvii] As premier, Kenney has continued to promise a referendum on equalization as part of Alberta's October 2021 municipal elections. Constitutional expert and long-time Morton collaborator Rainer Knopff has argued that in order to bring Ottawa and the other provinces to the table, the referendum should be followed by a resolution of the provincial Legislature. In any case, if the question had nothing to do with separation, Ottawa's response would not be conditioned by the Clarity Act. I cannot say what would come out of this scenario, but it is a strategy that has not yet been essayed and may be worth trying.

Leaving federal programs

It is well known that Albertans contribute more to many federal programs, such as equalization and pensions, than they get back. Most such programs are based on federal legislation, so Alberta has no way to alter the unfavourable terms except by persuading the federal government to change the legislation. The Canada Pension Plan (CPP), however, is based on agreements between the federal and provincial governments, because pensions were considered a provincial responsibility until 1951, when a constitutional amendment made them a shared jurisdiction.[xxix] There has been a Quebec Pension Plan since establishment of the CPP in 1966, and there could also be an Alberta Pension Plan (APP).

According to a recent analysis by Fraser Institute researchers, Albertans made a cumulative net contribution of $27.9 billion—the difference between what Albertans have paid in and what they have received in pension benefits—to the CPP in the years 2008-17.[xxx] This result occurred because Alberta has a younger age pyramid, a higher percentage of labour force participation, and higher average earnings than the rest of Canada. Workers' contribution rate for an Alberta plan would be lower, while it would rise for contributors to a CPP that no longer included Alberta. An internal analysis by the Alberta Investment Management Corporation (AIMCo), which would probably manage an APP fund, reached a similar but slightly less favourable result because of more conservative assumptions.[xxxi] A collateral benefit would be the enlargement of financial markets in Alberta if AIMCO managed APP investments.

Obviously, one would not rush into such a momentous change without an updated and thorough study by actuaries and economists to evaluate the risk of moving to a smaller pool of contributors. But at first glance, it seems like a promising step, providing economic benefits to Albertans while imposing higher costs on those people left behind in the CPP. That makes it a credible threat in bargaining with Canada over Alberta's place in confederation.

There may well be other areas of public policy where Albertans are subsidizing the rest of Canada but would be able to withdraw unilaterally. Supply management of dairy products may be one such area. The National Milk Marketing Plan did not apply in Alberta until the provincial government signed onto it.[xxxii] The consumer price of milk products is notoriously higher in Canada than in Australia, New Zealand, and the United States, yet most of the producers who are reaping the benefit of the supply-managed price are located in Quebec and Ontario. It would be worth studying whether Albertans would benefit by exiting from this cartel.

Another possibility worth studying would be greater provincial control over personal and corporate income taxes, which might be accomplished by replacing some federal transfers to Alberta by the transfer of tax points. Under such a scenario, Alberta might be able to change rates and deductibles to make its tax system friendlier to investment.

"Let the eastern bastards freeze in the dark."

Often wrongly attributed to Premier Ralph Klein, the above quote was said to be a popular bumper sticker in Alberta during the years of the National Energy Program, 1980-86. I cannot remember whether I ever saw the slogan on anyone's bumper, but I certainly heard about it.

In late 1980, the Alberta government led by Peter Lougheed announced that oil shipments would be curtailed by 180,000 barrels a day in 1981, to be implemented in three instalments. The cuts were part of what led to the agreement on pricing and revenue-sharing reached by Alberta and Ottawa on September 1, 1981, but they were not as effective as one might think. Alberta had announced that no Canadians would actually be left to suffer, international oil was not scarce at that moment, and Alberta producers complained to the provincial government that they were hurt because of diminished production and sales.[xxxiii] A private-sector oil economy such as Alberta's is not as well situated to absorb production cuts as the public oil corporations of OPEC, because the impact of the cuts falls most heavily on privately-owned Alberta companies.

In 2018, when the NDP was in power in Alberta, the Legislature passed Bill 12, giving the minister of energy sweeping power over the export of oil and gas.[xxxiv] It was meant to be a threat to the government of British Columbia, which had been trying to block the construction of the TMX pipeline. The legislation, however, was not proclaimed until the Conservative government led by Jason Kenney came into power. At that point, the government of British Columbia successfully sought an injunction in Federal Court forbidding Alberta to use its legislation until litigation over the bill's constitutionality could proceed.[xxxv] The judge found that the legislation might be in conflict with federal control over interprovincial commerce. He also found that, based on statements coming from both government and opposition, the legislation was discriminatory, i.e., intended to punish the single province of British Columbia.[xxxvi] Such discrimination seems to be forbidden by the language of the 1982 Resources Amendment: "…such laws may not authorize or provide for discrimination in prices or in supplies exported to another part of Canada."[xxxvii]

For the time being, the whole issue remains uncertain while the litigation over the merits of Bill 12 proceeds. Even if Alberta loses, it can probably draft constitutional legislation to reduce shipments of oil and gas out of the province, even if it cannot target particular regions or provinces.[xxxviii] However, the deeper problem remains, namely that production cutbacks may hurt Alberta energy companies and their workers more than anyone else.

Conclusion

"One Step Forward, Two Steps Back" is the title of a famous book by Vladimir Lenin. It could also apply to the development of Alberta's natural resources. Things seemed to be looking up for Alberta in early winter 2020. First the Federal Court of Appeal gave a green light to construction of the TMX pipeline to Pacific tidewater.[xxxix] Then the Alberta Court of Appeal ruled against the federal carbon tax.[xl] But just as Albertans began to feel there might still be a future for oil and gas, Teck Resources withdrew its proposal for the huge Frontier project in the oil sands.[xli] This project had passed ten years of regulatory review and had signed mutual benefit agreements with the surrounding fourteen First Nations and Métis communities. But it still required approval by the federal cabinet, and that seemed unlikely. Teck withdrew its proposal at the last minute (and wrote off a billion dollars in sunk costs) rather than provoke a confrontation with the Liberal government. As a Canadian company, it has other interests that it has to consider. But for Alberta it was yet another blow, signaling to potential investors that Alberta is not a reliable place to do business.

The Teck fiasco was soon followed by another blow when the investment house Berkshire Hathaway announced it was withdrawing its $4 billion investment on a $9 billion LNG export project in Quebec. The liquefaction facility was to be in the port of Saguenay and the new pipeline would run through Ontario and Quebec, but the natural gas would come from Alberta. In explaining why it would not continue with its proposed investment, the company cited the "current political context" in Canada[xlii]—code for the Trudeau government's hostility to the energy industry and its reluctance to rein in illegal blockades of railways and highways. The announcement was particularly damning because Berkshire Hathaway, led by the legendary "Oracle of Omaha," Warren Buffet, is famous for its long-term strategy of "value" investing. It is now unclear whether new investors can be found to resurrect Quebec's LNG project.

Conventional political strategies of party competition and pursuing constitutional amendments through executive negotiation have at times produced gains for Alberta, but as recent events show, those gains have always met the fate of Sisyphus. Perhaps new strategies of production cuts, withdrawing from federal programs, and using provincial referendums to seek constitutional change can strengthen Alberta's position within confederation. Maybe political leaders will invent other strategies not discussed here. If politics is a game, academic observers are like sportswriters: we observe, catalogue, and identify the effects of strategies, but we are not very inventive. It is the players themselves who possess creativity.

One way or another, Alberta's leaders must find strategies to improve the province's position in confederation. If not, the voices demanding separation from Canada are bound to get louder.[xliii] No province can be expected to remain passive while its livelihood is systematically attacked and denigrated by other governments in the same country.

Why do small regions secede from a federation (sometimes)?
Jack M. Mintz

An alliance between two equally big nations can be problematic enough. But even greater—yes, in practice, almost inextricable—are the difficulties which have to be faced in a union between a bigger and smaller country; at least if the latter is to retain an acceptable degree of independence and equality.

— Per Fuglum, *Norges Hisotrie*[i]

THIS CHAPTER is about conflict in federal countries between regions of different size and wealth. It is particularly focussed on economic factors, even though differences in language, culture and values often play a more significant role. Sometimes these conflicts lead to a devolution of powers to regional governments. Other times, they lead to outright separation. The question is why does separation take place in some cases but not others?

These questions are especially critical when less populated regions like Alberta are relatively more prosperous than the rest of the country. A small rich region is a significant contributor to federation simply because it pays more taxes and receives fewer spending dollars from a central government. Its economic and social development are influenced by central government policies catering to the more populated areas of the country which vote for parties that the majority prefers. Conflict arises when the large region supports policies contrary to the interests of the small region, especially if the small region is looked upon as the golden goose to support other regions.

Regions decide to secede from a federation only if the benefits from membership are less than the costs of remaining. Separation is unusual since it is never an easy process. Because of population mobility, a region shares a common heritage with others. As well, its mobile residents are linked to families and friends in other parts of the federation. Separation creates uncertainty about new governance rules and institutions, economic disruption, trade and immigration policies and security arrangement—often at high initial cost.

Yet at times federal conflict is so intense that voters express a desire to separate, as exemplified by the Catalan independence parties, the Western Australia Secession Movement, and the Quebec separatists. Or peaceful breakups occur such as Norway/Sweden in 1905, Malaysia/Singapore in 1965, and Czech Republic/Slovakia in 1992, which led to the smaller country prospering in later years even if the breakup imposed initial economic costs.

In the following discussion, I first describe two sources of conflict in a federal system. This is followed by a review of selected federations where conflict has been important. This provides some understanding of "lessons learned" as applied to Alberta.

Why do federations form and why do conflicts arise?

A federation brings several important economic benefits to a region. The first is access to a larger market enabling trade in goods and services. The second is freedom for people to move to the most advantageous region for financial or social reasons. The third is the ability to provide public services on a shared basis to reduce unit costs (economies of scale) or correct "spillovers" when actions by one region harm or benefit another. The fourth is risk-sharing, in which regions with different industrial structures can support each other in face of regional-specific shocks or a common shock like a pandemic.

I have elsewhere labelled two types of conflict in federal systems as differences in *tastes* and *claims*.[ii] Differences in taste are quite common since regions often have different priorities and values as a result of their culture, history, and industrial/demographic makeup. Even if two regions are equal in per capita wealth, they may still have different preferences with respect to government policies such as the degree of redistribution from rich to poor. Differences in claims are economic: the central government designs policies that affect the rich region's economic progress or lead to a transfer of wealth from a rich region to more populated and poorer ones.[iii]

If the rich region contains a majority of the federal country's population, it has the greatest political influence in designing central government policies. A rich region may support poorer regions because it is altruistic to do so, but it is also in its own interest to strengthen national unity. The rich region's transfers encourage the poor region to buy goods and services from the rich region as well as reduce migration of lower income households to the rich region. However, if the rich region has a small population, it may resent central government decisions over which it has no influence or if these decisions ultimately harm the rich region's economic and social prosperity. The region may still be altruistic in supporting other regions but be disappointed with the benefits derived from the federal union.

Federal conflict among regions is ameliorated under three types of mechanisms. The first is for the region to feel it has the ability to have its views represented at the national level beyond representation by population. This can be achieved by regional-based representation in the national legislature. For example, a bicameral legislature to approve legislation as in Australia and the United States includes equal regional representation in one elected chamber. The regionally represented body creates a different forum for bargaining among political representatives in national decision-making. In contrast, the Senate in Canada with its regional representation is neither equal for each province nor elected, therefore lacking political legitimacy to reject legislation.[iv]

The second is for certain powers to be devolved to sovereign regional governments that choose policies without direction from the central government. Federations often delegate responsibilities that are "closer to the people" such as education, health, and social services. The national government typically assumes responsibility where spillovers among regions require a common approach, including national security, justice, international trade and immigration, and the internal economic union.

The third is to make institutional arrangements between central and subnational governments to enable regions to have a role in designing policies directly. The joint administration of programs such as pension funds and tax systems help ease tensions. Joint central-subnational financial and banking arrangements enable regions including smaller ones to have a role in decision making.

Even with these various mechanisms, conflict in a federal state can still occur. Despite Australia's bicameral federal legislature, Tasmania and Western Australia looked to secede. Even though subnational states may have their own powers and responsibilities, federal conflict can still arise when national and regional interests differ. Jointly operated central-subnational institutional arrangements can still override the interests of a region as when Singapore was expelled from the Malaysian federation, as discussed below.

International experience with federal conflict

It is not unusual to find examples of conflict within federal countries. Table 1 lists selected jurisdictions, providing some data on regional incomes and population size in the year of a breakup or at the present time where conflicts are still ongoing. A brief discussion is provided for each case to emphasize the economic issues underlying conflicts.

Western Australia. A primary objective for creating the Australian federation was to create a common market but states like Tasmania and Western Australia, which were poorer and less populated, lost tariff revenues charged on imported goods from other states. Western Australia was initially reluctant to join the federation as it already had responsible government granted in 1890, but the promise of a rail link to the east and a gold rush boom brought many new workers from the east, supporting membership in the Commonwealth.

Tasmania, Western Australia and, to a lesser extent, South Australia, were disappointed with their membership in the first three decades. The Commonwealth of Australia was given a monopoly over the most important revenue sources. The widening financial gap and economic disparity between the small and large states eventually led to anti-federal feeling, especially in Western Australia. Western Australia voted in favour of

Table 1: Some Cases of Federal Conflict

Federal State	Dissolution	Richest	Poorest	Richest Share of Population	Richest Share of GDP	GDP per capita: Richest to Poorest
Australia/ Western Australia		Western Australia	Tasmania	10%	14%	1.7
Belgium		Antwerp	Hainaut	17%	18%	2.0
Canada/Alberta		Alberta	Prince Edward Island	12%	16%	1.7
Czechoslovakia	Breakup 1992	Czech Republic	Slovakia	66%	69%	1.1
Malaysia/ Singapore	Singapore cedes 1965	Singapore	Kelatin**	16%	24%	1.6
Norway/ Sweden	Norway cedes 1905	Sweden	Norway***	70%	76%	1.4
Spain/ Catalonia		Catalonia*	Extramadura	16%	19%	1.8
Yugoslavis/ Slovenia	Breakup in 1990-2	Slovenia	Bosnia	9%	16%	2.9

Notes:

1. Data based on 2017 for countries that have not broken up unless otherwise noted.

2. For those in which a dissolution occurred, data are based on the first year of the break-up.

* Catalonia per capita GDP in 2018 is $27.3 thousand, roughly 10 percent lower than Madrid, the Basque County and Navarre. Catalonia's share of Spanish population is 16% and share of GDP is 19%. https://www.worldatlas.com/articles/the-autonomous-communities-of-spain.html.

** Poorest states in the Federation of Malaysia were Kelantin followed by Kedah. Singapore was the richest state in 1965.

*** Norway-Sweden: For 2017, ratio of GDP per capita of Norway to Sweden is 1.2.

Source: Historical Statistics for the World (Angus Madison), various statistical agencies of governments.

separation in a referendum in 1933. The British Parliament was petitioned in November 1934 to enact legislation to enable Western Australia to be self-governing within the British Empire, but a Joint Select Committee of the British Parliament concluded that it did not have jurisdiction without the Commonwealth's agreement.

In 1933, under pressure from the states, Australia adopted new fiscal arrangements which included additional payments to the three poorer states. Currently, the system operates with an independent Commonwealth Grants Commission determining fiscal payments to the states. The Goods and Services Tax (GST) is collected by the federal government and given to the states according to their fiscal capacity—states with greater per capita revenues receive smaller GST revenues so that the national per capita revenues are the same across all states.

Western Australia has been particularly aggrieved by equalization because it has received far less GST revenue than other states, resulting in the formation of a non-partisan Western Australian Secession Movement in 2017. To help quell objections, the Commonwealth has moved away from full to "reasonable" equalization based on fiscal capacity of the two largest states: Victoria and New South Wales.[viii]

Belgium. Belgium is a federal state composed of communities and regions, dominated by the Catholic religion in all of Belgium. It gained independence in 1830 when it separated from the Protestant United Kingdom of Netherlands with French initially being the official language. It later adopted two official languages by the end of the nineteenth-century.

Today, Belgium's political governance is highly complex with separate institutions for linguistic communities (French, Flemish, and German), regions (Wallonia, Flanders and Brussels), provinces within each region and local governments (subdivisions and municipalities). French dominates Wallonia, Flemish dominates Flanders, and Brussels is officially bilingual.[ix]

Economic divisions also have created tensions between Flemish and Walloon areas. Flanders has become the richer region since 1975 with diversified strength in agriculture, diamonds, hi-tech, services, and textiles (Antwerp is its richest province). Wallonia is dominated by declining blue-collar industries (steel and coal) and it has the poorest province, Hainaut, with about half of the per capita income of Antwerp (Table 1). The Brussels Capital Region is richer than either Flanders or Wallonia with GDP per capita twice that of the Flemish region. The gap between Flanders and Wallonia has widened since 1965 even though Belgium is one of the most egalitarian states in Europe.[x]

Belgium's divisions flare up from time to time, sometimes leading to paralysis in government as in 2007 to 2010 when a stable governing coalition could not be created among thirteen parties divided by language and economic interests. The population generally favours unity even though recent polls show that roughly a third of both Francophone and Flemish voters would support partition.

Some of the federal conflict among regions in Belgium is related to legacy fiscal arrangements. Belgium operated as a unitary state until devolution in 1993. Devolved linguistic responsibilities have been given to communities (education, hospitals, social assistance, and cultural affairs) while economic responsibilities have been given to the regions. The federal government is responsible for relatively modest spending responsibilities (including defence, law and order social security, foreign relations, and debt management). Most tax powers belong to the federal government, resulting in only a fifth of autonomous tax policy given to the communities and regions that must depend on transfers from the federal government.[xi]

This vertical imbalance between federal and sub-national governments is an important cause of federal conflict in Belgium. Wallonia has insufficient revenues to cover its expenditures and therefore receives a partial equalization grant based on its personal income tax yield. In recent years, Brussels has also received equalization, leaving the smaller Flanders region contributing a higher share of the federal budget.[xii] This implicit transfer from Flanders to Wallonia has been estimated to be as much as 2.2 percent of national GDP in the 1990s, although expected to fall as Flanders' population ages more quickly than the rest of Belgium.

Belgium illustrates how conflict of claim can contribute to division. A relatively weak central government, elected by proportional representation, is divided along linguistic and economic lines. It is unable to easily bridge differences across the various regions and communities. Yet it still has significant powers over taxation resulting in Flanders contributing most to the federation. Devolution of spending powers has not been accompanied by a sufficient devolution of taxing powers, thereby contributing to tensions.

Czechoslovakia. An example of a peaceable breakup of a landlocked nation was Czechoslovakia in 1992, creating the Czech Republic and Slovak Republic (commonly referred to as Slovakia). Czechoslovakia was originally created in 1918 from remnants of the Austro-Hungarian republic and borderlands of Germany. The two regions had different languages (Czech and Slovak) but also different origins as Slovakia was formerly part of Hungary and the Czech Republic was taken from Austria and parts of Germany. Viewing themselves as more advanced, the Czechs opposed granting much autonomy to Slovakia. When the Nazis seized power in 1939, Slovakia agreed to become a separate state in 1939, which was resented by many Czechs.[xiii] These divisions resulted in cultural and historical differences that played an important role in the eventual dissolution of Czechoslovakia.[xiv]

As shown in Table 1, the Czech Republic had 69 per cent of GDP and 66 per cent of the population with per capita GDP about a tenth higher than Slovakia at time of dissolution. Slovakia was primarily agrarian with arms factories built in the Communist period while the Czech Republic had a more diverse and more advanced economy. By the end of 1992, unemployment in the Czech Republic was only 3 per cent but 11 per cent in Slovakia.[xv]

The central government collected almost half of the revenue but was responsible for only a fifth of public spending, resulting in large transfers to the republics that had insufficient revenues to cover their expenditure responsibilities.[xvi] Slovakia was provided greater subsidies (60 per cent of the budget) compared to the Czech Republic (40 per cent of the budget). This asymmetry became a point of contention after the Velvet Revolution in late 1989 when the Communist regime was overthrown.

These economic differences also played a role with the desired pace of privatization in the two republics.[xvii] The Czechs wanted most of the economy privatized as quickly as possible while the Slovakian population preferred a slower transition to capitalism, with maintenance of subsidies for ailing industries and state ownership for some sectors of the economy. The Czech rationale for secession became economic, including a resentment towards $300 million in subsidies paid to the Slovak Republic. For the Slovaks, it was a matter of national pride as they felt they were viewed as inferior. Without national or regional referenda, the two Republic legislatures decided to separate from each other after the 1992 elections.

In the aftermath, the two new countries agreed to a number of provisions. Assets were divided between the two countries based on the ratio of populations: two-thirds to the Czech Republic and one-third to the Slovak Republic. Federal real estate would be allocated to the country where it was located, while other assets (financial reserves, art collections and state debts) were divided according to the two to one ratio.[xviii] They agreed to a common currency but the post-independence downturn resulted in Slovakia adopting its own currency soon afterwards. Customs checks were adopted at the border and residents were effectively given the option of Czech or Slovakian citizenship.

At the beginning, separation led to economic losses especially for Slovakia. A quarter of Czech trade was with Slovakia and 40 per cent of Slovak trade was with the Czech Republic. Many Czech businesses no longer exported to Slovakia, which was experiencing foreign currency shortages. Slovak industrial production fell by 15 per cent and unemployment rose in the first three quarters of 1993. The Czech Republic fared better although foreign investment slowed down, given investor anxiety over separation. Even though the public was not given a direct opportunity to express support for separation through a referendum in 1992, today a majority of Czechs and Slovaks are at least comfortable with separation despite the initial poor start after independence.[xix]

Malaysia/Singapore. In 1957, the Federation of Malaysia became an independent country after operating as a British colony since 1771 (except for an interim period when the Japanese controlled what was then Malaya). Cultural, linguistic and economic divisions between Malays (55 per cent of the population) and the wealthier Chinese (25 per cent) were important factors leading to Singapore seceding from the federation in 1965. In 1965, Singapore was the richest state with 16 per cent of the population and 24 per cent of GDP (Table 1). Its GDP per capita was 60 per cent more than the poorest state in Malaysia.

With the expansion of Malaysia to include Singapore and the Borneo territories of Sabah and Sarawak, certain asymmetric features were introduced as concessions in 1963.[xx] While considerable accommodation was achieved to attract membership of the two Borneo states, the experience with Singapore was different. Singapore was granted certain concessions including authority over education, labour, social policy and health, as well as exemption from federal authority similar to Sabah and Sarawak. On the other hand, no agreement was reached with respect to tax arrangements. The federation wanted Singapore to contribute to the federal resources consistent with its fiscal capacity.[xxi] Singapore was reluctant to lose fiscal autonomy to the federal government and support weaker members of the federation. Although an agreement was reached, it was not finalized. This led the Malaysian Parliament to grant Singaporean independence in 1965. In announcing separation, the Malaysian prime minister specifically mentioned that Singapore would not agree to a financial contribution to the federation and development loans to Sabah and Sarawak.

The peaceful break-up was easy to manage because Singapore had been a member of the federation for only a few years with many provisions still subject to negotiation. Despite Malaysia providing significant representation in fiscal matters through the National Fiscal Council as well as providing asymmetric provisions to attract Sabah, Sarawak, and Singapore, Singapore balked at the financial terms. Singapore recognized that, as a small but relatively rich population, it had little political power to protect its interests within the federation.

At first, independence had its challenges. Unemployment was high, and Singapore lacked an industrial base, infrastructure, and natural resources. But it followed an aggressive economic agenda of export-led growth, industrialization, and education with a strong rule of law and low taxes.

Independence ended up being beneficial for Singapore, which now has the ninth highest per capita GDP in the world.[xxii]

Norway/Sweden. Although Norway and Sweden were united in the years 1319-43 and in 1449-50, Norway's history was closer to Denmark as a province with some limited autonomy. Denmark-Norway attempted to remain neutral during the Napoleonic Wars, but entered into an alliance with France after a British attack on the Danish navy in 1807. To compensate Sweden for its loss of Finland and its opposition to Napoleon, Great Britain and Russia consented to Sweden's annexation of Norway in the Treaty of Kiel signed by Denmark in 1814. Supported mainly by the upper-class, Norway then declared independence, adopted a new constitution and elected its own king. This led to the Swedish-Norwegian war, which resulted in the abdication of the king in favour of a single Norwegian-Swedish king. Norway was given a fair amount of autonomy under its adopted constitution, with the king responsible for foreign policy and defence. This enabled Norway to operate as an independent constitutional monarchy with its own political institutions and army in the nineteenth century.

Even before the nineteenth century, Norway's orientation was to the West, trading with Great Britain and Western Europe, while Sweden was more focussed on Germany and Russia.[xxiii] From 1840 to 1875, Norway boomed with expanding exports (4.8 per cent growth per year) in wood products, fish, and agriculture including cattle breeding, helped by international liberalization.[xxiv] Industrialization also took hold, enabled by cheap and plentiful waterpower that supported heavy machinery and textile production. But it was its expansion in merchant shipping from 1850 to 1880 that supercharged Norway's growth, with its share of world tonnage growing from 3.6 to 6.1 per cent. It is therefore no surprise that a single issue, independent foreign consular services, was the final straw that led to the peaceful separation of Norway and Sweden. With its growing merchant marine fleet, Norway wanted its own consular and foreign service, which Sweden opposed. Norway declared independence on June 7, 1905 and Sweden accepted separation on October 26.

Thus, the union lasted only ninety-one years before dissolution took place. Just prior to dissolution, Norway was the junior partner with a smaller population (2.3 million) compared to Sweden (5.3 million) and its per capita GDP was only 70 per cent of Sweden's (Table 1). Today, Norway is the richer cousin due to its oil wealth (fifth highest GDP per capita in the world[xxv]) although still less populated than Sweden (5.3 million versus 10 million respectively).

Spain/Catalonia. Catalonia's continuing desire for independence from Spain is an example of conflict of both taste and claim. Aragon and Catalonia entered into the unification of Spain in 1492. Even though Catalonia retained its autonomy and assembly, separatist movements began to form, culminating in a revolt against the Madrid government in 1640. The revolt was ended in the 1650s with the Catalan constitution and autonomy abolished by the Bourbon King Philip V in 1714.

The quest for autonomy never died. Periodically, Catalan nationalism led to hostilities, resulting in the granting or revoking of autonomy. When democratic rule was established in 1977, Catalans renewed their support for political parties pushing for autonomy. In 2006, Catalonia passed a referendum based on an agreement with the central government with two elements: (i) Catalonia would receive fifty percent of taxes collected in its territory and (ii) it would be granted "national status" (an ambiguous concept)[xxvi]. A later constitutional court decision downgraded national status to "nationality."

Catalonia's nationalism reflected mostly a conflict of taste, but it was conflict of claim that led to a resurgence of separatism after the 2008 global financial crisis. Catalans resented the large fiscal transfers made by the central government to poorer regions; the President, Artur Mas, ran a campaign in 2012 on the premise that "Spain is robbing us."[xxvii] Catalonia wanted fiscal powers similar to those historically enjoyed by Navarre and the Basque County, but the Madrid government rejected devolution.

As shown in Table 1, the Catalonian autonomous region accounts for 16 per cent of Spain's population and 19 per cent of its GDP. Its per capita GDP is 1.8 times that of the poorest region. It is close to having the highest per capita GDP in Spain (Madrid, Basque County, and Navarre are the richest, although the latter two have had their share of Basque separatist movements over the years). In recent years, the Catalans have paid roughly 25 per cent of federal revenues and received only 11 per cent of federal spending, equalling an annual transfer of 17 billion Euros.[xxviii]

Galvanized by the 2014 Scottish referendum in the United Kingdom, the Catalonian government called for a non-binding independence referendum on November 9, 2014. Its legality was under challenge at the Constitutional Court, but Catalonia's Mas held the vote anyway as an informal poll in which one-third of the electorate voted with 80 per cent in favour of separation. In 2015, the Catalan Parliament approved a measure for "peaceful disconnection from the Spanish state," which was immediately opposed by Madrid's government as illegal.

On October 1, 2017, under the new leadership of Carles Puigdemont, the Catalan government held a binding referendum. The vote was disrupted by the Spanish government, which tried to avert the referendum results by seizing ballot boxes from polling stations. Catalan officials stated that the turnout was 42 per cent with 90 per cent in favour of separation.

After a general strike against the Spanish government and encouraged by an October 22 Italian referendum that overwhelmingly backed local autonomy in Veneto and Lombardy, the Catalan Parliament voted to declare independence. The Spanish government then invoked Article 155 of the constitution to take over Catalan's police force, finances and media. The Catalan Parliament was dismissed, and criminal charges were laid against the leaders seeking independence. Puigdemont fled to Belgium for sanctuary (and later was elected to the European Parliament). A snap election was held in Catalonia on December 2017, with the independence parties winning a majority of seats. Autonomy today remains unresolved with continuing demonstrations and calls for independence.[xxix]

Yugoslavia/Slovenia. Yugoslavia is an example of a breakup that resulted in subsequent hostilities soon afterwards between nationalistic groups. Slovenia was the most successful and least affected jurisdiction, which, as we will see below, was first to declare independence in 1990. As is shown in Table 1, Slovenia accounted for 9 per cent of Yugoslavia's population, 16 per cent of its GDP and had a per capita GDP 2.9 times more than Bosnia, the poorest of the republics.

With the end of Ottoman rule and defeat of Austria-Hungary after the First World War, the Paris Peace conference created a single country comprised of former Balkan territories. The Kingdom of Yugoslavia was officially proclaimed in 1929, lasting until the Second World War, after which it became the Socialist Republic of Yugoslavia composed of northern (Serbia, Croatia and Slovenia) and southern parts (Bosnia and Herzegovina, North Macedonia and Montenegro). Kosovo and Vojvodina were given autonomous provincial status as part of Serbia to satisfy Albanian and Magyar interests. Yugoslavia then dissolved by 1992 with only two republics left, Serbia and Montenegro. They abandoned the name Yugoslavia by 2003, when the two countries became separate.

The federal government, following its socialist principles, viewed it as a paramount obligation to reduce economic inequality among the republics. Article 122 of the 1963 constitution required the federation to finance development in the under-developed parts of Yugoslavia.[xxx] The allocation of these funds to achieve equalization between republics and areas in the 1960s switched from pre-1960 attempts to industrialize the south to diversification of the economy, economic integration of the south and north, and provision of social services. Under-developed areas received funds equal to two percent of national income. The richer republics criticized these schemes for being unproductive and uncoordinated with industries in the north.

With the collapse of communism in Eastern Europe in 1989, Yugoslavia began to disintegrate. Slovenia was the first to declare independence in 1990, supported by Germany. Although the declaration of independence provoked a war with Yugoslavia, it ended after ten days.[xxxi] No doubt the breakup of Yugoslavia was largely related to historical, religious and cultural rivalries. However, economic differences led to conflict of claim tensions especially with respect to Slovenia, the richest republic. The north had benefited from its transport and communication linkages with other parts of Europe while the south was always much less developed. These differences in economic development played a role in the eventual breakup of Yugoslavia.

Alberta. Alberta's tensions in confederation are an example of what I call "conflict of claim." It has only 11 per cent of Canada's population, but 16 per cent of Canada's GDP and the highest per capita income of all the provinces. As Mansell notes in this volume, Alberta has contributed $631 billion or an average annual $3,700 per capita during the years 1961-2018 as fiscal transfers in through the federal budget (all values here and below are in 2018 dollars). This amount is equal to an "effective tax rate" on Albertan personal incomes equal to 10 percent.

To understand Alberta's conflict of claim it is also important to relate it to the "conflict of taste" that involves Quebec and the rest of Canada. For much of its history, Canada has been vexed with the issue of accommodating Quebec, which has its own language, culture and values. Even though Quebec has had two referendums in 1980 and 1995 that rejected separation (by a slim majority the second time), Canada adopted several policies to accommodate Quebec's aspirations since 1867.

These accommodations included the following. Constitutional powers sensitive to cultural, religious or linguistic differences were delegated to the provinces including education, hospitals and property rights. French and English were guaranteed in Parliament and the Quebec legislature. Quebec, with its civil rather than common law, was given two judges (later three of nine judges) when the Supreme Court of Canada was created in 1895. In the 1960s, the federal government allowed Quebec to opt out of certain conditional cash grants by reducing federal personal income tax points instead. Quebec also has more autonomy over taxation powers: it collects its own personal and corporate income tax and it collects both the federal Goods and Services Tax and Quebec Sales Tax under a tax harmonization agreement. Quebec has its own pension plan (benefits are harmonized with the Canada Pension Plan) and control over immigration and labour market training. Bilingualism has been introduced for the federal civil service providing an advantage to Quebecers to enter the civil service compared to those from more unilingual parts of Canada.

Most important, Quebec has received substantial financial support in that federal spending in the province far outstrips federal taxes paid. As Mansell shows, Quebec received $497 billion in federal support from 1961 to 2018 or an annual average of $1200 per capita (the four Atlantic provinces have received $761 billion and Manitoba $184 billion in the same period). From 2009-2018, the best-known source of this federal contribution to Quebec has been via equalization (32 per cent) although it is second to redistribution through the progressive personal income tax (53 per cent).

In the case of Alberta's conflict of claim, its ownership of oil and gas has been a major point of contention for over a century. When Alberta and Saskatchewan were created as provinces in 1905 (as well as Manitoba in 1870) the federal government did not grant them ownership of public lands. All other provinces did receive these public lands upon their creation. Federal politicians argued that Rupert's Land was purchased by the federal government and the revenue from land sales was needed to cover migrant settlement costs and the construction of the CP Railway under Macdonald's National Policy. Westerners saw this as making them second-class provinces and contested this policy from the start. Their campaigns were finally successful in 1930, when the British North America Act was amended to transfer the ownership of crown lands and resources to the three prairie provinces.

However, resource wealth continued to be a constant source of tension in the Canadian federation. After the Leduc oil discovery in 1947, Alberta's economy began to boom and by 1966, it became a net contributor to the federal budget. After the oil price shocks of the 1970s, the Trudeau government established the National Energy Program in 1980 to subsidize a domestic oil price for consumers below the international price with an oil export tax largely collected from Alberta. Mansell estimates the net fiscal transfer from Alberta to the rest of Canada totalled $68 billion (2018 dollars) in 1980 and 1981. Although the NEP was reversed by the Progressive Conservative Mulroney government in 1986, Albertans still bitterly remember the experience to this day.

Alberta economy reached a peak with a booming oil sands industry and high oil prices during the years 2000 to 2014. However, the collapse of the commodity boom and the election of the Liberal government in 2015 led to a new round of regional tensions. Alberta and Saskatchewan were particularly upset with the Liberal government's climate-inspired regulatory and tax policies that hurt industry competitiveness. Liberal policies also partly contributed, directly and indirectly, to the failure to build new export pipelines for the growing production of oil from the oil sands.[xxxii] The province's economy was weakened as Alberta oil prices were heavily discounted and foreign investors shifted investments to other parts of the world due to political risk. Despite the weakening economy, the province remained the largest contributor to the federal budget: $17 billion in 2018 alone. With rising anger in Alberta and Saskatchewan, the federal Liberal government lost all of its seats in the two provinces in the 2019 election.

The use of asymmetric federalism has enabled Canada to accommodate Quebec's "conflict of taste" but, much less so, Alberta's "conflict of claim" in confederation. Ontario has played a critical role as the largest province in Canada supporting Quebec's accommodation. Ontario voters have covered this financial cost with $768 billion from 1961-2018 although its contribution virtually disappeared from 2010-18 (only $74 million). Thus, the financial cost to Ontario would have been much greater had it not been for Alberta's largesse. Perhaps, without Alberta, Ontario voters would not have been so magnanimous in transfers to Quebec (as well as to Atlantic Canada and Manitoba). In other words, it was much easier Ontario to support federal policies with Alberta voters picking up most of the share in recent years.

Key lessons for Alberta in thinking about its future

Alberta polls have shown a rising interest in separation or at least a Fair Deal from the rest of Canada. While Albertans debate their future, what lessons can they take from the international experience described above? Here are five.

1. *Less populated but wealthier regions have limited political power to protect themselves from predatory policies supported by national majorities.* Small regions have less ability to influence central government decision-making since they do not have sufficient representation in the national government to modify or block harmful policy decisions. This vulnerability has typically been resolved by three types of reforms: devolution of more powers/revenues to the disaffected region; increased power/influence/representation of the smaller regions in the national government; or secession of the disaffected region from the larger nation. The asymmetry between size and wealth has led to movements in favour of devolution of spending, tax and regulatory powers in Australia, Belgium, Italy and Spain. In Norway, Singapore and Slovenia, this conflict led to separation.

Alberta's situation is similar to these examples. At different times and with different leadership Alberta has attempted all three. Albertans advocated for devolution of power in the 2001 "Alberta Agenda" and Premier Kenney's more recent "Fair Deal" panel. At other times, Alberta (and other Western provinces) have supported political parties and policies that would increase their representation and influence in the national government such as equal and elected Senate reform. Finally, there have been sporadic attempts to form separatist parties in Alberta almost from the start, the most recent being the WEXIT party.

2. *Large fiscal transfers from rich to poor regions can be a major source of regional tension if the rich region feels exploited (Catalonia, Flanders, Singapore, Slovenia, and Western Australia).* Fiscal transfers provide the glue needed to keep a country unified when rich regions are willing to share their wealth with poorer regions. However, if the rich region feels that it is being exploited, voters build up resentment towards equalization and other similar programs. They may feel that the transfers lead to dependency if the poorer region does not try to improve itself (as in the cases of Catalonia, Flanders, Singapore and Slovenia). Or they may be unhappy with transfers that are not sensitive to sudden economic shifts (such as Western Australia's complaints over equalization after the oil price collapse). Alberta faces similar issues today with calls for a reform of equalization. Many Albertans feel aggrieved that they have supported the rest of Canada through the federal budget while receiving little accommodation for its aspirations, unlike Quebec.

3. *Weak central government institutions make devolution or outright separation more tenable (Belgium, Czechoslovakia and Norway/Sweden).* If regional interests are insufficiently represented in federal institutions or the central government is weak, regions will push for more devolution of powers in a federation or separate. The weak central government in Belgium under proportional representation has been unable to accommodate Flemish and Walloon interests, leading to devolution except in taxing powers. Many of the spending and regulatory powers already belonged to the republics in Czechoslovakia before dissolution. The union between Norway and Sweden left little power in the hands of the king except for foreign policy, thereby enabling Norway to rely on well-developed public institutions when it separated. In Australia, regional interests represented in the Senate and an independent fiscal grants commission have given more voice to regional interests in national decision-making.

In Canada, regional representation in federal decision-making has been weak, resulting in greater decentralization compared to Australia. An unelected Senate has little credibility to overturn House of Commons decisions. As Donald Savoie points out in this volume, regional representation in the cabinet has much less impact today, given that decision-making is largely centralized in the prime minister's office, making cabinets less relevant. The provinces have therefore become the main voice on behalf of the regions. Quebec has been especially successful in achieving transfers of jurisdictional powers from Ottawa. Its example is the model for dissatisfied Albertans with initiatives like the "Fair Deal."

4. *A lack of strong economic linkages can lead to greater tensions (Belgium, Malaysia Norway/Sweden, Western Australia and Yugoslavia).* Federations with relatively free mobility of labour and internal trade are more likely to stick together than fall apart. Norway is a perfect example of weak economic linkages. Despite similar culture, Norway's trade was western with Britain and Western Europe while Sweden's trade was southern and eastern with Germany and Russia. Further, migration was limited between Norway and Sweden, even though many Norwegians moved to North America in the mid-nineteenth century. Western Australia was distant from the more heavily populated parts of Australia (Perth is closer to Singapore than Sydney), but a strong internal union encouraged migration and trade. In the case of Yugoslavia, its breakup reflected deep religious, cultural and economic divisions that limited any desire for a unified country. Belgium and Malaysia also have populations that interact less with each other for linguistic or cultural reasons, making unity more difficult to achieve. For Alberta, language and culture is similar to other parts of Canada, but distance matters as with Western Australia. Labour is quite mobile in Canada, although east-west trade has weakened relative to north-south trade with the United States (see Emery in this volume).

5. *Separation can be peaceful if both parties are mutually in agreement (Czechoslovakia, Malaysia/Singapore and, Norway/Sweden).* The peaceful breakup of Czechoslovakia, Malaysia and Norway/Sweden was accommodated on friendly terms. Parliaments in the two Czechoslovakian republics each voted for separation even though neither had a referendum seeking public approval. The Malaysian Parliament formally agreed to Singapore's secession without conflict after being unable to work out fiscal terms. Norway and Sweden peacefully separated once the king agreed in 1905. On the other hand, Yugoslavia's breakup resulted in wars and a lack of protection of minority groups, and Catalonia's unresolved push for independence has been blocked by Spain's constitution. If Alberta were to opt for separation rather than devolution or re-confederation, would Canada try to block it as in Spain? Unlike Spain, both Canada's constitution and now the Clarity Act (2001) allow for a province to secede, at least in theory.

Conclusions

Conflict of claim is an important source of federal tensions especially when smaller, richer regions are expected to support larger, poorer regions. The issues can be sorted out with accommodation in a federal system, typically involving a devolution of powers to the sub-national governments or greater regional say in federal political institutions. Alternatively, a jurisdiction may find it better to separate even if some initial costs are involved. The international experience is replete with examples of accommodation and separation, which is to say there is no single outcome to predict when conflict arises in a federal state.

Canada's national political institutions wear blinders

Donald J. Savoie

P OLITICAL AND administrative institutions matter. They create incentives, both positive and negative, that shape the behaviour of politicians and career officials, as well as policy outcomes.[i] Canada's national political institutions have been ill-fitted to the country's political-economic circumstances from the very beginning. Canada was born to deal with a crippling political impasse between Canada East and Canada West (Quebec and Ontario). The fathers of confederation did not spend much time designing political institutions that would accommodate regional interests, other than those of Canada East. They also ensured that the Canadas would be top dogs in confederation. They did this by importing political institutions lock, stock, and barrel from Britain. Therein lies the problem, at least for Western Canada and Atlantic Canada.

Geography never dominated politics in Britain to the extent it has and still does in Canada. British-inspired political institutions are essentially spatially blind because it suits British, or at least England's history and national character. Britain remains a unitary state, though on shaky ground of late, and its main political cleavages have been around economic class rather than geography.

Being spatially blind in Britain is one thing. Being spatially blind in Canada is quite another. Ramsay Cook explained: "The question of Canadian identity is not a Canadian question at all but a regional question."[ii] Being spatially blind explains in no small measure why Canada's national institutions have not been able to act as the arena for reconciling regional and national interests. The failure is built into the system.[iii]

In the beginning

Geography explains virtually everything Canadian and it is central to understanding the workings of Canadian democracy. Canadians continue to think in spatial terms. We have English and two or three French Canadas, Indigenous peoples with many living in designated communities, the Laurentian consensus, Western alienation, the Maritime Rights Movement (established to influence national policies to better accommodate the region's economic circumstances), the north, rural Canada, urban Canada, the prairies, and the country's industrial heartland. Yet, the 1867 British North America Act made no reference to space or territory. The focus is on language and denominational rights, revealing code words for the two-nation concept or a treaty signed between two peoples or between Ontario and Quebec.

Some countries, like the United States, are born out of revolution. Revolutions force political and intellectual elites to think of new approaches and define new institutions. That is what revolutions are good at. The founding fathers of the United States could hardly duplicate British political institutions after they had fought a war of independence, pledging to build vastly different institutions. Alexander Hamilton and James Madison invented the modern form of federalism as they set out to put an end to the concentration of power in the hands of the monarch, in one level of government or even in one branch of government.[iv]

America's founding fathers came from large and small states. Delegates from small states at the Philadelphia constitutional convention insisted that representation in Congress be established on an equal basis, no matter the size, while the larger states insisted on representation by population. The disagreement came close to preventing the union. But, by the end of the summer of 1787, the constitutional convention reached what Americans call the "great compromise." Small and large states got equal representation in the Senate and large states got a form of representation by population in the

House of Representatives. Leaving aside Canada, other federations from Australia, which also has a Westminster-inspired parliamentary system, to Germany and Russia, have adopted essentially the same model. I note that Canada was the first political community to combine the Westminster model of parliamentary government with federalism.

Canada was not born out of a revolution but rather out of a compromise between Canada West and Canada East. Canada's "great compromise" was between the two Canadas, Ontario and Quebec. The main architects, John A. Macdonald, George-Étienne Cartier, George Brown, and Alexander Galt, all got what they wanted in bringing together two colonies constantly at odds with one another. Macdonald wanted Canada to retain its strong ties to Britain and a strong central government with subordinate provincial governments; Cartier wanted the use of French in Parliament and in the courts, and the continuation of a Code Civil in Quebec; Galt designed the new country's financial arrangements, which favoured Canada West and Canada East while Brown insisted on representation by population to establish political power in Canada and an appointed and essentially ineffective Senate.

The four looked to the four colonies to the east to break the political deadlock between Canada West and Canada East.[v] However, all four colonies resisted the proposed deal. Newfoundland rejected the proposal outright and only joined confederation in 1949. Prince Edward Island, initially at least, withheld support for confederation, convinced that true political power would always reside in the House of Commons and that it would always favour Ontario and Quebec. It only joined in 1873 after Macdonald sweetened the deal. New Brunswick's premier of the day, A.J. Smith, rejected the deal, asking that "small provinces" be given "at least the guard which they have in the United States (an equal and effective Senate) although we ought to have more because, here, the executive branch is all-powerful." He reminded Macdonald that confederation "is not a Legislative Union and we have sectional and local differences."[vi] Opposition to confederation became widespread in Nova Scotia as soon as the terms of the Quebec Resolutions became known. Premier Charles Tupper pledged to fix the problems by introducing measures to counterbalance representation by population at the 1866 London conference.

Nova Scotia voted twice on the merits of confederation and said no on both occasions. Nova Scotia sent a clear message when it elected eighteen anti-confederation MPs to Canada's first Parliament out of nineteen; thirty-six out of thirty-eight provincial seats in the 1867 provincial election went to anti-confederation candidates. The anti-confederation movement endured in the Maritimes for decades. For example, William S. Fielding led his Liberal party to victory in Nova Scotia in 1886 on a campaign to take Nova Scotia out of confederation. He successfully secured a resolution from the legislative assembly to ask Ottawa to help the province leave confederation. Federal politicians did not respond.[vii] Joseph Howe, as is well known, led the anti-confederation forces in Nova Scotia, insisting that the province would become a neglected member of Canada, given how national political institutions would be structured.

Nothing came out of Tupper's commitment to fix things at the London conference. Ged Martin sums up the negotiations: "The Maritimers were smacked into line by the British acting on appeal from the Canadians." Calls for referenda in New Brunswick or Nova Scotia were ignored. Both the colonial office and Macdonald saw no need for them. Delegates from Ontario and Quebec also rejected the call for an elected Senate to give it legitimacy to speak on behalf of the smaller provinces. An elected and effective Senate speaking on behalf of the smaller provinces was simply a non-starter because Ontario delegates insisted that the two houses would be at loggerhead, and because Quebec delegates feared that the Senate would not protect their cultural and linguistic position if it had the same number of elected senators as the smaller provinces.[viii]

Western Canada did not have a voice at the negotiation table. If it had, one can only assume that it would have joined forces with those from Atlantic Canada to ensure that British North America would have strong federal components.

It will be recalled that when Alberta joined confederation in 1905, it initially sought to do so as one province that would have included Saskatchewan and parts of the then Northwest Territories. Sir Frederick Gordon Haultain, the driving force behind Alberta and Saskatchewan efforts to join Canada, wanted to create a large western province called Buffalo that would unite a large swath of Western Canada before joining confederation. The Laurier government said no, fearing that it would give "too much power to Western Canada."[ix] Well-known historian Bill Waiser explains Prime Minister Wilfred Laurier's reasoning: "because of the fear that one large western province might upset the balance of confederation."[x] Neither the four key fathers of confederation nor any prime minister since have ever expressed concerns that two large provinces, Ontario and Quebec, would upset the balance of confederation, a classic case of *deux poids, deux mesures*.

The above makes the point that the treaty that Macdonald and Cartier negotiated between 1864 and 1867 lives on. In a true federal state, the central government would not have objected to Alberta and Saskatchewan joining forces to join Canada as one province. The fear that a large western province could in time challenge the dominant position of Ontario and Quebec and somehow compromise the treaty that Macdonald and Cartier had carefully negotiated forced Alberta and Saskatchewan to drop plans to join confederation as one province.

Both Macdonald and Cartier frequently employed the terms "pact," "treaty," or "compact" to describe the deal struck in Quebec in 1864. George Stanley explains: "The Canadian delegates to Quebec and London were thoroughly convinced that their bargain was a treaty or a pact; however, this conviction was always weaker among the Maritimers." Stanley concluded that their view continues to influence both the political thinking and the political vocabulary.[xi]

Federalism in name only

John A. Macdonald, the main architect of Canadian federalism, had no intention of establishing a federal structure. He wanted a unitary system built around the Westminster model and said so. Donald Creighton maintains that Macdonald got his unitary state in all but name or that, in the end, he was able to secure a legislative union in a federal disguise.[xii] Macdonald explained his position, hardly an endorsement of federalism: "The true principle of a confederation lies in giving to the general Government all the principles and powers of sovereignty, and in the provision that the subordinate or individual states should have no powers but those expressly bestowed upon them. We should thus have a powerful central Government, a powerful central Legislature, and a powerful decentralized system of minor Legislatures for local purposes."[xiii] Macdonald was so confident that provincial governments would be minor players and that Canada would, in time, evolve into a unitary state, that he did not even see the need to include an amending formula in the British North America Act, a basic requirement of a federal constitution.

The British North America Act (BNA) gave the provincial lieutenant-governors the power of reservation to stop provincial legislation from coming into force until the central government had approved it. It also gave the central government the authority to veto provincial legislation through its power of disallowance. The right to dismiss provincial acts by the federal government does not square with the true principles of federalism and it also undermines the concept of the sovereignty of the provinces in their sphere of jurisdiction.[xiv]

The Western provinces strongly opposed Ottawa's national policy (circa 1878) and passed legislation designed to attenuate its impact. However, between 1867 and 1920, Ottawa disallowed ninety-six provincial laws with the bulk from Western Canada dealing with the national policy.[xv] In sharp contrast, Ottawa only disallowed a handful of acts from Ontario and Quebec between 1867 and 1943.[xvi] There is now a tacit agreement that the federal government will not use its power of disallowance and it has not, in fact, been used since 1943.[xvii]

The four leading architects of confederation, in particular Macdonald and Brown, also did not see the need to modify the Westminster parliamentary model to square with Canada's political and economic realities other than those of Ontario and Quebec. Britain had an unelected House of Lords and so Canada would have an unelected Senate. An unelected House of Lords was well suited to Britain with its established families, landed gentry and aristocracy which, in 1867, feared democracy. Canada then was a pioneer society more open to democracy. I note that, contrary to the widely held perception in Ontario and Quebec, responsible government first came to Nova Scotia in January 1848 and later that year in Canada. Historica Canada's Heritage Minutes, for example, report that it was Lafontaine and Baldwin who brought responsible government to the British North American colonies.[xviii]

The four key architects of confederation decided that an elected Senate did not square with "the principles of British cabinet government."[xix] Cabinet, they insisted, was all that was needed to look after the regions or the interest of the smaller provinces. In the pre-confederation discussions, it was agreed that the Maritimes would have one-third of cabinet posts to compensate somehow for representation by population in the Commons. Maritime delegates pressed to have this enshrined in the constitution. Canadian delegates, however, firmly rejected this idea, insisting that this could never square with the Westminster-inspired parliamentary system.

Macdonald and Brown saw first hand how regionalism had brought the two Canadas to their knees, forcing them to look to the Maritime colonies to break their political impasse. They and the other fathers of confederation also saw a civil war raging in the United States, fuelled by regional tensions, precisely at the time they were trying to craft a federal system for Canada. In short, given Macdonald's bias for British institutions, the strong opposition to an elected and equal Senate from the four key architects of confederation, and the view that regional interests had not only led to the failure of the two Canadas but also fuelled a civil war south of the border, measures to promote the interests of the smaller provinces in national institutions held little currency in the negotiations, at least with the four key architects of confederation.

Big dogs eat first

The 1867 Macdonald-Cartier two-nation treaty has been stretched beyond recognition and Canada has become a federation in spite of its constitution. Canada embraced a form of hyphenated federalism rather than introduce change through constitutional amendments. Hyphenated federalism has enabled Ottawa and the provinces to sidestep the constitution in launching a multitude of federal-provincial programs. We now have federal-provincial agreements in virtually every sector, ignoring the warning that it is never wise for one government to raise revenue for another to spend.

Hyphenated federalism has enabled Ottawa to distribute wealth all the while leaving intact its ability to influence where and how wealth is created. Atlantic Canada has benefitted greatly from federal transfer payments, a form of guilt money from Ottawa as compensation for its central-Canadian economic policies.

Ottawa's national policy (circa 1878-1950s) is hardly the only example where the federal government policies were able to direct economic development to central Canada. It will be recalled that the Western provinces had to struggle until 1930 to secure jurisdiction over national resources, a jurisdiction that the four founding provinces have enjoyed since 1867. The National Energy Program (NEP) is another, as is Ottawa's decision to award the CF-18 maintenance contract to a Montreal-based firm, even if Winnipeg-based Bristol won the bid. The head of Bristol went to the heart of the issue when he said: "If this is the way Canada wishes to do business, we will avoid smaller provinces; they have too little political clout. It's better for us to choose provinces like Quebec or Ontario, they can pull the political strings."xx

There are many more such cases. The federal government played a critical role in promoting the country's manufacturing sector through the war efforts for the Second World War. It established twenty-eight crown corporations which gave rise to aircraft manufacturers, synthetic rubber producers and research-and-development firms. All were established in Ontario and Quebec and many stayed in business after the war was over.

Ottawa decided to concentrate the bulk of its war efforts in Ontario and Quebec when, at times, both economic and military considerations suggested otherwise. After a visit to Canada in 1940, the British Admiralty Technical Mission concluded: "Political issues weigh heavily" in military decisions. They underlined problems with building ships in yards cut off from the Atlantic Ocean for five months and questioned the need for vessels to make the long trip down the St. Lawrence. American military advisors also made the same point. The first ten ships built for Britain barely escaped getting trapped in the St. Lawrence in the winter freeze-up and "required substantial work in the Maritimes before they could risk an Atlantic crossing." The British tried, as best they could, to convince Ottawa to make Halifax the logical naval headquarters for their Canadian convoys and the repair centre for the larger vessels. They were not successful.[xxi] This was one occasion where geography favoured Atlantic Canada but the federal government decided otherwise. These are hardly the only examples when the federal government favoured Ontario and Quebec through its policies and economic development efforts.

National institutions with blinders on

The treaty Macdonald and Cartier struck in 1867 put blinders on national institutions to ensure that they would focus on Ontario and Quebec, and would limit regional considerations to Quebec. Quebec was guaranteed a number of MPs in the Commons set at sixty-five in 1867, adjusted at seventy-five in 1974 and again to seventy-eight in 2011. Quebec is also guaranteed, by law, three Supreme Court judges. The same does not apply to the other regions. It will be recalled that Justin Trudeau publicly contemplated in 2016 replacing Nova Scotia's Justice Cromwell with someone from outside Atlantic Canada.[xxii]

The Senate has had a confused mandate from the beginning, with its regional voice all but lost in the mist. Macdonald saw it as a house to protect Canadians from the excesses of democracy, hence his label, the chamber of "sober second thought," which has met the test of time, notably in Ontario. The Supreme Court has added new responsibilities when it ruled that "The Senate also came to represent various groups that were under-represented in the House of Commons. It served as a forum for ethnic, gender, religious, linguistic, and Aboriginal groups that did not always have a meaningful opportunity to present their views through the popular democratic process."[xxiii] In short, the Senate has no widely accepted mandate. It all depends on how individual senators define their role.

Some premiers have suggested that there is no need for the Senate to speak on behalf of the regions—that is their responsibility. Brad Wall maintains that "The Senate was to be a voice for the regions, specifically the provinces. We have that without the Senate, constitutionally known as the provinces."[xxiv]

Wall's argument does not hold water, as Montreal mayor Denis Coderre made clear. Wall pressed Coderre to support the Energy East Pipeline, suggesting it was in the interest of the national economy. Coderre dismissed Wall's position out of hand by saying that "metropolitan Montreal has a population of 4 million, Saskatchewan has 1.1 million—end of story."[xxv] No mayor or elected politician from a large city or state within a federation having an effective upper house speaking for the regions would likely make this argument. In any event, in other federations there is an important component in their national political institutions to challenge the mayor's view. In addition, provincial premiers are invariably busy dealing with the details of the day at home and always far removed from Ottawa where important policy and program decisions first take shape.

Macdonald and Brown's argument that cabinet would look after the regional perspective has fallen flat on its face, even from day one. Writing about the first Cabinet, Richard Gwyn, who wrote a highly sympathetic biography of John A. Macdonald, reports: "The intent was to give the regions a voice at the centre in Cabinet, as a substitute for the U.S. system of a powerful Senate with equal representation for all states. In fact, most ministers functioned principally the other way around—as voices speaking to their regions on behalf of the federal government."[xxvi] Things have only deteriorated further in recent years. In the words of a senior cabinet minister in the Chrétien government, cabinet is no longer a decision-making body, it has been turned into a kind of "focus group" for the prime minister.[xxvii]

I invite those who believe that Canada still has cabinet government to ponder this point: "Two key decisions regarding Canada's deployment in Afghanistan—one by a Liberal government, one by a Conservative government—were made in the Prime Minister's Office with the help of a handful of political advisers and civilian and military officials. The relevant minsters of National Defence and Foreign Affairs were not even in the room." Cabinet was later told of the decision. Former cabinet minister Lowell Murray adds that this is "far from atypical illustration."[xxviii]

I recall that as recently as the early 1980s, cabinet ministers were free to appoint their senior political advisors. No more. The Prime Minister's Office today appoints all chiefs of staff.[xxix] I note that virtually all ministerial chiefs of staff in the Trudeau government (2015-19) were from Ontario and Quebec as were all the senior staff in Justin Trudeau's PMO. I also note that prime ministers appoint deputy ministers or the permanent head of government departments often without consulting the relevant ministers.

There was a time when the cabinet was home to powerful regional ministers: think of Clifford Sifton, Allen J. MacEachen, Don Jamieson and Don Mazankowski, among others. No more. Justin Trudeau even did away with regional ministers in 2015. For some unexplained reason, he decided to re-introduce the position in 2019 but only for Quebec when Pablo Rodriguez was made "Quebec lieutenant."[xxx] It is difficult to understand why Trudeau saw the need for a regional minister for Quebec and not for any other province, given that he is from Quebec.

Students of federalism look to "interstate" and "intrastate" federalism to assess a federal system. Interstate speaks to the constitutional distribution of power between central and provincial governments while intrastate federalism channels the central government itself.[xxxi] I know of no student of federalism that makes the case that Canada's national political and administrative institutions have an effective capacity to accommodate regional circumstances in shaping national policies but many that argue that they are much weaker than is the case for all other federations.[xxxii] It is worth repeating that John A. MacDonald, Cartier, Brown and Galt simply saw no need for intrastate federalism capacities in national institutions.

In short, the idea of confederation came from Canada West and Canada East as a solution to their ingrained and unsolvable political problems and was designed by their delegates to give full advantage to the economic interests of the two Canadas. First the Atlantic provinces and then the Western provinces were added, more as appendages than as partners.

The machinery of government falls into line

The federal public service is even more Ottawa-centric than the political institutions it serves. Canada stands out among Anglo-American countries in locating more public servants in its National Capital Region (NCR). This has been true down through the ages, and the pace has only accelerated in recent years. This is all the more surprising, given that Canada is a federation and its national political institutions have very weak intrastate requirements. In Australia, 38 per cent of federal public servants work in the Australian Capital Territory; in England, only 18.6 per cent work in London; in France, 22 per cent work in Paris and in the United states 16 per cent of federal government employees work in Washington, D.C. In Canada over 40 per cent of federal public servants work out of the NCR. Forty-five years ago, only about one in four public servants worked in the NCR.[xxxiii]

Prime Minister Stephen Harper became concerned with the concentration of public servants in the NCR. He pledged in 2012 to look more to Ottawa-Gatineau than to the other regions in pursuing his commitment to eliminate 19,200 public service positions. He, or rather the machinery of government, failed to deliver on his commitment. The Parliamentary Budget Office reported on 26 February 2015 that, after Harper made this commitment, "almost two-thirds of employment reductions have fallen outside of the NCR."[xxxiv] This makes the point that when it is in its interest, the federal public service has a well-honed capacity to give the appearance of change while standing still.

It will be recalled that the federal government launched a program in the mid-1970s to promote national unity, regional economic development, balanced urban growth and enhanced delivery of services to Canadians by moving some of its administrative units to the regions. Ottawa killed the program a few years later. A report from the Library of Parliament gives three reasons why the program was killed: cost, opposition MPs from the NCR, public servants and their unions. The last two reasons resonate but not the first. A strong case can and has been made that federal government units are less costly to operate in the regions. For one thing, the cost of office accommodation in many urban areas is less than in the NCR. For another, advances in information technology, from FaceTime to Zoom, now enable easy and inexpensive communications between offices. Studies also report that decentralized units are more efficient and less costly to operate than units in the NCR in part because of substantially lower staff turnover.[xxxv]

No one has taken the public service to task for moving more and more public servants by stealth to the NCR. The Senate has remained silent on this matter, as it has on many other issues that speak to regional concerns.

To Western and Atlantic Canadians, national policy is a code phrase for the economic interests of Ontario and Quebec. Liberal Member of Parliament David McGuinty spoke directly to the problem in his remarks that Alberta politicians in Ottawa were being too "provincial" when they focused on the energy sector. He said, "They are national legislators with a national responsibility, but they come across as very, very small-p provincial individuals who are jealously guarding one industrial sector, picking the fossil-fuel business and the oil-sands business specifically, as one that they're going to fight to the death for."[xxxvi]

The "one industrial sector," or the oil, gas and coal sector, matters greatly to British Columbia, Alberta, Saskatchewan, Nova Scotia, New Brunswick, and Newfoundland and Labrador (six out of ten provinces). No matter, in the eyes of McGuinty, it is a regional sector and politicians who focus on it are parochial, unable to pursue a national perspective. McGuinty, other MPs from Ontario, and the national media, however, view the automobile sector as a "national sector." Yet, for nine of Canada's ten provinces, the automobile industry is a regional sector, far more so than fossil fuel. I remind McGuinty that growth in the auto sector is not a product of Adam Smith's invisible hand. Ontario's auto sector is tied directly to federal government intervention, when it signed the Canada-U.S. Auto Pact in 1965. In addition, when the auto sector confronted serious financial difficulties in 2008-09, the federal government rushed in to save G.M. and Chrysler from bankruptcy, in the end costing $3.5 billion.[xxxvii]

Quebec-based Davie Shipbuilding has been living on a federal government lifeline for over forty years. In a competitive bidding process, Davie lost in its bid to build frigates for the Canadian navy to Irving's Saint John shipyard. However, the Quebec Liberal caucus successfully pressured the federal government to allocate part of the contract to Davie Shipyard located outside of Quebec. Davie again lost the $25 billion contract to build navy ships in 2011. It was later awarded a sole-source contract to provide a supply vessel to the navy only weeks before the 2015 general election.[xxxviii] These are hardly isolated cases when it comes to Quebec and Ontario. I challenge readers to come up with examples where Ottawa ignored the bidding process to direct contracts to firms from either Western or Atlantic Canada.

I have raised the issue with a number of journalists. Few of them dispute the point, but some add that it is to be expected because the majority of Canadians live in Ontario and Quebec, conveniently ignoring that Canada is a federation. One of Canada's leading journalists remarked: "A country that argues over such matters as federal-provincial relations and the shape and powers of the Senate is funneling emotions into time-consuming but rather harmless pursuits." Jeffrey Simpson goes on to quote "an old friend" to describe Canada as having a "malignant sense of regional envy." It is easy to dismiss the problem as simply "regional envy."[xxxix] This diagnosis does not require any changes to the country's national political institutions, just a change of attitude on the part of the regions other than Ontario and Quebec, at least on economic issues, and all will be well. This is a classic case of misdiagnosing the patient. A change in attitude that would matter can only take place in Canada's national political institutions, and that can only happen if the institutions themselves change.

Western and Atlantic Canadians know that Canada's national political institutions are ill-suited to speak to their interests. To be sure, these institutions would be ill-suited for any federation, but all the more for Canada, given its size and the reality that it is home to six time zones and several distinct economies. A recent public opinion survey reports on "a persistent malaise in Atlantic Canada" and that "Western alienation has gotten worse."[xl]

Atlantic Canadians know that the treaty that Macdonald and Cartier put together in 1867 has been detrimental to their region's economic interests. K.C. Irving, Canada's leading entrepreneur of the twentieth-century explained: "Over the years the federal government, regardless of party, has been responsible for policies which have resulted in New Brunswick being a forgotten section of Canada. When these national, or federal policies are changed, then the economy of the province of New Brunswick will change."[xli] K.C. Irving was never one to play the victim card.

Leaving aside guilt money flowing to Atlantic Canada in the form of transfer payments, a strong central government has never been in the economic interest of either Western or Atlantic Canada. It always has and remains in the economic interest of Ontario and Quebec and our national political institutions have a lot to answer for, given their central-Canadian bias. The inability of national institutions to accommodate regional interests, other than those from Ontario and Quebec, may well explain why Canada has only met modest success over the years in abolishing internal trade barriers.

Atlantic Canada, with only thirty-two seats in a 338-seat House of Commons, knows that it does not have the political clout to bring their issues to a head as they did in the 1920s through the "Maritime Rights Movement." But the region's patience is running thin. I do not think, for example, that thousands of Atlantic Canadians would walk the streets of Montreal asking Quebeckers to vote no in another referendum, as they did in the days leading up to the 1991 referendum.

What now?

Western and Atlantic provinces have common interests when dealing with Ontario-Quebec-centric national institutions. Atlantic Canada should be supportive of Western Canada in its efforts to bring structural changes to our national political institutions. I had difficulty understanding why only one out of four Atlantic provinces supported Western Canada's efforts to move to a Triple-E (effective, elected, equal) Senate during the 1990s and until the issue went to the Supreme Court in 2014. I take some credit in helping to convince the then New Brunswick Premier David Alward to support Senate reform. The other three Atlantic premiers stayed silent.

The battle for a Triple-E Senate is now lost in light of the 2014 Supreme Court decision. The debate over Senate reform also enables Ottawa to underline the point that Western and Atlantic Canada can have different interests and promote a divide and conquer strategy. Unwittingly or not, a cabinet minister from Quebec, Stéphane Dion, spoke to a divide and conquer strategy when he wrote that there was a basic problem in the Triple-E logic "because of the unequal distribution of senators per province. To elect senators with the current distribution of seats would be unfair for the under-represented provinces, Alberta and British Columbia, who have only six senators each, whereas New Brunswick and Nova Scotia, with about one quarter of their population, have ten."[xlii]

Western and Atlantic Canada have at least one common interest: the need to press the point that national unity concerns can no longer be just about Quebec. Mathieu Bouchard, former senior advisor to Justin Trudeau explained that, "If Quebeckers don't feel represented by the government for a period of time, unlike in other provinces, it becomes a question of national unity. We always have to be conscious of the fact." For Bouchard, much of the national media and senior public servants, which for the most part are located in Ottawa, that logic somehow can only apply to Quebec. If Western Canada threatens to separate, the logic may start to apply to other regions than Quebec, but that suggestion is not without risks.

Western and Atlantic Canadians need to make the case that Canada can never develop to its full economic potential unless the economic circumstances of their regions are brought into the mix when national economic policies take shape. With only 136 seats in the 338-seat House of Commons, and given the importance of party discipline, I hold little hope that prime ministers, always with their eyes on the next election, will want to initiate the required changes to give the regions greater voice in the Commons by initiating electoral reform or in cabinet by embracing it as an effective decision-making body where the voice from the regions are allowed to carry weight. If the status quo is to be reformed, it will only happen by a bottom-up challenge from the Western and Atlantic provinces. In short, those at the top are too beholden to the beneficiaries of the status quo to change.

The Senate, however, is a different story. Western and Atlantic Canada hold a majority of seats (54) in the 105-seat Senate. Recent changes to the appointment process may offer hope, though even here time will tell. A group of eleven senators recently joined forces to establish a new group to speak to Canada's regional interests. The group's central purpose is to ensure that "the will of the majority does not always trump regional interests."[xliii] This squares with the role that the upper house should have in a bicameral Parliament in a federation and Western and Atlantic Canadians should pressure current and future senators from their regions to join the group.

Leaving the above aside, Western and Atlantic Canadians will have to make do with modest reform to the Senate. Quebec and Ontario hold the key to more substantial Senate reform and there is no indication that they have an open mind on the matter. They remained silent, for example, when both the Chrétien and Martin governments refused to appoint Alberta's elected senators and when the Harper government introduced legislation to formalize the appointment of elected senators. The Supreme Court, with six of its nine members from Ontario and Quebec, ruled that the proposed Harper Senate reform was an attempt to amend the constitution by ordinary statutes, making the point that it should not be allowed. However, the ruling conveniently ignored the 1996 Regional Veto Act that returned to Quebec the veto power over constitutional amendments that was removed by the Constitution Act, 1982.[xliv]

It is one more case of *deux poids, deux mesures*. It also makes the point that Canada's national political, administrative and judicial institutions all have blinders on when it comes to the interests of the outer Canadas. Much like a tiger doesn't lose its stripes, Ontario and Quebec see no reason to see national institutions lose their blinders. These blinders have and continue to serve their political and economic interests. Change can only come from two sources: from central Canadians who are able to see that Canada can only develop to its full economic potential if national institutions can better accommodate regional economic circumstances, and from Western and Atlantic Canadians joining forces to ensure that the country's national institutions incorporate strong intrastate federalism requirements, as is the case in other federations.

Alberta's fiscal contribution to confederation
Robert Mansell

Introduction

THE HIGH degree of regional dissonance is a distinctive feature of Canada. As detailed by Donald Savoie, this is quite predictable given that the national governance institutions are and always have been tuned primarily to the interests of central Canada, and there are no effective checks to ensure the interests of the other provinces and territories are reflected. The result is regional tensions, particularly in the Atlantic and western regions, that regularly tug at the fragile fabric of confederation.

Jack Mintz argues that these tensions can generally be categorized as those that arise from conflicts of tastes and those arising from conflicts of claims. The former reflect differences in political tastes related to culture, values and history that are most applicable to Quebec. In the peripheral provinces, however, it is conflicts of claim that dominate. Broadly speaking, these concern federal tax, expenditure and transfer policies, along with those in areas such as transportation, trade, energy and regional development that impair the economic prosperity, growth and stability of those regions.[i]

Many of the original opponents of confederation in the Maritime provinces, for example, centred on such concerns. We see similar but amplified sentiment in the West. A common thread is that interregional transfers via federal tax and expenditure policies are unfair or otherwise disadvantageous to particular regions. For example, in a recent IPSOS poll, well over 60 per cent of Alberta and Saskatchewan residents feel they are not getting their fair share from confederation. The comparable percentage of residents in Atlantic Canada is 54 per cent, while Manitoba is 42 per cent, B.C. is 36 per cent, Quebec is 34 per cent, and Ontario is 20 per cent (Braid, IPSOS November 2019). These mirror the results of the most recent (2019) federal election where the governing Liberal party won only fourteen seats west of Ontario and none in Alberta or Saskatchewan.

Alberta is typically the centre of western alienation. During times when its economy has been strong, there has been a general view and acceptance that it is the cash cow of confederation. However, in the difficult periods, such as those since 2014, there tends to be much more concern that there is no quid pro quo for its large fiscal contributions that benefit other regions. One reflection is the recent establishment in Alberta of a Fair Deal panel focused on these concerns.

To better understand the veracity and nature of these tensions, the focus in this chapter is on quantifying Alberta's fiscal contributions to confederation over the long run, along with comparative information for the other provinces. This is done by examining the net federal fiscal balances for each province over the period 1961 to 2018. These balances show the amount each province has contributed to federal revenues compared to how much comes back to the province in the form of federal expenditures or transfers. As well, the objective is to unpack the policies behind the level and differences in these balances and the implications in terms of redistribution of incomes, employment and population across provinces.

At the outset a misplaced criticism of this type of analysis should be noted. It is that the impacts of federal tax, expenditure and transfer policies most importantly affect the welfare of individuals or groups regardless of the region they reside in. As such, it is argued that regional boundaries do not matter. While this argument may be valid in a unitary state, it is not in a federation. In Canada, the regions (read provinces and territories) are a very important part of the constitutional arrangement. As a federation of provinces (and territories), the governments of those regions are independent constitutional units which are assigned specific responsibilities. Two of the paramount are the protection and promotion of the economic interests of the residents in the region. Even more important, unlike the federal systems in other industrialized democracies, there is no serious or effective form of regional representation at the federal level to counterbalance the concentration of power in Parliament that arises from the large regional differences in population size. Clearly, to the extent federal policies differentially affect the provinces, they also differentially affect individuals and general levels of well-being of the residents of the provinces.

Estimating the regional impacts of federal fiscal policies

The federal fiscal balance for each province (and territory) is the total federal revenues collected in all forms in each region less the total of all types of federal expenditures in and transfers to each region. The federal revenue for each region is the sum of direct taxes (such as personal and corporate income taxes, withholding taxes, employment insurance premiums and contributions to social insurance plans), indirect taxes (for example, the federal GST, taxes on fuel and on banks and insurance companies, excise taxes, custom import duties and royalties), and investment income (such as interest, other investment income and remitted profits of government business enterprises) collected from the region. Federal expenditures for each region include all final federal expenditures on goods and services in the region (including such things as the salaries and benefits of federal civil servants, agents and other personnel in the region, and various other operating and capital expenditures in the region related to defence and non-defence activities) and interest payments on the public debt to residents of the region[ii] Federal transfers include all current transfers to households (for example, family and youth allowances, child tax benefits, childcare benefits, employment insurance and CPP payment, old age security, and GST credits), all subsidies on products and imports (for example, subsidies to agricultural and other industries), and all federal transfers to businesses and provincial /

territorial and local governments in the region (such as, equalization, and transfers to local and aboriginal governments).

A positive net fiscal balance or gap means that the combination of federal taxes, expenditures and transfers generates a net transfer out of the region while a negative balance indicates a net fiscal transfer to the region.

In the former case, the effect is to reduce income, employment and population in the region, while the values of these variables are increased in the region with a negative balance. Here the focus is on quantifying the distribution of these balances over a long period of time, namely 1961 to 2018. The starting year is as far back as is possible given available data. Note that the largest federal social programs capable of producing significant interregional fiscal transfers were created just before 1961 or in the mid-1960s.[iii] Others, such as those related to energy policy occurred later. The end year (2018) represents the most recent year for which the required data are available.

Quantifying the federal fiscal balance is not a trivial undertaking, especially given the long period of time covered in this study and the detailed analysis of the regional balances associated with each major federal fiscal policy. However, this long-term, detailed analysis addresses common shortcomings in evaluations of this type. First, unlike the latter where the focus is on just a few years, this takes into account the possibility, for example, of positive net federal fiscal balances for a region in some years being offset by negative balances in other years. In such cases, a shorter-term evaluation will likely give a distorted view of the fundamental patterns in terms of regional net fiscal contributions. Second, public attention is often focused on just one or two elements of federal fiscal policies (such as equalization) directly aimed at redistribution across regions. However, to draw valid conclusions about the overall net federal fiscal contributions or benefits for each region it is important that all tax, expenditure and transfer policies be considered, as is done here using measures of overall federal fiscal balances for each region. As noted later, while attention is often focused on fiscal equalization policies, other policies typically account for significantly larger components of the total net fiscal redistribution across the regions.

Details on the data sources and the adjustments required to obtain a consistent series over time are outlined in Mansell and Schlenker (1992, 1995), Mansell, Schlenker and Anderson (2005) and Mansell, Khanal and Tombe (2020)[iv]. It will suffice to note that core data are from the Provincial Economic Accounts (PEA), now the Provincial and Territorial Economic Accounts (PTEA), that use the national accounting conventions. In order to produce a consistent time series, some adjustments are required in the earlier years (1961-1995). These are to take account of factors such as the incidence of indirect taxes, the allocation of energy-related transfers (such as those during the National Oil Policy, Domestic Energy Pricing Controls and National Energy Program eras[v]), and the provincial allocation of interest on the federal public debt. The more recent data published by Statistics Canada under the PTEA, and now integrated with the Canadian Government Finance Statistics, uses similar methodology to allocate such things as indirect taxes and interest on the public debt so no further adjustments are required. Finally, for comparability over time, all estimates are adjusted for inflation using the Consumer Price Index and expressed in terms of the value of year 2018 Canadian dollars.

It is important to note the regional distribution of federal fiscal balances (or fiscal gaps) computed as outlined above does not indicate the net benefits or costs associated with regional autarky or independence from the federation. That is a much more complicated exercise requiring numerous assumptions about the division of assets and liabilities (including the national debt), the costs of replicating various federal programs, and the arrangements regarding such things as trade and migration (See Mansell and Schlenker, 1992).

Also note that redistribution across regions via programs such as equalization, Employment Insurance, or the Canada Pension Plan does not involve direct payments from the net contributor to net beneficiary regions. Rather, these take place indirectly through the federal treasury, using a combination of net federal fiscal flows from the contributor regions and funds borrowed by the federal government. In the latter case of federal debt the redistribution occurs through the regional allocation of federal expenditures and transfers supported by borrowed funds, through the regional allocation of interest paid on those funds, and through the regional allocation of federal revenues used to pay the interest on the debt. These allocations are incorporated in the methodology used to estimate the regional distribution of federal fiscal balances.

Regional distribution of federal fiscal balances

The federal fiscal balances for each region are expressed in per capita terms to take account of the large differences in region population size. The values for each region and each year (1961-2018) are provided in Appendix Table 1. The average annual per capita balances for selected periods are summarized in Table 1 and in Figure 1. Recall that a positive balance indicates a net fiscal outflow from the region (that is, the region is a net contributor) while a negative balance indicates a net fiscal inflow (that is, the region is net beneficiary).

Taking all federal tax, expenditure and transfer policies into account, there were only five years (1961-1965) when Alberta was a net beneficiary.[vi] During this period the average annual net fiscal benefit to the province amounted to $483 per person. In every other year since then Alberta has been a net contributor. Indeed, it was by far the largest net fiscal contributor over the period 1974-1985, with an average annual net contribution of $7512 per person, and over the period 1993-2018, with an average annual net contribution of $4546 per person.[vii] The large net transfers from Alberta in the earlier period were primarily related to the interregional transfers associated with federal energy policies. These substantial transfers from Alberta would appear to constitute the largest interregional transfer in Canadian history. The factors behind the large net transfers from Alberta in more recent periods are outlined in a later section.

Table 1: Average Annual Per Capita Federal Fiscal Balances (in 2018$) by Province and Territory for Selected Periods. Net inflows or negative values are shown in brackets, net outflows or positive values are unbracketed.

Province	1961-69	1970-79	1980-89	1990-99	2000-09	2010-18	1961-2018
NL	(2,231)	(4,710)	(8,370)	(8,264)	(6,124)	(3,128)	(5,567)
PEI	(3,507)	(6,430)	(7,960)	(6,982)	(7,080)	(8,673)	(6,795)
NS	(3,283)	(5,707)	(8,218)	(6,360)	(5,949)	(7,474)	(6,192)
NB	(2,127)	(4,436)	(6,801)	(5,290)	(4,987)	(6,493)	(5,047)
QC	208	(1,400)	(2,523)	(1,032)	(412)	(1,979)	(1,200)
ON	1,326	1,322	348	1,467	2,492	585	1,267
MB	(777)	(1,691)	(3,651)	(3,439)	(3,410)	(3,641)	(2,787)
SK	(1,174)	(1,235)	(3,221)	(3,186)	(1,740)	149	(1,777)
AB	(136)	4,323	5,029	1,986	5,645	5,243	3,720
BC	686	575	(1,122)	947	1,566	1,016	603
TERR	(13,217)	(12,578)	(26,559)	(23,701)	(26,509)	(34,714)	(22,842)

Source: Estimates by author using sources and methods described in text.

As indicated in Table 1, the net federal fiscal contribution by Alberta has averaged $3,700 per person per year over the entire 1961-2018 period, and averaged over $5,000 per person (or approximately $20,000 per family of four) each year during the 1980s and over the period since 2000. By way of comparison, Ontario has been a net contributor as well, except for the years 1980-1985 and 2009-2011, with annual per capita balances ranging from an annual net benefit of $942 per person to an annual net contribution of $4,132 per person. For the entire period Ontario's net contribution has averaged $1,267 per person per year. Although British Columbia was a net beneficiary in 1961, 1977 to 1990, and in 2010, for the period as a whole it has had an average net contribution of $603 per person per year, ranging from a net annual benefit of $2,060 per person in 1985 to a net contribution of $2,233 per person in 2000.

Figure 1: Average Annual Per Capita Federal Fiscal Balance (in 2018$) by Province for Selected Periods

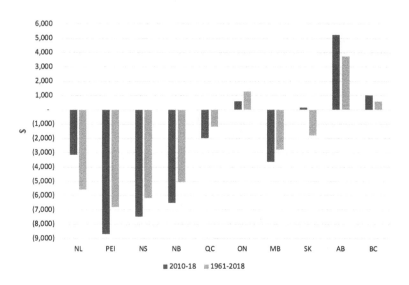

It is noteworthy that Saskatchewan became a net contributor in 2012 and this lasted until 2016. As well, Quebec was a minor net contributor from 1961-1967 and from 1997-2004. In all other years it has been a net beneficiary. By far the largest net beneficiary has been the Territories, but this largely reflects the very small and widely dispersed population resulting in the very high costs per person of providing federal services. This aside, the largest net beneficiaries on a per capita basis have tended to be the Atlantic provinces, Manitoba, and Quebec.

The per capita values outlined above are derived by dividing the total net federal fiscal balances for each region by that region's population. The annual total balances for Alberta and the other regions are provided in Appendix Table 2. They are summarized for selected periods in Table 2 and portrayed in Figure 2.

Table 2: Total Federal Fiscal Balances (in billions 2018$) by Province and Territory for Selected Periods

NL	-9.8	-26.1	-48.3	-46.7	-31.7	-14.8	-177.4
PEI	-3.4	-7.6	-10.1	-9.3	-9.8	-11.4	-51.5
NS	-22.3	-47.2	-72.1	-58.8	-55.7	-63.5	-319.7
NB	11.8	-30.1	-48.9	-39.6	-37.3	-44.4	-212.1
QC	10.5	-89.3	-167.5	-73.5	-32.6	-144.8	-497.2
ON	82.8	106.6	36.2	163.4	304.8	74.3	768.1
MB	-6.7	-17.4	-39.2	-38.6	-40.2	-41.9	-183.9
SK	-10.0	-11.5	-32.9	-32.2	-17.4	1.5	-102.5
AB	-1.5	82.0	115.6	55.9	189.1	189.8	630.9
BC	12.0	12.9	-33.2	37.0	65.4	44.3	138.3
TERR	-5.0	-8.0	-20.6	-22.4	-27.8	-36.7	-120.5
Prov Total	34.7	-35.6	-321.0	-64.8	306.9	-47.6	-127.5

Source: Estimates by author using sources and methods described in text.

Alberta was the largest net fiscal contributor in terms of total dollars over the periods 1973-1985 and 2007-2015.[viii] The net contribution to other regions over the earlier period (1973-1985) amounts to $193.8 billion, with a large part of this related to federal energy policies.

Measured over the entire 1961-2018 period Alberta's total net fiscal contribution was $631 billion, compared to Ontario at $768 billion and British Columbia at $138 billion. All other provinces and territories were net beneficiaries over this period. The largest net recipients were Quebec ($497 billion), Nova Scotia ($320 billion), New Brunswick ($212 billion), Manitoba ($184 billion), Newfoundland and Labrador ($177 billion) and the Territories ($121 billion). Over the most recent period (2010-2018), Saskatchewan became a net contributor, the net benefits to Newfoundland decreased significantly and the net benefits to Quebec increased substantially.

Figure 2: Total Federal Fiscal Balances (in billions 2018$) by Province for Selected Periods

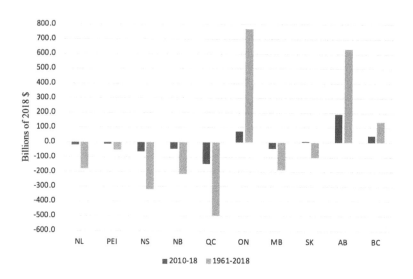

Unpacking federal fiscal balances

There are numerous national policies driving the differences across regions in federal fiscal balances. As noted earlier, in some earlier periods a major factor behind the outsized net contributions by Alberta was federal energy policy involving taxation, price controls and the redirection of expenditures. This policy was very effective in transferring activity and funds primarily to central Canada from Alberta and, to a lesser extent, from Saskatchewan and British Columbia. With the phasing out of those policies by the mid-1980s, the main drivers of the regional differences in fiscal balances have been a combination of general taxation, expenditure, and transfer policies. Of particular note are the policies related to personal and corporate income taxes, fiscal equalization payments, contributions and payments under the Canada Pension Plan (CPP) and Employment Insurance (EI) programs, GST and excise taxes, and the regional allocation of federal defense and non-defense procurement.

The focus here is on decomposing the federal fiscal balances for Alberta over the period 2009-2018, with comparative data for the other regions. The approach is outlined more fully in Mansell, Khanal, and Tombe, 2020. Basically it involves an evaluation of each region's average revenue contributed per capita and federal spending and transfers received per capita relative to the national average level. This provides a consistent benchmark for comparisons among the regions. The contributions of the various policies to the per capita federal fiscal balances for Alberta and the other regions are indicated in Table 3.

Table 3: Average Annual Contribution to Per Capita Federal Fiscal Balances by Province and Source, 2009-2018 (2018 Dollars)

	AB	BC	MB	NB	NL	NS	ON	PEI	QC	SK
Personal Income Taxes	2,069	3	(723)	(1,052)	(190)	(843)	294	(1,239)	(1,171)	18
Equalization and Stabilization	508	508	(1,095)	(1,885)	508	(1,413)	368	(2,145)	(711)	514
Corporate Income Taxes	951	(86)	(370)	(599)	(294)	(505)	7	(635)	(268)	295
CPP Net Contributions	735	73	82	(253)	(237)	(557)	(19)	(289)	(292)	112
Non-defense Purchases	670	385	(45)	(618)	(416)	(1,128)	(229)	(1,923)	59	221
OAS Benefits	384	(17)	71	(328)	(399)	(255)	68	(230)	(221)	55
EI Payments less Receipts	141	78	102	(702)	(1,335)	(409)	99	(1,111)	(90)	96
GST and Excise Taxes	372	89	(101)	(117)	66	(53)	(7)	(112)	(205)	99
Defense Purchases	121	207	(66)	(714)	201	(2,223)	(78)	153	224	351
Other Policies	129	(106)	(1,413)	(404)	(1,422)	(558)	103	(1,485)	468	(1,471)

Source: Authors' calculations as outlined in Mansell, Khanal and Tombe, 2020

The positive values (shown in bold) indicate the amount contributed by the particular policy to the region's overall federal fiscal balance. For example, in the case of Alberta, of the province's average annual net per capita fiscal contribution over the period 2009-2018, $735 is due to the higher net CPP contributions by Alberta residents (that is, CPP contributions minus CPP payments received). Similarly, $670 is due to the below average federal non-defense purchases in Alberta and $121 is due to below average federal defense purchases in Alberta. The negative numbers (indicated in brackets) on the other hand show the average net per capita gain to a region associated with each of the main policy areas. For example, equalization and stabilization policies accounted for an average annual net per capita benefit of $2,145, $1,885 and $1,413 respectively in the cases of Prince Edward Island, New Brunswick and Nova Scotia.

In the case of Alberta all ten major federal tax, expenditure and transfer policies indicated in Table 3 contribute to the net outflow from the province and the size of the per capita contributions under each policy area is much larger than those in any other province. Further, in comparison, most provinces, except British Columbia and Saskatchewan, see net fiscal gains associated with at least four of the policies.

These differences are related to the design of the various federal tax, spending, and transfer initiatives combined with regional economic and demographic differences. Without going into great detail, a summary of the factors at play is provided below.

Given the nature of federal personal income taxes,[ix] the personal income taxes contributed to Ottawa by Alberta are much higher because the province has tended to have incomes above the national average. This accounts for a federal fiscal contribution by Alberta averaging $2,069 per person per year. In most periods this is mainly due to higher wages and longer hours worked, combined with higher labour force participation rates in the province.[x] The above average incomes in turn translate into higher personal expenditures[xi] and this results in larger GST and Excise tax revenues for the federal government. This additional revenue contribution by Alberta to the federal government amounts to an average of $372 per person per year. Corporations in Alberta also contribute an outsized proportion of federal revenues from application of the corporate income tax. For the period shown, on average these account for about $951 per person per year to Alberta's total net per capita fiscal contribution. Turning to the expenditure side, the significantly below-average defense and non-defense expenditures in Alberta by the federal government account for an average of $791 (that is, $670 + $121) per person per year of the province's net fiscal contribution.

The design of other major programs such as equalization, revenue stabilization, the Canada Pension Plan (CPP), Old Age Security (OAS) and Employment Insurance (EI) is such that under each Alberta is also a substantial net fiscal contributor. The formula used for the allocation of fiscal equalization payments is such that Alberta does not qualify for any of these payments and is unlikely to qualify under most future scenarios (see Tombe, 2018). As noted in Table 3, this translates into a net fiscal outflow from Alberta averaging $508 per person per year. The revenue stabilization program is intended as an insurance policy for provinces in cases where their government revenues show sharp declines due to economic shocks. The particular formulas for this program have meant that, in spite of numerous cases of substantial declines in Alberta government revenue, it has only received minimal payments (capped at $60 per capita) on two occasions.[xii]

In the case of the CPP, Alberta's net annual federal fiscal contribution amounts to an average of $735 per person. In general, this mainly reflects the relatively lower percentage of the Alberta population over sixty-five years of age. This, combined with the higher average incomes in the province, is also largely behind the net annual federal fiscal contribution averaging $384 per person associated with the OAS program. The employment insurance program results in an average net annual fiscal contribution by Alberta of $141 per person. In general, the design of the program favors the provinces with generally lower labour force mobility, a smaller share of employment in industries where self-employment is more common, and higher average unemployment rates. Finally, we estimate for Alberta an average annual net contribution of $129 per person per year associated with other region-specific policies such as those focused on agriculture or on resource development.

To find the total (versus, per capita) redistribution across Canada as a whole, the per capita balances shown in Table 3 are multiplied by each province's population. The results are indicated in Table 4.

Table 4: Average Annual Contribution to Federal Fiscal Balances by Province and Source, 2009-2018, (Millions 2018 Dollars)

	AB	BC	MB	NB	NL	NS	ON	PEI	QC	SK
Personal Income Taxes	8,279	12	(922)	(799)	(100)	(796)	3,992	(180)	(9,507)	20
Equalization and Stabilization	2,032	2,379	(1,396)	(1,431)	267	(1,333)	4,999	(312)	(5,771)	567
Corporate Income Taxes	3,805	402	(472)	(455)	(154)	(477)	99	(92)	(2,176)	325
CPP Net Contributions	2,941	342	105	(192)	(125)	(525)	(257)	(42)	(2,371)	123
Non-defense Purchases	2,681	1,805	(57)	(469)	(219)	(1,064)	(3,117)	(280)	476	244
OAS Benefits	1,536	(82)	91	(249)	(210)	(241)	920	(33)	(1,792)	61
EI Payments less Receipts	564	364	130	(533)	(702)	(386)	1,348	(162)	(729)	105
GST and Excise Taxes	1,490	419	(129)	(89)	35	(50)	(101)	(16)	(1,668)	109
Defense Purchases	485	970	(84)	(542)	106	(2,098)	(1,063)	22	1,818	387
Other Factors	516	(498)	(1,802)	(306)	(748)	(527)	1,399	(216)	3,802	(1,621)

Source: Authors' calculations as outlined in Mansell, Khanal and Tombe, 2020

For example, as indicated in the first column, of the average net annual transfer out of Alberta of about $24 billion, 8.3 billion was accounted for by personal income taxes, $3.8 billion by corporate taxes, $2.9 billion by CPP, $2.7 billion by non-defense purchases, $2 billion by equalization and stabilization, $1.5 billion by OAS, $1.5 billion by GST, and $1.6 billion by a combination of employment insurance, defense purchases and other policy areas.

Overall, these deviations between revenue and spending across all provinces and programs represent an implicit redistribution of fiscal resources through the federal budget amounting to over $38 billion per year—or nearly 2 per cent of national GDP.

Regional impacts

The provincial distribution of federal fiscal balances has direct impacts on the distribution of income, employment and population across the regions. Aggregate demand is redistributed from the regions with positive federal fiscal balances to those with negative balances. For example, over the 1961–2018 period there has been $1.54 trillion in aggregate demand transferred from Ontario, Alberta, and BC to the other provinces and territories (see Table 2). These direct impacts, measured as a percentage of each province's GDP and total personal income, are shown in Tables 5 and 6. Note that the negative values indicate a net inflow to the region as a percentage of its GDP and personal income while the positive values indicate a net outflow as a percentage of these two measures.

Table 5: Average Annual Direct Impacts of Federal Fiscal Balances by Region Relative to GDP

Province	1961-69	1970-79	1980-89	1990-99	2000-09	2010-18	1961-2018
NL	-19%	-26%	-34%	-29%	-12%	-5%	-17%
PEI	-31%	-36%	-32%	-23%	-19%	-20%	-24%
NS	-22%	-27%	-29%	-20%	-14%	-17%	-20%
NB	-15%	-21%	-25%	-16%	-12%	-14%	-16%
QC	1%	-5%	-7%	-3%	-1%	-4%	-3%
ON	5%	3%	1%	3%	5%	1%	3%
MB	-4%	-6%	-10%	-9%	-7%	-7%	-8%
SK	-6%	-4%	-9%	-8%	-3%	0%	-4%
AB	0%	10%	9%	4%	7%	6%	7%
BC	3%	1%	-3%	2%	3%	2%	2%
TERR	-51%	-31%	-45%	-42%	-33%	-39%	-39%

Source: GDP data for 1961-2002 is from Mansell, Schlenker and Anderson (2005) and for 2003-2018 from Stats Can Table 36-10-0222-01 (formerly CANSIM 384-0038)

In the case of Alberta the net direct fiscal transfers from the province have averaged 7 per cent of GDP over 1961-2018, with an average of almost 10 per cent over the 1970-1989 period. In comparison, for the entire period, the average transfer from Ontario has amounted to 3 per cent of its GDP while that from BC is 2 per cent. At the same time the net fiscal transfers to the Atlantic provinces have averaged around 20 per cent of GDP in the most recent decade, but with a much smaller percentage for Newfoundland in recent years. The net transfers to Quebec for the same period represent an average of 3 per cent of its GDP. The comparable values for Manitoba and Saskatchewan have been, respectively, between 8 per cent and 4 per cent.

There are substantial differences across the regions in the percentage of GDP or value added in the region that is received as personal income by residents of the region.[xiii] This discrepancy is particularly large for regions such as Alberta and Saskatchewan (and the Territories) owing to their economies being resource and capital intensive. For example in 2018 personal income amounted to 90 per cent of GDP in Quebec, 85 per cent in Ontario, but only 72 per cent in Alberta. In the latter case, the much higher capital intensity means, for instance, larger payments to capital, the owners of which disproportionally reside in other regions. Further, it should be noted that, particularly in the most capital and resource intensive regions, the relationship between income received and GDP is highly variable.[xiv]

A measure of income received, such as personal income, is a better indicator of the economic welfare of residents in the region than is GDP or total value added through payments to labour and capital in the region.[xv] The direct impacts of the regional redistribution associated with federal fiscal policies on personal incomes in each province are shown in Table 6. It is apparent that the direct impacts of the interregional fiscal transfers are significantly larger when measured against total income received rather than against GDP (compare the results to those in Table 5).

Table 6: Average Annual Direct Impacts of Federal Fiscal Balances by Region Relative to Personal Income

Province	1961-69	1970-79	1980-89	1990-99	2000-09	2010-18	1961-2018
NL	-22%	-27%	-38%	-31%	-17%	-7%	-21%
PEI	-33%	-35%	-32%	-24%	-20%	-21%	-25%
NS	-26%	-28%	-30%	-21%	-16%	-17%	-21%
NB	-18%	-23%	-27%	-18%	-14%	-15%	-18%
QC	1%	-6%	-8%	-3%	-1%	-4%	-4%
ON	7%	4%	1%	4%	6%	1%	3%
MB	-5%	-7%	-12%	-11%	-9%	-8%	-9%
SK	-8%	-5%	-11%	-11%	-5%	0%	-6%
AB	-1%	17%	14%	6%	11%	9%	10%
BC	4%	2%	-3%	3%	4%	2%	2%
TERR	-81%	-49%	-81%	-61%	-52%	-59%	-60%

Source: Personal Income data for 1961-2002 is from Mansell, Schlenker and Anderson (2005) and for 2003-2018 from Stats Can Table 36-10-0226-01 (formerly CANSIM 384-0042)

Using this measure, the redistribution away from Alberta averaged 10 per cent over the 1961-2018 period, reaching a high of 17 per cent in the 1970-79 period and 14 per cent in the 1980s. In comparison, the redistribution away from Ontario has averaged 3 per cent per year over the 1961 period, with a high of 7 per cent over 1961-1969 and a low of 1 per cent over 1980-89 and 2010-2018. The amount of redistribution toward Saskatchewan, Newfoundland and the territories is also significantly larger when measured in terms of personal income. For the provinces of Nova Scotia, Prince Edward Island and New Brunswick the net fiscal inflows as a percentage of total personal incomes have tended to decline over time but still amount to between 15 and 21 percent in the most recent decade.

There are, however, indirect effects that must also be taken into account.[xvi] These strongly interact with federal fiscal policy. In the case of international trade, only Alberta and Saskatchewan have generally run international trade surpluses (that is, on balance they export more to international markets than they import from those markets). It is also apparent that, in general, Ontario and Quebec have tended to run large interprovincial surpluses with the other regions. That is, they export more to the other provinces than they import from them. In the case of Ontario, at least until more recent decades, the large federal fiscal surpluses for the province were not seen as a particular burden. This is because the fiscal redistribution from Ontario to recipient provinces typically meant larger exports from Ontario to those regions as their imports expanded. In turn, this would tend to offset the negative impacts of the federal fiscal surpluses on Ontario's income, employment and population.

An analysis suggests that these trade linkages can result in as much as a 35 per cent gain for Ontario and an 8 per cent gain for Quebec in the redistribution associated with federal fiscal balances (Mansell and Schlenker, 1995). A more recent analysis that takes into account the regional trade patterns and effects on prices and interprovincial movements of population has been undertaken by Tombe and Winter (2020). They use a computable general equilibrium model and data for the period 2007-2016 to trace the direct and indirect effects of the regional distribution of federal fiscal balances on GDP, real incomes, employment, and migration flows among the provinces. Their analysis indicates for that period, the net federal fiscal balances served to lower real incomes in Alberta by over 8 per cent and lower its population by over 12 per cent. The largest gains are by PEI with an uplift of 30 per cent in its real income and 50 per cent in its population.

Summary

There is no doubt that over the lengthy 1961-2018 period considered, Alberta has been the cash cow of confederation. The province's annual net federal fiscal contribution has averaged $3,700 per person for this period, or about $5,400 per person (or $21,600 per family of four) over the period since 2000. The comparable figures for Ontario are $1,270 per person per year for

1961-2008, $2,500 over the period 2000-2009 and $585 over the period 2010-2018. BC has been a net contributor for five of the six decades covered with an average net contribution of $600 per person per year. Averaged over almost six decades, all of the other provinces have been net beneficiaries, ranging from a net federal fiscal inflow of $1,200 per capita in Quebec to $6,800 in Prince Edward Island.

In terms of total dollars, Alberta has been a net fiscal contributor in every year since 1965, amounting to a net contribution of $630 billion. Ontario has been largest net contributor overall at $768 billion in spite of being a net beneficiary over 1980-1985 and 2009-2011. British Columbia's net contribution is $138 billion. All other provinces and territories were net beneficiaries over 1961-2018. The largest net recipients were Quebec ($497 billion), Nova Scotia ($320 billion), New Brunswick ($212 billion), Manitoba ($184 billion), Newfoundland and Labrador ($177 billion) and the Territories ($121 billion). Over the most recent period (2010-2018), Saskatchewan became a net contributor, the net benefits to Newfoundland decreased significantly and the net benefits to Quebec increased substantially.

These fiscal transfers continue to result in a significant redistribution of incomes, employment and population across provinces. The redistribution from Alberta is by far the largest, amounting to an average of about 10 per cent of its personal income. The comparable values for Ontario and B.C. are, respectively, 3 per cent and 2 per cent. The annual average redistribution to the Atlantic provinces equals about 20 per cent of total personal income. For Manitoba, Saskatchewan and Quebec, this redistribution amounts to between 4 per cent and 9 per cent of personal income.

When the indirect effects are taken into account, the amount of redistribution is significantly increased. For example, the redistribution away ·from Alberta in the most recent decade has worked to lower employment and population by over 12 per cent and reduce real incomes by more than 8 per cent.

There are numerous factors accounting for the pattern of federal fiscal balances across regions. These include the transfers associated with federal personal and corporate income taxes, equalization and stabilization payments, CPP net contributions, Defense and Non-Defense purchases, EI payments less receipts, and OAS benefits. Of the ten policies analyzed, all ten result in a net fiscal outflow from Alberta. For Saskatchewan, nine produce net outflows and one generates a net inflow. For BC, seven generate a net outflow and three produce a net inflow. In the case of Ontario, six generate outflows and four generate net inflows, while for Quebec, Manitoba, and Newfoundland there are three policies producing a net outflow and seven contributing to net inflows. It is interesting that, contrary to the common view that fiscal equalization payments constitute the largest source of redistribution across the regions, they actually account of only about one-quarter of the redistribution. Rather, it is the other fiscal policy components that account for the majority of the redistribution across regions.

In summary, taking account of the direct and indirect impacts associated with the regional pattern of federal fiscal balances, the redistribution of income, employment, and population is disproportionately from Alberta. While the federal government has also run large fiscal surpluses with Ontario in some periods, these balances have been more modest considering the size of the province's economy and the indirect effects from federal fiscal deficits with other regions that are net importers of goods and services from Ontario. The greatest redistribution has been and continues to be to Quebec, the Atlantic region, Manitoba and the territories.

APPENDIX Table 1: Per Capita Net Federal Fiscal Balances by Province (in 2018 dollars), 1961-2018

	NL	PEI	NS	NB	QC	ON	MB	SK	AB	BC	TERR
1961	(1,967)	(2,522)	(3,016)	(2,058)	232	755	(1,037)	(1,477)	(629)	(268)	(13,968)
1962	(2,171)	(2,939)	(3,087)	(2,021)	146	640	(1,067)	(1,730)	(531)	70	(13,882)
1963	(1,964)	(3,183)	(3,010)	(1,970)	200	770	(929)	(1,249)	(465)	202	(13,048)
1964	(1,790)	(3,057)	(2,903)	(1,932)	362	1,236	(553)	(1,118)	(401)	612	(13,918)
1965	(2,254)	(4,087)	(3,116)	(2,055)	382	1,449	(557)	(1,130)	(388)	738	(13,283)
1966	(2,255)	(3,922)	(3,236)	(2,084)	306	1,612	(648)	(966)	38	985	(13,214)
1967	(2,587)	(3,883)	(3,668)	(2,497)	85	1,601	(706)	(924)	157	1,032	(14,588)
1968	(2,477)	(3,871)	(3,861)	(2,375)	(32)	1,669	(851)	(845)	428	1,059	(12,565)
1969	(2,615)	(4,097)	(3,654)	(2,152)	194	2,205	(648)	(1,129)	566	1,746	(10,491)
1970	(2,821)	(4,571)	(3,131)	(2,317)	(69)	1,929	(791)	(1,628)	437	1,281	(9,117)
1971	(3,255)	(5,099)	(3,346)	(2,690)	(411)	1,955	(884)	(1,862)	288	1,225	(9,456)
1972	(3,550)	(5,204)	(3,732)	(2,959)	(656)	1,949	(964)	(2,072)	444	1,119	(12,760)
1973	(3,699)	(5,223)	(4,138)	(3,114)	(485)	2,124	(983)	(1,705)	1,453	1,594	(9,217)
1974	(4,633)	(5,485)	(5,391)	(3,936)	(1,088)	1,819	(884)	156	8,272	1,278	(7,650)
1975	(5,683)	(6,803)	(6,719)	(5,409)	(2,041)	898	(1,655)	(706)	7,435	339	(12,909)
1976	(4,775)	(7,440)	(6,808)	(5,262)	(1,616)	1,109	(1,669)	(388)	5,971	333	(15,375)
1977	(5,834)	(7,976)	(7,853)	(5,966)	(2,327)	645	(2,589)	(973)	5,877	(346)	(16,837)
1978	(6,797)	(8,801)	(8,114)	(6,527)	(2,756)	598	(3,181)	(1,903)	4,644	(675)	(16,848)
1979	(6,054)	(7,697)	(7,835)	(6,184)	(2,550)	192	(3,307)	(1,268)	8,412	(396)	(15,615)
1980	(6,477)	(7,606)	(9,059)	(8,339)	(3,227)	(754)	(3,758)	27	15,161	(778)	(17,837)
1981	(5,847)	(6,605)	(8,269)	(7,873)	(3,027)	(392)	(2,555)	424	15,231	(309)	(19,695)
1982	(7,747)	(7,615)	(8,411)	(7,410)	(3,427)	(523)	(3,121)	(1,561)	9,770	(1,245)	(25,327)
1983	(8,674)	(7,542)	(8,795)	(6,505)	(3,125)	(299)	(3,344)	(2,884)	4,094	(1,495)	(26,957)
1984	(9,034)	(8,887)	(9,567)	(6,827)	(3,200)	(334)	(3,830)	(3,959)	3,063	(1,939)	(29,639)
1985	(10,679)	(8,941)	(8,684)	(7,326)	(3,115)	(264)	(4,182)	(4,483)	2,218	(2,060)	(30,395)
1986	(9,902)	(8,011)	(7,780)	(5,944)	(1,857)	1,195	(3,796)	(5,397)	266	(1,294)	(34,699)
1987	(8,575)	(7,616)	(7,036)	(5,844)	(1,501)	1,510	(3,880)	(5,455)	269	(902)	(25,464)
1988	(8,457)	(8,283)	(7,334)	(5,893)	(1,375)	1,713	(4,131)	(4,978)	78	(675)	(25,917)
1989	(8,312)	(8,489)	(7,248)	(6,050)	(1,377)	1,631	(3,913)	(3,938)	135	(520)	(29,661)
1990	(8,948)	(8,679)	(7,512)	(6,356)	(1,567)	1,231	(3,887)	(4,405)	508	(341)	(26,251)
1991	(8,332)	(7,793)	(6,852)	(5,805)	(1,705)	611	(4,150)	(4,593)	600	102	(28,516)
1992	(9,114)	(8,231)	(6,860)	(6,243)	(1,674)	648	(3,744)	(4,356)	634	384	(23,602)
1993	(8,985)	(7,607)	(7,175)	(5,860)	(2,026)	172	(3,820)	(3,979)	1,165	364	(28,120)
1994	(9,191)	(7,360)	(7,504)	(5,646)	(1,727)	412	(4,194)	(3,563)	1,491	664	(23,749)
1995	(8,356)	(6,793)	(6,980)	(5,303)	(1,622)	745	(3,797)	(2,543)	1,667	900	(20,546)
1996	(7,771)	(5,401)	(6,225)	(4,995)	(757)	1,440	(3,730)	(3,635)	2,152	1,507	(20,224)
1997	(6,619)	(5,558)	(5,060)	(4,026)	297	2,728	(2,445)	(1,320)	3,708	2,110	(19,390)
1998	(7,760)	(6,009)	(4,818)	(4,349)	169	3,122	(2,138)	(1,391)	3,981	1,979	(19,786)
1999	(7,561)	(6,391)	(4,613)	(4,311)	294	3,561	(2,484)	(2,075)	3,951	1,803	(26,824)
2000	(5,890)	(5,560)	(4,287)	(3,457)	755	4,132	(2,190)	(1,658)	4,693	2,233	(22,122)
2001	(6,484)	(7,152)	(5,554)	(4,531)	130	3,478	(2,744)	(2,075)	4,463	1,714	(24,141)
2002	(6,380)	(6,175)	(5,476)	(4,264)	184	3,181	(2,735)	(1,431)	4,623	1,407	(16,762)
2003	(5,511)	(5,921)	(5,017)	(4,359)	188	2,959	(3,114)	(1,996)	4,344	1,580	(25,369)
2004	(4,725)	(5,486)	(4,726)	(4,103)	489	3,120	(2,752)	(2,916)	4,799	1,666	(25,189)
2005	(11,634)	(6,707)	(7,413)	(5,358)	(77)	2,877	(3,849)	(2,463)	5,729	1,522	(31,564)
2006	(5,466)	(6,403)	(5,324)	(4,872)	(319)	2,875	(3,431)	(1,871)	7,314	2,257	(28,947)
2007	(5,446)	(7,984)	(6,520)	(5,911)	(1,084)	1,702	(4,058)	(1,459)	7,558	1,851	(27,848)
2008	(3,874)	(9,067)	(7,454)	(6,171)	(1,962)	822	(4,451)	(943)	7,317	1,185	(30,477)
2009	(5,835)	(10,345)	(7,721)	(6,846)	(2,420)	(227)	(4,778)	(585)	5,606	247	(32,676)
2010	(5,703)	(10,468)	(7,914)	(7,306)	(2,669)	(942)	(5,009)	(944)	5,096	(467)	(34,146)
2011	(3,986)	(9,104)	(7,712)	(6,864)	(2,192)	(83)	(4,397)	(278)	5,253	335	(31,733)
2012	(3,520)	(8,403)	(7,866)	(6,566)	(2,010)	104	(3,917)	47	5,442	775	(32,314)
2013	(2,512)	(8,715)	(7,668)	(6,354)	(1,975)	204	(3,454)	770	6,417	746	(33,971)
2014	(2,187)	(7,983)	(7,187)	(6,101)	(1,949)	695	(3,044)	1,216	7,059	1,072	(34,799)
2015	(2,472)	(7,851)	(7,272)	(6,192)	(1,810)	1,038	(2,953)	1,011	6,294	1,346	(35,327)
2016	(2,730)	(8,073)	(7,090)	(6,232)	(1,809)	1,224	(3,180)	115	3,951	1,540	(36,285)
2017	(3,007)	(8,613)	(7,199)	(6,413)	(1,867)	1,508	(3,385)	(328)	3,679	1,757	(36,722)
2018	(2,032)	(8,842)	(7,361)	(6,411)	(1,533)	1,519	(3,429)	(271)	3,994	2,046	(37,128)

APPENDIX Table 2: Net Federal Fiscal Balances by Province (in millions of 2018 dollars), 1961-2018

	NL	PEI	NS	NB	QC	ON	MB	SK	AB	BC	TERR
1961	(900)	(264)	(2,220)	(1,229)	1,219	4,703	(955)	(1,364)	(837)	(437)	(527)
1962	(1,015)	(315)	(2,300)	(1,222)	781	4,060	(997)	(1,608)	(727)	117	(548)
1963	(934)	(344)	(2,256)	(1,198)	1,093	4,990	(882)	(1,163)	(652)	344	(528)
1964	(864)	(333)	(2,189)	(1,180)	2,018	8,191	(530)	(1,052)	(573)	1,069	(581)
1965	(1,098)	(445)	(2,352)	(1,263)	2,170	9,828	(537)	(1,073)	(561)	1,328	(561)
1966	(1,112)	(426)	(2,445)	(1,285)	1,767	11,213	(623)	(922)	55	1,845	(568)
1967	(1,291)	(423)	(2,786)	(1,548)	498	11,400	(679)	(884)	234	2,009	(642)
1968	(1,253)	(427)	(2,961)	(1,485)	(188)	12,115	(825)	(811)	651	2,122	(572)
1969	(1,343)	(455)	(2,832)	(1,350)	1,157	16,282	(634)	(1,081)	882	3,596	(496)
1970	(1,459)	(504)	(2,447)	(1,452)	(417)	14,565	(776)	(1,532)	697	2,726	(451)
1971	(1,728)	(574)	(2,668)	(1,728)	(2,523)	15,342	(883)	(1,735)	479	2,744	(524)
1972	(1,914)	(590)	(2,994)	(1,920)	(4,049)	15,517	(966)	(1,908)	752	2,577	(752)
1973	(2,018)	(599)	(3,361)	(2,045)	(3,013)	17,151	(990)	(1,555)	2,507	3,774	(571)
1974	(2,546)	(636)	(4,414)	(2,617)	(6,818)	14,924	(900)	141	14,514	3,122	(476)
1975	(3,163)	(801)	(5,553)	(3,662)	(12,919)	7,472	(1,696)	(648)	13,448	848	(836)
1976	(2,687)	(883)	(5,686)	(3,628)	(10,340)	9,332	(1,722)	(361)	11,161	844	(1,027)
1977	(3,298)	(956)	(6,596)	(4,152)	(14,967)	5,488	(2,686)	(919)	11,449	(890)	(1,127)
1978	(3,858)	(1,071)	(6,854)	(4,566)	(17,750)	5,137	(3,311)	(1,812)	9,392	(1,764)	(1,153)
1979	(3,451)	(946)	(6,655)	(4,348)	(16,491)	1,663	(3,430)	(1,217)	17,639	(1,056)	(1,073)
1980	(3,710)	(941)	(7,725)	(5,889)	(20,996)	(6,590)	(3,887)	26	33,219	(2,137)	(1,238)
1981	(3,364)	(816)	(7,069)	(5,562)	(19,816)	(3,456)	(2,646)	414	34,896	(873)	(1,404)
1982	(4,445)	(941)	(7,225)	(5,242)	(22,552)	(4,668)	(3,262)	(1,540)	23,154	(3,580)	(1,874)
1983	(5,024)	(944)	(7,637)	(4,650)	(20,633)	(2,698)	(3,544)	(2,888)	9,799	(4,348)	(2,006)
1984	(5,240)	(1,125)	(8,394)	(4,919)	(21,218)	(3,060)	(4,105)	(4,017)	7,333	(5,714)	(2,260)
1985	(6,186)	(1,141)	(7,693)	(5,299)	(20,762)	(2,453)	(4,527)	(4,595)	5,334	(6,130)	(2,389)
1986	(5,707)	(1,029)	(6,917)	(4,309)	(12,460)	11,278	(4,143)	(5,552)	647	(3,887)	(2,744)
1987	(4,933)	(980)	(6,288)	(4,253)	(10,182)	14,554	(4,262)	(5,634)	657	(2,751)	(2,055)
1988	(4,862)	(1,071)	(6,580)	(4,304)	(9,398)	16,852	(4,553)	(5,119)	192	(2,103)	(2,137)
1989	(4,792)	(1,105)	(6,551)	(4,447)	(9,533)	16,479	(4,319)	(4,015)	338	(1,663)	(2,503)
1990	(5,166)	(1,132)	(6,840)	(4,705)	(10,965)	12,674	(4,297)	(4,439)	1,295	(1,121)	(2,281)
1991	(4,830)	(1,016)	(6,269)	(4,328)	(12,050)	6,372	(4,605)	(4,605)	1,555	343	(2,559)
1992	(5,287)	(1,077)	(6,308)	(4,671)	(11,901)	6,852	(4,166)	(4,374)	1,668	1,332	(2,180)
1993	(5,211)	(1,005)	(6,629)	(4,388)	(14,496)	1,839	(4,270)	(4,007)	3,106	1,299	(2,635)
1994	(5,280)	(982)	(6,955)	(4,236)	(12,421)	4,457	(4,711)	(3,597)	4,028	2,442	(2,248)
1995	(4,741)	(913)	(6,478)	(3,982)	(11,708)	8,154	(4,287)	(2,579)	4,557	3,399	(1,990)
1996	(4,349)	(733)	(5,798)	(3,758)	(5,486)	15,964	(4,230)	(3,704)	5,972	5,839	(1,998)
1997	(3,647)	(756)	(4,718)	(3,029)	2,157	30,634	(2,778)	(1,343)	10,493	8,333	(1,926)
1998	(4,189)	(816)	(4,490)	(3,264)	1,235	35,487	(2,432)	(1,415)	11,541	7,881	(1,945)
1999	(4,032)	(871)	(4,307)	(3,236)	2,155	40,964	(2,838)	(2,106)	11,667	7,231	(2,635)
2000	(3,110)	(759)	(4,003)	(2,594)	5,556	48,271	(2,513)	(1,671)	14,099	9,020	(2,177)
2001	(3,385)	(977)	(5,179)	(3,398)	962	41,375	(3,159)	(2,075)	13,650	6,988	(2,393)
2002	(3,315)	(845)	(5,121)	(3,195)	1,367	38,472	(3,164)	(1,426)	14,464	5,770	(1,691)
2003	(2,857)	(813)	(4,705)	(3,267)	1,406	36,230	(3,623)	(1,989)	13,829	6,517	(2,610)
2004	(2,445)	(755)	(4,440)	(3,075)	3,683	38,661	(3,229)	(2,908)	15,543	6,924	(2,635)
2005	(5,984)	(926)	(6,953)	(4,008)	(583)	36,050	(4,535)	(2,447)	19,031	6,387	(3,334)
2006	(2,791)	(883)	(4,993)	(3,633)	(2,432)	36,407	(4,060)	(1,857)	25,023	9,572	(3,076)
2007	(2,772)	(1,100)	(6,097)	(4,406)	(8,341)	21,732	(4,826)	(1,462)	26,562	7,944	(2,989)
2008	(1,982)	(1,258)	(6,976)	(4,609)	(15,229)	10,584	(5,331)	(960)	26,311	5,154	(3,302)
2009	(3,015)	(1,447)	(7,244)	(5,134)	(18,979)	(2,944)	(5,774)	(605)	20,623	1,090	(3,578)
2010	(2,977)	(1,483)	(7,456)	(5,502)	(21,165)	(12,379)	(6,115)	993	19,020	(2,087)	(3,798)
2011	(2,093)	(1,311)	(7,282)	(5,187)	(17,544)	(1,103)	(5,424)	(296)	19,902	1,508	(3,589)
2012	(1,852)	(1,215)	(7,423)	(4,980)	(16,200)	1,393	(4,896)	50	21,084	3,537	(3,702)
2013	(1,324)	(1,256)	(7,211)	(4,820)	(16,016)	2,755	(4,368)	847	25,548	3,452	(3,929)
2014	(1,155)	(1,152)	(6,746)	(4,631)	(15,888)	9,463	(3,893)	1,353	28,828	5,047	(4,071)
2015	(1,306)	(1,135)	(6,810)	(4,699)	(14,797)	14,223	(3,817)	1,134	26,086	6,428	(4,183)
2016	(1,445)	(1,186)	(6,685)	(4,757)	(14,884)	16,979	(4,179)	131	16,580	7,482	(4,360)
2017	(1,589)	(1,296)	(6,842)	(4,918)	(15,495)	21,222	(4,519)	(377)	15,610	8,654	(4,486)
2018	(1,068)	(1,358)	(7,063)	(4,942)	(12,856)	21,750	(4,641)	(315)	17,175	10,231	(4,593)

References

Alberta 2020. *Fair Deal Panel*. See https://www.alberta.ca/fair-deal-panel.aspx

Braid, Kyle / Ipsos, 2019. "Canadians across all regions feel country more divided than ever." *IPSOS News & Polls*, November 5.

Dahlby, Bev. 2019. "Reforming the Federal Fiscal Stabilization Program," *The School of Public Policy Briefing Papers* 12(14): 1- 16.

Mansell, Robert L. and Ronald C. Schlenker. 1992. "A Regional Analysis of Fiscal Balances Under Existing and Alternative Constitutional Arrangements." In *Alberta and the Economics of Constitutional Change*, edited by Paul Boothe (Edmonton: Western Centre For Economic Research, University of Alberta).

_____. 1995. "The Provincial Distribution of Federal Fiscal Balances." *Canadian Business Economics* 1-18, Winter.

Mansell, Robert, Ron Schlenker, & John Anderson. 2005. "Energy, Fiscal Balances and National Sharing." *Research Report*. Institute of Sustainable Energy, Environment and Economy. November 18.

Mansell, Robert L., Mukesh Khanal & Trevor Tombe. 2020. "The Regional Distribution of Federal Fiscal Balances: Who Pays, Who Gets and Why it Matters." *The School of Public Policy Research Paper* 13 (14): 1-43. June.

Mintz, Jack M. 2019. "Two Different Conflicts in Federal Systems: An Application to Canada." *The School of Public Policy Research Paper* 12(14):1-21. April.

Ruggeri, G.C. & Weiqui Yu. 2000. "Federal Fiscal Balances and Redistribution in Canada, 1992-1997." *Canadian Tax Journal* 48(3): 626-655.

Savoie, Donald J. 2019. *Democracy in Canada, The Disintegration of Our Institutions*. Montreal and Kingston: McGill-Queen's University Press

Statistics Canada. 2019. Tables 36-10-0221 to 36-10-0482-01, including Table 36-10-0450-01: "Revenue, expenditure and budgetary balance—General governments, provincial and territorial economic accounts." https://www150.statcan.gc.ca/n1/daily-quotidien/191107/dq191107a-cansim-eng.htm. See also: Statistics Canada sources referenced in Mansell and Schlenker (1992, 1995); "Deriving revenue, expenditure and budgetary balance of the government sector by province and territory," May 16, 2016, http://www.

statcan.gc.ca/pub/13-605-x/2016001/article/14627-eng.htm; and Tables 11-10-0054-01 and 12-10-0088-01.

Tombe, Trevor. 2018. "Unpacking Canada's Equalization Payments for 2018-19". *The School of Public Policy*, (January 17).

Tombe, Trevor and Jennifer Winter. 2020. "Fiscal Integration with Internal Trade: Quantifying the Effects of Federal Transfers in Canada." *Canadian Journal of Economics, forthcoming. See also Department of Economics Working Paper*, August 2019.

Whalley, John and Irene Trela (1986). *Regional Aspects of Confederation, Vol. 68, Research Studies for the Royal Commission on the Economic Union and Development Prospects for Canada.* Toronto: University of Toronto Press.

The economic importance of Alberta to Canada

Herb Emery & Kent Fellows

BEYOND THE large and sustained contributions to federal finances and programs, what is the economic importance of Alberta to the rest of Canada?

And to what extent are the costs Alberta bears through federal transfers to be part of confederation offset by the economic benefits of being part of the national Canadian economy?

The answers to these questions can provide a better understanding of Alberta's interest in a fairer deal from confederation, and of the rest of Canada's belief that Alberta's energy exports are a regional interest but not a national interest.

We will examine the thesis put forward by Tom Courchene (1999, 2013) for the structural changes to Canada's economy since the 1989 Canada-U.S. Free Trade Agreement (CUSTA) and the 1993 North American Free Trade Agreement (NAFTA). We will also consider how those changes may have altered the perceived value proposition of Alberta's energy resources, and its economic growth, for the rest of Canada. Historically, Alberta and its resource-based exports created an important market for the products of other provinces. Prior to 1985, Alberta's supply of oil and gas were a source of competitive advantage for central Canadian manufacturers and buffered residents of energy consuming provinces from energy price shocks of the 1970s and early 1980s. Since the CUSTA and the NAFTA, the relative importance of Canada's historical east-west trade axis has weakened in favor of larger trade values with the U.S. This trend is perhaps even more acute for oil and gas due to dramatic changes in federal energy policy and regulation.

Of late, Canadians do not seem to perceive trade with Alberta as important. Canadians see Alberta's energy exports and resource sector development as benefiting Alberta and leaving the rest of the country with economic challenges and environmental liabilities. Albertans seem frustrated and confused as to why the rest of Canada does not see the value of a growing Alberta economy driven by energy exports.

In fact, consistent with the views of Albertans, and at odds with the narrative in the rest of Canada, Alberta's energy exports and the market for interprovincial exports they sustain, are creating economic benefits for the rest of Canada. Alberta offers a sizeable, and stable, market for other provinces. For Alberta, trade with other provinces provides a benefit of being part of confederation that roughly offsets the value of net fiscal transfers it makes to the rest of Canada.

Courchene and the old cow

Tommy Douglas offered a vivid description of Canada's old transcontinental economy: "Canada is like an old cow. The West feeds it. Ontario and Quebec milk it. And you can well imagine what it's doing in the Maritimes."[i] With the old cow economy, a prosperous and diversified national economy was driven by specialization in natural resource exports in the periphery provinces, west and east. Resource exports increased the incomes and populations of the resource-based regions which created a domestic market for central Canadian manufactured goods and services. The east-west axis of the economy was created with national tariffs and other protectionist barriers, transportation investments and policies directing trade through Canadian corridors, and (at least in principle) free trade in goods and mobility of people across provinces (Norrie, Owram and Emery 2008). The national interest was served by growing natural resource exports.

Tom Courchene (1999) shows that as late as 1981 interprovincial trade was about equal to the value of Canada's international trade, demonstrating the importance of the domestic Canadian market. Free trade agreements with the U.S. and Mexico were turning points for the Canadian economy as growing trade values with the U.S. diminished the relative importance of the domestic market for Canadian producers through the 1990s.

Updating Courchene's numbers on trade by provinces, Figure 1 shows the ratio of the value of international exports to the value of interprovincial exports since 1981. The constant dollar value of interprovincial trade was relatively flat since 1990 but international trade, primarily with the United States, increased the ratio of exports to interprovincial trade until 2001. After 2001, an appreciating dollar reduced the value of trade with the United States while interprovincial trade values remained stable. Obviously for Ontario, autos and auto parts are important contributors to the value of international trade but even netting these out, international exports grew much more than interprovincial trade. A similar picture is apparent with international imports to interprovincial imports. In addition, interprovincial labour mobility trended down in Canada and much of the population growth that provinces have experienced has come from immigration. Overall, the Courchene thesis for the dismembered old cow national economy interprets these changing trade values as demonstrating that provinces are less linked and less dependent on each other for income growth.[ii]

Figure 1:

NOTES: 1981, 1983, 1988 and 1990 ratios are from Courchene (1999, Table 1). Ratios constructed with data from Statistics Canada Table: 12-10-0086-01 (formerly CANSIM 386-0002) for 1997 to 2008, and Table: 12-10-0088-01 (formerly CANSIM 386-0003) for 2009 to 2016.

As the economic prosperity of Canada's provinces became relatively less dependent on the domestic market, the extent to which the economic benefits from a region's growth are shared by other regions may have changed. In the past, income generated through resource exports in the periphery regions supported trade with Central Canada's industrial heartland. In addition, federal transfers from `have' to `have not' provinces would have resulted in "'second round' spending impacts that tended to end up somewhere in Ontario, since trade largely flowed east-west and Ontario was the principal north-south conduit. With generalized north-south trade, however, these second-round spending impacts may now end up in North Carolina or Minnesota and not in Ontario." (Courchene, 1999)

While the regions have always been economically distinct, Courchene argues that the rising importance of north-south trade creates a new challenge of competing interests in terms of preferred policies and processes on the part of the Federal government and provincial governments. Where regional interests are in conflict then there will be challenges for the federal government in determining what is in the "national interest". The size of the Ontario economy, its population and electoral representation in Ottawa, and the perceived and largely self-declared "dynamism" of its economy makes it increasingly likely that the interests of Ontario and Ontarians define the national interest insofar as federal policy is concerned.[iii]

Ontario's economic base has been largely in manufacturing and services, and unlike the resource-rich provinces (Alberta, British Columbia, and Newfoundland among other provinces), its industrial base is inherently footloose. Given the large size of the Ontario economy in relation to Canada overall, Courchene believes that the "national interest" is in "preserving and promoting Ontario as a preferred location within the NAFTA umbrella necessarily" and requires "a greater sensitivity to issues relating to North American comparative advantage." This perspective justifies "policies and processes designed to enhance the ability of Ontarians and Ontario to compete within the North American and global marketplace."[iv] For example, Alberta's energy boom after 2000 was interpreted as a situation where Alberta's "regional interest" is not necessarily aligned with Courchene's view of the "national interest" because energy exports have been associated with an appreciating Canadian dollar.[v] From Courchene's perspective, rather than allocate resources to resource exporting "backward regions," national competitiveness to attract "transnational-enterprise capital" will require government favoring "their most dynamic sectors and locations." Unlike with the Old Cow economy, today the federal government may see the "national interest" as being served by restraining natural resource exports.

Alberta oil as an export rather than an input

Historically, Canada and its provinces have developed and used energy resources, including hydroelectricity, to create competitive advantages for industrial producers through low energy costs. With oil and natural gas, taxes and restrictions on export have been lifted since the 1980s and since 1985, the practice of maintaining a Canadian price below the world price is no longer in place.

Despite the 1947 oil discovery at Leduc and robust investment in discovering and developing Alberta's oil resources, the high cost of producing and distance from major markets initially limited the market for Alberta oil. With the National Oil Program of 1961, and the completed construction of the IPL oil pipeline system connecting Leduc to Sarnia, Ontario in 1958, Alberta's oil industry had a market in Ontario despite its higher price for Ontario consumers than imported oil. The price of Canadian oil before 1973 was based on the U.S. market price, which was higher than the world price in order to protect domestic U.S. producers.[vi] Whereas the National Oil Program split the Canadian market along the Ottawa River Valley: consumers west of the valley were restricted to Canadian oil while those to the east continued to use imported oil that was priced below the prevailing United States and Canadian prices.[vii]

The economic benefit for Ontario and the rest of Canada from Alberta's energy resources emerged after 1973 when world oil prices started to rise with the first OPEC oil crisis. Alberta oil allowed for a made-in Canada oil price that was typically below the world price sheltering Ontario's manufacturing sector and energy consumers from the price shocks that were hammering manufacturers and oil consumers in the United States. As world prices for oil climbed and energy security based on Middle East imports declined, Alberta's oil supply was a clear benefit for Ontario and Canada. World oil prices rose abruptly from $3 (U.S.) per barrel in 1972 to just over $12 (U.S.) in 1974. The Canadian government responded by regulating the domestic price of oil, initially freezing prices to keep the Canadian price at half the level of the world price in order to protect petroleum consumers in central Canada. From 1973 to 1978, world oil prices stabilized at $12 (U.S.) to $14 (U.S.) per barrel. While prices remained regulated in Canada, they were expected to rise towards 75 to 85 per cent of the world price and had reached $12 (U.S.) per barrel in 1978.

This benefit of Alberta oil for Ontario was even greater with the 1980 National Energy Program which sheltered the energy consuming provinces from the sharp oil price increases after 1978 with the political upheaval in Iran. Despite the enormous gains for the Alberta economy from the first OPEC oil shock, the Iranian revolution in 1979 and the Iran-Iraq war in 1980 resulted in sharp reductions in oil production from those countries and caused world oil prices to rise from $14 (U.S.) per barrel in 1978 to $32 (U.S.) per barrel in 1981.[viii]

The oil boom of the 1970s made Alberta more populous, wealthier, and changed the balance of power within confederation. By 1981, Alberta, through the Alberta Heritage Savings and Trust Fund, had extended $1.5 billion in long term loans to the governments of Manitoba, Quebec, New Brunswick, Nova Scotia, Prince Edward Island, and Newfoundland and/ or their agencies. As Alberta became a lender to the have-not provinces of Canada, it was perceived by the federal Liberal government to have gained bargaining power within confederation potentially creating an undue influence of the energy exporting province on policy development for the national interest.[ix]

As oil prices started to rise in 1978-79 because of the destabilizing situation in Iran, Alberta Premier Peter Lougheed offered to sell Alberta's oil in Canada for 75 per cent of the world price.[x] The Trudeau government that had been recently returned to power in February 1980 ignored the Lougheed offer and instead introduced the National Energy Program (NEP) as part of its October 1980 federal budget. The NEP had several goals concerning Canadian energy supply, and its control and development, but the notorious aspect of the NEP was that it unilaterally imposed a Canadian price of oil of around $17 per barrel in 1981, roughly half of the world price at the time, along with an oil export tax that funded the subsidy but also prevented Alberta from selling oil to the world market instead of Canada. The NEP was a massive transfer of wealth from oil producing Alberta to the oil consuming provinces of Canada and the cost to Alberta is estimated to have been around $100 billion between 1981 and 1985.[xi]

The severity of the downturn of the early 1980s for Alberta coincided with historically high world oil prices that were expected to continue. Thus, as Alberta watched many of its economic gains from 1973 to 1980 diminish, it is easy to see why Albertans would blame this economic hardship on the NEP. Had the price of oil for Canadian producers not been held so far below the world price, investment levels, employment and population growth may have been sustained, or at least not so severely impacted. It is also the case that an immediate deregulation of oil prices that would have moved the price of oil in Canada closer to the world price would have been an obvious way to aid Alberta's recovery from the downturn. After a brief but bitter dispute between Alberta and Ottawa, the two governments in September 1981 reached an agreed schedule for the deregulation of oil prices that would see the price of oil return closer to world levels.

Despite the difficult times experienced in the early 1980s with the NEP and the 1982 recession, it was expected that elevated oil prices would continue for the foreseeable future. As Robert Mansell notes, the petroleum boom of the 1970s was not seen as a transitory, short-lived boom that would be followed by an inevitable bust, but as a permanently higher growth path for the Alberta economy.[xii] Even though some observers, including the federal government, did not expect oil prices to increase indefinitely, few would have expected that world prices would not remain at around $35 (U.S.) per barrel that prevailed in the early 1980s. The 1981 Canada-Alberta Energy Agreement set out a schedule for oil prices in Canada to rise from $17 per barrel in 1981 to $77 per barrel in 1986.[xiii]

It is worth highlighting that the NEP led to a transfer from oil and gas producing regions to oil and gas consuming regions. Examining government revenues in particular, by some estimates the NEP resulted in a transfer of $5.4 billion (in 1990 dollars, equivalent to $9.5 billion in 2020 dollars) from the Alberta government to the federal government.[xiv] In that context, Alberta's anger with rising separatist sentiments was dismissed at the time as "oil tantrums" and a sign that Albertans were selfish in not seeing the larger national interest. After all, Prime Minister Joe Clark's short-lived minority government failed after trying to raise the fuel excise tax to encourage energy conservation. The succeeding Trudeau Liberal government used the NEP to pursue "national interest" goals including lengthening and smoothing the Canadian economy's adjustment to higher energy prices and pushing for increased Canadian ownership in the petroleum industry.

With respect to the first of these goals, NEP pricing protected Canadian consumers from some of the cost-push inflation and gave a competitive advantage to Canadian exporters through low input energy prices relative to international competitors. With respect to the second goal, a series of acquisitions totalling $10 billion (in 1990 dollars, equivalent to $17 billion in 2020 dollars) had increased the Canadian share of ownership in the petroleum sector from 6.7 percent to 34.7 per cent by 1982.[xv]

Since the Western Accord and the end of the NEP in 1985, there is no longer a domestic oil price below the world price. Thus Western Canadian energy exports are the means by which Alberta and Canadian incomes are driven by the oil economy rather than western Canadian oil being used as a low-cost input to create advantages for Central Canadian producers and consumers. For Alberta, energy exports have reduced the relative importance of interprovincial energy sales for its GDP growth. At the same time, the end of the pricing of oil to serve national interests has eliminated a visible benefit of Alberta energy resources for the rest of Canada which may contribute to the interpretation that today Alberta's energy economy is a "regional interest" but not a "national interest".

How important is Alberta to Canada today (and vice versa)?

Given the changes in the national economy, how important is Alberta for income and growth in other provinces? How important is the rest of Canada for Alberta?

Have Alberta's energy exports been an economic driver for the rest of Canada beyond the federal fiscal transfers from Alberta?

Carbone and McKenzie (2016) use a model of the Canadian economy to assess the impact of oil prices on Alberta the rest of Canada. Even accounting for the negative influence of the exchange rate on tradeable sectors like manufacturing, they found that a 10 per cent increase in the price of oil raised output in Alberta by 3.7 per cent and by around 1 per cent in Canada overall. The gains to the rest of Canada arise from the higher value of oil exports and higher wealth/income for consumers with an appreciating exchange rate. Their work also shows that most of the benefits with respect to higher income from higher oil prices accrue to Alberta, Saskatchewan and Newfoundland and Labrador. For the rest of the country, the increases in GDP from higher oil prices are relatively small (0.16 per cent in Ontario). In other words, it would take a sustained 40 per cent increase in oil prices to generate a 1 per cent increase in GDP in the non-oil producing provinces. As many in Alberta believe, a case can be made that energy exports are driving national growth but Carbone and McKenzie (2016) show that the benefits of that growth are concentrated in the oil producing provinces and not as strongly benefiting other provinces through interprovincial trade. At the same time, Carbone and McKenzie's work refutes the claims of Courchene that energy exports harm Ontario's economy:

> Our analysis makes an important contribution to the Dutch Disease debate as it relates to Canada. A key aspect of the "disease" that is the focus of much discussion is the implications of an exchange rate appreciation associated with a resource boom. It is claimed that the resulting hollowing out of the export-oriented manufacturing sector can have negative effects on the economy. Our results suggest that matters are more complicated than this and that the "disease" may be overwhelmed by other, positive impacts associated with a positive oil price shock." ... "while the Manufacturing sector benefits from the reduction in energy prices and increased international exports due to a depreciation of the Canadian dollar, on balance Ontarians suffer from the higher international prices of consumer goods and from the lower demand for the goods that they export to other parts of Canada, most particularly the oil-producing regions".

Beyond the direct impact of energy exports on the national economy, Alberta is important to the economies of the other regions in Canada as a market for their goods. Alberta imports from other provinces and territories goods and services for consumption, and intermediate inputs into Alberta's production of goods and services. To give a few examples: in 2015, Alberta imported $322 million worth of processed meat products from Ontario and $210 million worth of processed dairy products from Quebec. Alberta also imported $2.2 billion worth of natural gas from British Columbia (the majority of which is likely exported from Alberta along with Alberta produced gas, mostly to the United States with smaller but significant volumes going to Ontario).[xvi]

Where Carbone and McKenzie assessed the impact of oil prices on the economies of Canadian provinces, we investigate the impact of higher trade barriers between Alberta and the other provinces. We suggest that the scenario we model, a doubling of trade costs, could represent the potential impact of Alberta seceding, or having greater independence, from the rest of Canada. Our modelling assumes that Alberta maintains the Canada dollar, and that the trade cost increases have no impact on the Canada-U.S. dollar exchange rate. We use an established economic model from Fellows et al. (2018) and a simulation methodology from Fellows and Tombe (2018) to answer this question.

We simulate the impact of imposing 100 per cent tariffs on interprovincial imports into Alberta and 100 per cent tariffs by other provinces on imports from Alberta.[xvii] To see the relative importance of oil and gas exports to other provinces, we also model increases in interprovincial export costs applied only to crude oil and natural gas from Alberta to other Canadian provinces.

The importance of the Alberta market for domestic trade is not just from oil and gas. A doubling of the trade costs for export and import delivered goods result in Alberta's interprovincial exports falling by $47 billion, or around 75 per cent. While not complete autarky, this is as close as can be reasonably modelled given our assumptions about the Alberta and Canadian economies and the observable data on interprovincial trade.[xviii] If interprovincial trade in oil and gas alone were restricted via a 100 per cent tariff, then the value of exports from Alberta would be $12 billion less (20 per cent).

If there was only a restriction on Alberta exports to the rest of Canada, Alberta would lose $15 billion in GDP and the rest of Canada would lose $8 billion in GDP. Alberta's loss in GDP is due to lost export values with other provinces, while the rest of Canada's GDP loss results from other provinces relying on more expensive supply imported from each other or from international markets. If Alberta were to also impose higher trade costs on interprovincial imports, then Alberta's GDP loss increases to $20 billion compared to an increased loss of $24 billion for the rest of Canada. Overall, this experiment shows that the aggregate impact of trade with Alberta is higher for the rest of Canada than for Alberta but the lost GDP for the rest of Canada is spread over a larger economy and population. Alberta's GDP loss is around 7 per cent of the province's GDP but the $24 billion loss for the rest of Canada is around 2 per cent of GDP.

While many might expect that these GDP losses arise from reductions in interprovincial energy exports from Alberta, the model suggests that this is not the case. Oil and gas exports from Alberta to the rest of Canada are small relative to its exports to the United States.[xix] When oil and gas exports are restricted from Alberta, the rest of Canada (particularly Ontario) suffers more than Alberta. Alberta loses $1.8 billion from the reduced export values from oil and gas and the rest of Canada loses $3.5 billion in GDP, of which $2.4 billion is lost to Ontario due to higher oil and gas import costs and lower overall oil and gas imports. Alberta's loss is only 1.3 per cent of GDP, whereas Ontario's GDP loss is only 0.35 per cent.[xx]

The rest of Canada clearly benefits from relatively unfettered trade with Alberta. Our model suggests that for the rest of Canada, the value of trade attributable to having Alberta as part of a national market is around 2 per cent of GDP. The value of annual GDP attributable to interprovincial trade with Alberta is 20 per cent higher than the value Robert Mansell estimates is the annual federal fiscal transfer from Alberta to the rest of Canada over the past 20 years (nearly $20 billion per year). Those fiscal transfers from Alberta, in addition to the trade values, come in large part from the higher incomes and tax collections arising from international energy exports. It is clear that Alberta and its energy sector benefit the rest of Canada.

On the other side of relationship, Alberta's GDP is 6 per cent higher with interprovincial trade than if it were excluded from the national market. This value is approximately equal to the loss of GDP represented by the federal fiscal transfers to the rest of Canada shown by Robert Mansell in this volume. Our numbers can be used to illustrate a cost-benefit case for Alberta's demands for a fairer deal from confederation, or even secession from Canada. The rest of Canada stands to lose $20 billion in annual fiscal transfers from Alberta and $24 billion in interprovincial trade value. Alberta would lose $20 billion in interprovincial trade value but keep an equal value in net taxes no longer transferred to the federal government. Should Alberta successfully negotiate a tariff with the rest of Canada less than 100 per cent, then Alberta would have a net gain from independence from the rest of Canada. Put another way, the rest of Canada has much more to lose from an independent Alberta than does Alberta, meaning it might make sense the rest of Canada to consider a fair deal for Alberta to keep confederation whole.

Why don't other Canadians value Alberta's economy?

If the Canadian economy were simply the collection of several regional economic engines, then the national interest would be served by setting policy to maximize regional growth along with policies and institutions that ensure that the benefits are shared across Canada. Fiscal federal transfers from Alberta to the rest of Canada are highly visible arrangements for sharing the benefits of Alberta's economic prosperity, but it seems to be the case that Canadians do not see Alberta's economic growth as benefiting non-Albertans. We have shown that there are clear benefits for the rest of Canada from Alberta's energy export driven economy through interprovincial trade so it must be the case that they are not viewed as large enough to be important, or large enough to compensate for the perceived costs of resource exports for Canadians. For example, Courchene (2007) argues that Western Canada's "premier energy clusters" generate opportunities for Alberta and economic challenges for the rest of Canada.

Central Canadian perceptions that Alberta energy exports are a regional interest and not in the national interest probably had their clearest statement in 2012. David McGuinty, Liberal Natural Resource critic and MP from Ottawa, publicly accused Conservative MPs from Alberta of being "shills" for the province's oil sands saying that "they really should go back to Alberta and either run for municipal council in a city that's deeply affected by the oil sands business or go run for the Alberta Legislature".[xxi] Interim Liberal Leader Bob Rae sought to distance himself and his party from that view but claimed that while McGuinty's comments came out the wrong way, he was expressing frustration at trying to get the Commons natural resources committee to discuss a study on energy innovation "from a national perspective."

Michelle Rempel, Conservative MP from Calgary, fired back with an assertion that Alberta energy development is in the national interest. "It's a lack of respect for the contributions from people in the province, the fact that our industries within Alberta generate jobs and growth for the entire economy. I am proud to stand up for that."

Eight years later with the Liberal party in power in 2020, the view of Alberta's energy sector being a regional but not a national interest persists. With a recent collapse in oil prices with a Saudi Arabia-Russia price war and a global Coronavirus (COVID19) pandemic, Alberta has called for a federal bailout for its energy sector. The Trudeau government, however, is pursuing ways to support businesses in Canada that are, in the words of the Finance Minister Bill Morneau, "sector agnostic" and which avoid being regionally targeted.[xxii] Much like MP Rempel argued in 2012, in 2020 Alberta Senator Paula Simons argued that with strong sector specific headwinds policy aimed at addressing the profitability of energy companies is in the national interest: "Alberta's energy sector doesn't just power Alberta's economy, it drives a lot of the federal economy.... This is not just an Alberta problem, it's to an extent a Saskatchewan problem and to a huge degree a Newfoundland problem... So we need to come up with solutions that are transnational, that help all of our key sectors."

National interest has been focused of late on the climate crisis. David Emerson (2012) argues that campaigns to brand Canada as an environmental pariah and producer of "dirty oil" play to old insecurities and sensitivities. Oilsands development, even with an improving emissions and environmental record, is seen by many in central Canada as incompatible with Canadian environmental aspirations. Many outside of the province, and even in the province, see the crisis as the opportunity to reduce Alberta's dependence on oil and transition the economy a greener alternative from a dying industry.[xxiii] John Ivison suggests that the Trudeau government's aversion to provide help to get Canada's Alberta based energy industry through a period of expected prolonged instability reflects the "queasiness about bankrolling an industry that some members regard as a stain on the nation's reputation."[xxiv] While Ivison's interpretation is that this lack of federal empathy for Alberta's energy companies reflects the Trudeau government's climate change virtue signaling to woo left-of-centre voters who are not as prevalent in Alberta, climate change is just the latest reason Alberta's energy resources have been painted as a regional interest and national problem.

Emerson (2012) also observes that "in spite of the enormous contribution of energy natural resources to our fiscal and economic well-being, our national psyche continues to be torn by ambivalence toward this unique endowment of nature… The thought of being 'hewers of wood and drawers of water' has tormented Canadian thinkers and writers for much of our history. For many, it adds to a deeply ingrained international view that staple economies tend to underperform compared with more balanced industrial economies over time."

Brunnen and Kmiec (2013) assess that many Canadians see energy and resource dependence as a "harbinger of great calamity—we are a one trick pony, we're a 'staple' economy, unstable, dependent, a single resource producer." According to Courchene (2000), "we Canadians are finding it difficult to make the transition from a resource-based behind-the-tariff-walls economy to a human capital based economy (i.e. from boards and mortar to mortar-boards).[xxv] Financial Post columnist Kevin Carmichael (2019) stated that "there are some Albertans who seem to think they would be better off as their own country. Maybe, but only because the province has enjoyed the benefits of being a member of a stable, diversified economy for more than a century... Places that are overly reliant on resources tend to be poorer; the booms never quite outweigh the busts, but the good times are so good that no one ever gets around to doing anything unrelated to harvesting that resource. Alberta has a decent social safety net, good universities, and options outside of oil and gas because its place in Canada kept the resource curse from fully taking hold."[xxvi]

Even the defenders of resource exports quoted by Brunnen and Kmiec (2013) do not provide inspiring rebuttals. Jim Prentice, before becoming premier of Alberta, argued that "there's no shame hewing wood and drawing water as long as you are the best in the world at it."[xxvii] Bank of Canada Governor Mark Carney in 2012 stated that "high commodity prices were unambiguously good for Canada and, rather than debate their utility, we should focus on minimizing the pain and maximizing the benefits of our resource economy."

The costs for the resource industries of these debates are real. Brunnen and Kmiec (2013) argue that political squabbling in Canada over resource development has resulted in Canada failing to become an energy or natural resource superpower and is at best a "second-rate supplier that is unable to resolve deep-seated division about our economic future." The anger many Albertans express in 2020 makes sense in that the loss of export income coming from the lack of pipeline capacity to tidewater and the resulting loss of investment are reducing incomes and reducing government revenues. One estimate of the annual losses implied by inadequate pipeline capacity is $7.2 billion for the Alberta provincial government, $5.3 billion for the private sector and $0.8 billion for the federal government.[xxviii]

What is not adjusting, enough, are the sizes of fiscal transfers to the rest of Canada. Clearly the Fair Deal panel report that provides options to bring greater fairness to the treatment of Alberta by the federal government will find political support and a strengthening economic case. In seeking a fair deal from confederation with its panel struck in 2019, Albertans will test the foundations of Canadian confederation. As Heaman (2017) points out, fairness can only exist among equals and the federal government's treatment of Alberta of late appears more about a return to its pre-NAFTA exercise of power than concerns for regional fairness.[xxix] Should the federal government choose not to bring more balance between the costs that federal policies, decisions and inactions impose on Alberta and the rents it extracts from Alberta through its fiscal arrangements, Alberta separatists could find growing political support in the province. Secession, if it occurs, will result if enough Albertans find being treated like a disrespected cash cow intolerable.

References

Bunner, Paul ed., *Lougheed & the War With Ottawa 1971-1984, Volume XI Alberta in the 20th Century: A Journalistic History of the Province* (Edmonton: History Book Publications Ltd., 2003).

Brunnen, Ben & Tom Kmiec, "Energy superpower or second rate supplier?" Policy Options March 2013.

Carbone, Jared C., & Kenneth J. McKenzie, 2016. "Going Dutch? The Impact of Falling Oil Prices on the Canadian Economy," Canadian Public Policy, University of Toronto Press, vol. 42(2), pages 168-180, June.

Courchene, Thomas (1999) Ontario as a North American region state, Regional & Federal Studies, 9:3, 3-37, DOI: 10.1080/13597569908421096Courchene (1999)

Courchene, Thomas (2007) "Alberta: the new dominant player in Confederation," Policy Options.

Courchene, Thomas (2013) Policy Signposts in Postwar Canada: REFLECTIONS OF A MARKET POPULIST (Montreal: IRPP

Doern, Bruce and Glen Toner (1985) *The Politics of Energy: The Development and Implementation of the NEPG* (Toronto: Methuen)

Emerson, David (2012) "Reversing the curse: Starting with energy," Policy Options.

Emery, J.C. Herbert (2006) "Alberta 1986: The Bloom Comes off of the Wildrose Province," in Michael Payne, Donald Wetherell and Catherine Cavanaugh eds. *Alberta Formed – Alberta Transformed*. Calgary: University of Calgary Press.

Fellows, C. Michael and Manual Mertin (1990) "The NEP: a national economic panacea?" in Roger Gibbins, Keith Archer and Stan Drabek, ed. *Canadian Political Life: an Alberta perspective* Kendall/Hunt Publishing Company

Fellows, G. Kent *"The Invisible Cost of Pipeline Constraints"* School of Public Policy Energy and Environmental Policy Trends https://www.policyschool. ca/wp-content/uploads/2018/03/ENERGY-trends-advisory-March.pdf

Fellows, G.K., Patterson, M., MacFarlane, A., Marriott, L., Carrothers, A. and Krause, J., (2018). Economic loss analysis to Prince Edward Island resulting from a prolonged closure of the Confederation Bridge. Canadian Journal Regional Science, 29-41

Fellows, G.K. and Tombe, T., (2018) "Opening Canada's North: A Study of Trade Costs in the Territories." SPP Research Papers 11:17

Heaman, E. A., Tax, Order, and Good Government: A New Political History of Canada, 1867–1917. Montreal: McGill-Queen's University Press, 2017.)

James Laxer, *Oil and Gas: Ottawa, the Provinces and the Petroleum Industry* (Toronto: James Lorimer & Company, 1983), 118-119

MacFadyen, A. J., & Watkins, G. C. (2014). Petropolitics: Petroleum Development, Markets and Regulations, Alberta as an Illustrative History. University of Calgary Press.

Robert Mansell, "Fiscal Restructuring in Alberta: An Overview," in A Government Reinvented: A Study of Alberta's Deficit Elimination Program, ed. Christopher J. Bruce et al. (Toronto: Oxford University Press, 1997)

Robert L. Mansell and Ronald Schlenker, "The Provincial Distribution of Federal Fiscal Balances," *Canadian Business Economics* (Winter 1995), 3-19.

McRae, R. N. (1982). A Major Shift in Canada's Energy Policy: Impact of the National Energy Program. *The Journal of Energy and Development*, 173-198.

Tammy Nemeth (2005) Continental Drift: Canada—U.S. Oil and Gas Relations, 1958-1988. (PhD., diss, University of British Columbia)

Kenneth Norrie, Douglas Owram and J.C. Herbert Emery (2008) *A History of the Canadian Economy* Fourth Edition. Toronto: Thomson-Nelson.

Andrei Sulzenko and G. Kent Fellows (2016) PLANNING FOR INFRASTRUCTURE TO REALIZE CANADA'S POTENTIAL: THE CORRIDOR CONCEPT, School of Public Policy Research Papers 9(22).

Watkins, G. C. (1984). The National Energy Program—or Pogrom. *In Convention of the Canadian Society of Exploration Geophysicists and the Canadian Society of Petroleum Geologists, Calgary, June* (pp. 17-20).

Alberta has viable trade options
Derek H. Burney &
Fen Osler Hampson

I T IS axiomatic that free trade and accessible markets are essential to the health of the Albertan economy.[i] When demand for Alberta's key exports, especially in the energy sector, softens and prices fall, the Albertan economy suffers and with it the rest of Canada. In a post COVID-19 economic recovery, this will be even more true. The importance of Alberta's energy sector will be of paramount significance in the transition period to Canada's full economic recovery just as Canada's requirement for energy will enhance Alberta's capabilities and leverage.

More so than ever before, the health of Alberta's economy and the province's ability to trade with the rest of Canada and the world is not simply dictated by the laws of supply and demand, but also critical considerations of public regulation, judicial decision-making, political stability, and market access, which, in recent years, have posed major challenges and risks to Alberta's economic health, growth, and development. This chapter discusses those risks and the options available to mitigate them, either by negotiating a closer, more balanced trade and investment strategy within the Canadian federation or by pursuing a more independent path.

In this chapter, we offer three options for Alberta to promote its economic and trading interests in what is now a dire, post COVID-19 environment, one that poses an existential threat to the province's social and economic future.

In the first scenario, clearly the one we would prefer, Alberta's leadership uses this unprecedented crisis to seek a new, strategic grand bargain by negotiating hard like Quebec in the federation, especially as Alberta gives substantially more to the federation than it receives. It should use its imbalanced contribution to the equalization formula as leverage to secure a new pipeline eastward to the Atlantic Ocean. This option would require changes to the regulatory environment, in particular. A second priority would be a firm commitment to full internal trade liberalization.

Failing that, the second option would be to seek the expansion of western oil and gas pipelines to Ontario coupled with the development of new refinery capacity in Sarnia, Ontario and Edmonton, Alberta. This option would not only contribute to domestic job creation (as in the first scenario), but also allow Canada to break the stranglehold that American-based refineries in Texas and Louisiana have on North American petroleum product supply chains, which have systematically used their monopsony power to suppress prices for Canadian crude in the U.S. market.

If neither of these options is successful and the economic situation continues to worsen without any prospect of firm support from Ottawa, Alberta might conclude it has no option but to pursue a more independent path that would start with common market arrangements with the United States. This would be preceded by a six-month MacDonald Royal Commission-style study and analysis of the precise terms to be established for a common market association and for independence.[ii] Assuming favorable recommendations on both, the results would be put to a referendum in Alberta. Formal negotiations on both would follow, starting with the terms of the common market association.

Unlike a free trade agreement, a common market arrangement (such as the EU) allows for the free movement of capital and labour as well as goods and services. Also, because rules on trade remedy, e.g. antidumping and countervail, would be harmonized, Alberta would be exempt from protectionist U.S. trade remedy measures. Under this scenario Alberta would gain unprecedented and unfettered access to U.S. markets for all its goods and services including notably energy supplies, and would almost certainly become a magnet for U.S. investment without the regulatory shackles and indifference it now faces from Ottawa. A closer economic association would certainly appeal to President Donald Trump, but also to Democrats and Republicans in Congress alike, given longstanding American aspirations of "manifest destiny" on the North American continent. Such an association would also strengthen U.S. efforts to develop a stronger U.S. bulwark against China. While recognizing the formidable political challenges this would pose, Alberta's leaders and its people may well conclude they have no choice but to take steps leading to a closer association with the United States, especially if unemployment levels rocket to 30 or 40 percent of Alberta's labour force with little prospect of economic recovery and/or major economic assistance or attention from Ottawa.

Statistical overview

Alberta's economic relevance to Ottawa is a bit like the proverbial iceberg. What you do not see is what really matters to the rest of Canada, which is the nub of Alberta's problem. Relative to its population, Alberta plays a disproportionately important role in the Canadian economy though most Canadians are blissfully ignorant of some simple facts.

With a population of just four million, or 11.6 percent of Canada's total, Alberta generates 15.5 percent of Canada's GDP (pre-COVID, 2018 figures). When combined with Saskatchewan and Manitoba, the total (27.4 percent) exceeds that of Quebec and is second only to Ontario. Because the economies of Alberta and Saskatchewan rely heavily on the extraction and export of natural resources, they produce the highest per capita GDP in the country (Quebec, Manitoba, and the Maritime provinces have the country's lowest per capita GDP).

The energy sector alone, primarily oil and gas, contributes roughly 10 per cent of Canada's GDP, more than that of the country's finance and insurance industries combined. The importance of the energy sector is also reflected in the strong correlation between the Canadian dollar and the price of oil because the largest portion of Canada's total foreign exchange earnings comes from crude oil sales. In 2018, Canada was the world's fourth-largest producer and exporter of crude oil in the world.

During the first decade-and-a half of this century, Alberta enjoyed strong levels of sustained economic growth buoyed by a booming oil and gas sector, strong global demand and external investment. In January 1997, Alberta's GDP was $184.3 billion. Ten years later in 2007, it had grown by more than 50 per cent to $270 billion. In 2018, it stood at $363.3 billion, almost double the size of where it stood twenty years earlier. (Adjusted for inflation the numbers are $278.1 billion, $328.8 billion and $ 378.9 billion respectively in current [2020] Canadian dollars.) Mining, quarrying, and oil and gas extraction contributed 26.9 per cent of Alberta's GDP and were the most important sectors in the economy followed by real estate and rental leasing (10 per cent), construction (8 per cent), and manufacturing (7.6 per cent). Although Alberta's economy has become more diverse in recent years, it remains dependent on the energy sector for capital investment.[iii] And Canadians as a whole benefitted. As Ben Eisen observes: "The economic growth in Alberta that comes in large measure from the resource sector and development... people all across the country... an economically vibrant Alberta makes for an economically vibrant Canada.[iv]

Alberta has also played a critical role in balancing the books on Canada's trade and balance of payments accounts with the United States and the rest of the world. What is striking is that international exports are more important than inter-provincial exports. Without Alberta and its energy exports, which have also been a major source of capital and investment inflows, Canada's overall balance sheet would run in the red. Energy exports alone accounted for 22 per cent of Canada's exports to the U.S. in 2019, well above any other sector including autos (13 per cent). Alberta's major export destinations are as follows: United States (87.1 per cent), Asia (8.0 per cent), Americas (excluding U.S., at 2.1 per cent). In dollar terms, Alberta's major export destinations are: United States ($87.6 billion), China ($3.9 billion), and Japan ($1.8 billion). Alberta's highest-valued exports in 2017 were crude oil and hydrocarbon gases, which accounted for 67.7 per cent of the total value of provincial exports. The remaining exports were divided among the following categories: machinery and equipment, cereals, plastics, and organic chemicals.[v]

What many Canadians also fail to appreciate is the degree to which Alberta's exports and imports of goods and services are important for sustainable economic growth in other provinces, especially in recent years. A 2018 report on Alberta's exports of goods and services to the other provinces and territories finds that its exports to other provinces are "quite substantial and totaled $63 billion in 2016. Between 2006 and 2016, exports to international markets grew by only 7 per cent but exports to Canadian markets rose a much stronger 28 per cent. The top Canadian markets for Alberta exports are Ontario, British Columbia and Saskatchewan."[vi] Quebec, Manitoba, and the Atlantic provinces are further down the list and that's the nub of the problem.

Although Quebec is dependent on Alberta's natural gas exports and propane for its continuing energy needs, it has traditionally imported its oil from abroad as a result of a political decision made many decades ago under the National Oil Policy to divide the Canadian market into two along the Ottawa River. Ask any driver from Ottawa or the City of Gatineau on the Quebec side what the price is for gas on any given day in their respective provinces and you usually get two different answers.[vii] However, in recent years, the reality is that Albertan oil is of growing important to refineries in Quebec, although public perceptions in Quebec are not aligned with this. As one study notes, "Quebec's supply of crude oil from Western Canada ballooned from less than one per cent in 2012 to 44 per cent in 2017. Some of this western crude, according to Suncor, comes from the oilsands in Alberta." This was due to the reversal of Enbridge's Line 9 pipeline in 2015 to bring discounted western crude via North Westover to Montreal (Line 9B) to access Quebec refineries. In the first decade of this century, "92 per cent of oil supplied to Quebec's refineries was imported, mostly from Kazakhstan, Angola and Algeria" but by the end of the second decade, roughly "82 per cent was sourced from North America."[viii]

Similarly, Alberta is also a major importer of goods and services from other provinces. But again, the numbers lie below the perceptual waterline. As one study notes, "In 2016, imports of goods and services from the other provinces and territories totaled $67 billion in 2016, actually exceeding Alberta's inter-provincial exports of $63 billion in that year....The top Canadian suppliers of Alberta imports are Ontario, British Columbia, and Quebec."[ix]

Given the degree of acrimony between Alberta and British Columbia in recent years, you would also never know that the two provinces in economic terms are joined at the hip.[x] According to British Columbia Business Council chief economist Ken Peacock: "The functioning of labour markets and inter-provincial migration flows also suggest B.C. and Alberta share the closest economic ties of any two provinces in the country." B.C. politicians should also take careful note of the fact that "B.C. exports more merchandise to Alberta than it does to China. In 2015, it also exported $16 billion to Alberta, more than any other province—even Ontario, with an economy two and a half times larger."[xi] British Columbia is also Alberta's second largest source of imports, accounting for 23 per cent of inter-provincial imports. In 2014, imports from B.C. amounted to $17.6 billion compared to $13.1 billion in 2010. Mineral fuels, mainly natural gas, accounted for 18 per cent of imports and were followed by transportation services at 11 per cent.[xii]

One of Alberta's biggest contributions to the rest of Canada is reflected in a yawning fiscal gap between federal revenues and federal transfers to the province, as Robert Mansell points out in his chapter in this volume, although again this is something that most Canadians don't see. Mansell calculates that Alberta was "by far the largest net fiscal contributor [of any province] over the period 1974-1985, with an average annual net contribution of $7,512 per person, and over the period 1993-2018, with an average annual net contribution of $4,546 per person." A report by the Fraser Institute, which reached similar conclusions, showed that Alberta contributed an astronomical $221.4 billion more in total revenues to the federal government than it received in transfer payments and services between 2007 and 2015.[xiii] In comparative terms that is slightly less than one-eighth of Canada's total annual GDP, but also a trend cannot be sustained in the current economic environment.

Turmoil in the global economy coupled with recent developments have blown a hole into Alberta's economic fortunes. Alberta's economy experienced a major, two-year-long recession in 2015-2016, which was brought on by plunging oil prices and exacerbated by the introduction of a new carbon tax by Rachel Notley's NDP government and the cancellation of the Keystone XL pipeline to the United States in 2015 by the Obama administration (a decision which was reversed by the Trump administration in March 2017, but then dealt another setback after a Montana judge revoked a key permit issued by the U.S. army corps of engineers in April 2020).[xiv] By 2017, the economy was slowly recovering and outgrew every other Canadian province (+4.6 percent). However, the growth spurt was short-lived. By 2019, Alberta's economy contracted again because of continuing uncertainty over pipeline construction, heavy discounting of bitumen prices, and the fate of the province's energy exports. As the Conference Board of Canada reported, the biggest declines in 2019 were in the construction and drilling sectors in the realm of "10.4 per cent and 30.3 per cent, respectively."[xv] Job losses—150,000 and rising—have been catastrophic and investment, both domestic and foreign, has virtually disappeared. This downward trend has been exacerbated by the COVID-19 pandemic, which has wreaked further havoc on Alberta's main resource because of reduced demand worldwide for hydrocarbons, along with plunging global oil prices brought on by the Russian-Saudi price war. The one bright light has been Alberta's bold decision to backstop the Keystone XL pipeline with a one-billion-dollar investment even though certain outstanding legal hurdles remain.

Political and regulatory risks in the energy sector

Alberta's principal challenges as an energy exporter are the regulatory roadblocks, judicial decision-making, and the attendant political risks that have come from the actions of the United States government, the federal government in Ottawa, and other provinces, particularly British Columbia and Quebec, on pipelines.[xvi] In recent years, these risks have grown dramatically with little prospect of diminishing.

To recap briefly: under the government of Stephen Harper, efforts to boost Canada's oil exports to the United States were stymied by the administration of President Barack Obama, which rendered a political decision to stop the Keystone Pipeline, which would have taken oil from Alberta through Nebraska down to refineries in Louisiana, a move that was applauded by

American environmentalists. When Obama denied a permit for the project in 2015, the newly elected government of Justin Trudeau acknowledged the decision without comment, to the deep consternation of western oil producers. The project was resuscitated by President Donald Trump days after his inauguration in January 2017, but it still hinges on a few court challenges in the United States.

Although the Harper government gave its approval to Enbridge Inc. and its oil industry partners to proceed with construction of the Northern Gateway Pipelines project, which was to carry 525,000 barrels of bitumen from Bruderheim, Alberta to Kitimat, British Columbia, the permit was revoked by the Federal Court of Appeal in June 2016 on the grounds that the government had failed to consult properly with First Nations about the project.[xvii] Trudeau had already promised that he would introduce legislation banning tanker traffic in the coastal waters of northern British Columbia, so it came as no big surprise when he permanently shelved the project in late November of that year.

Canada's other major pipeline builder—TransCanada Pipelines (now known as TC Energy)—had been developing a proposal, Energy East, for a 4,500-kilometre pipeline "to carry 1.1 million barrels of crude oil per day from Alberta and Saskatchewan to refineries in Eastern Canada."[xviii] It would have reduced Quebec's reliance on foreign oil. The proposal involved converting an existing natural gas pipeline to an oil transportation pipeline. It ran into stiff opposition in Quebec from environmentalists and the then-mayor of Montreal, Denis Coderre. Frustrated with a hostile political environment and an inconclusive regulatory process, TransCanada Pipelines abandoned its Energy East project after spending more than $1 billion on an inconclusive regulatory process.[xix] Instead, it paid $10.2 (U.S.) billion to acquire Columbia Pipeline Group—a leading network of natural gas pipelines in the United States.

Two days after terminating Northern Gateway Pipelines, Trudeau gave his government's approval to Kinder Morgan's Trans Mountain Pipeline expansion project to carry oil from Alberta to Vancouver along Kinder Morgan's existing pipeline route, and to Enbridge's proposed replacement of Line 3, a fifty-year-old pipeline from Alberta to the United States. Both plans involved expanding pipeline capacity along existing routes to allow for exports of more than 1.1 million additional barrels of oil per day.[xx]

But TMX also ran into stiff political, judicial, and regulatory headwinds. Facing political pressure from the Green Party, which propped up his minority NDP government, the then newly elected premier of British Columbia, John Horgan, joined the court challenge against the project.[xxi] As political and legal challenges against the project mounted, Kinder Morgan announced on 8 April 2018 that it was halting construction and all "non-essential" spending on the project unless it could break the deadlock with the B.C. government. Finance Minister Bill Morneau offered to indemnify Kinder Morgan against its losses and then, just two days before Kinder Morgan's deadline expired, made an offer to buy the pipeline outright for a generous sum of $4.5 billion and put the entire project under the control of a crown corporation.[xxii]

With exquisite timing, Kinder Morgan's shareholders voted to approve the federal buyout on 30 August, just as the Federal Court announced its decision against the pipeline's environmental approval, sending the National Energy Board back to the drafting table to conduct further consultations with the First Nations and a proper environmental assessment of the project's impact on the local killer whale population in Burrard Inlet, through which oil tankers would transit. The court ruled that consultations were not sufficient, hardly, but it failed to say what would be sufficient.

After conducting more hearings and consulting with potentially affected parties, the National Energy Board recommended on 22 February 2019 that the federal government approve for a second time the long-stalled Trans Mountain Pipeline expansion.[xxiii] Noting that the project might have "significant adverse" impacts on the endangered killer whale population and local Indigenous communities, the 700-page report touted the project's compensating benefits for energy export diversification and economic growth.[xxiv] Faced with a political hot potato in an election year, the government announced that it would conduct further consultations before making a final decision by June 2019 about whether to proceed with the pipeline. Cabinet gave its approval for construction of the pipeline on June 18, 2019, but stipulated that eight new additional "accommodation measures" had to be met to address specific Indigenous concerns, including measures to limit the impact of increased tanker traffic on the southern resident killer whale population in the Salish Sea as well as noise pollution. The project faces additional hurdles, including regulatory hearings to finalize its route and further litigation in the courts from environmentalists and First Nations. Finally, in February 2020 the Federal Court of Appeal approved the latest round of consultations.

Two other elements in the Trudeau government's legislative strategy will have an important impact on future pipeline projects and energy exports from Canada's West Coast. The first is Bill C-48, "An Act Respecting the Regulation of Vessels That Transport Crude Oil or Persistent Oil to or from Ports or Marine Installations Located along British Columbia's North Coast,"[xxv] legislating a crude-oil tanker moratorium on the North Coast of British Columbia and setting penalties for contravention of the moratorium.

It is worth noting that Bill C-48 would affect less than 15 per cent of the tanker traffic into Canada. The vast majority of tankers land on the East Coast and sail up the Saint Lawrence River to refineries in Montreal. Additionally, the bill would not restrict U.S. tanker traffic through the Dixon Entrance and Hecate Strait. The sovereignty of both are matters of dispute between Canada and the United States.

The second important piece of legislation is Bill C-69, "An Act to Enact the Impact Assessment Act and the Canadian Energy Regulator Act, to Amend the Navigation Protection Act and to Make Consequential Amendments to Other Acts."[xxvi] It changes the way major infrastructure projects are reviewed and approved, replacing the National Energy Board with a new Canadian Energy Regulator and establishing new environmental review assessment processes to be carried out by a new federal Impact Assessment Agency.

A direct consequence of many years of political, judicial and regulatory uncertainty is that Canada has gone from being a "low-risk, high-reward" place for energy investment to the reverse—"high-risk, low-reward"—diminishing the potential of a sector that, for decades, had been a major growth engine for Canada, especially Alberta. The exodus is not confined to pipeline companies. The $2.8-billion fire sale of Devon Energy Corp—an asset esti-mated to be worth $5 billion to $6 billion—to Canadian Natural Resources is a telling example of the foreign exodus from Alberta's tailspin. Devon is a U.S. company that was run by a Canadian. Encana's $7.7 billion purchase of Newfield Exploratory followed in the wake of similar strategic acquisitions in the Permian and Eagle Ford fields in the United States in recent years. Enerplus has made significant investments in the Bakken Formation, the Marcellus Formation, and the Denver Basin. Crescent Point is spending more on its Uinta and Bakken properties than in Canada. Baytex is doing the same in the Eagle Ford field in Texas. Even energy service companies like Precision Drilling and Akita Drilling are following the trend with increasingly more activity in the United States than in Canada. That is not surprising. Fourteen applications for new pipelines were submitted to U.S. regulators for approval in the period 2017-19. Only one, Imperial Oil's Aspen project, was submitted in Canada, and then put on hold until the termination of Alberta oil curtail-ment program. The C.D. Howe Institute estimates that Canada lost $100 billion in potential oil and gas investment in the same period.[xxvii] And in early 2020 Teck Resources Limited abandoned a $20-billion investment in the oil sands because of political uncertainty, notably tepid support from Ottawa.

In the midst of the Coronavirus pandemic the government chose to increase the carbon tax by 50 per cent, adding to the aggravation. Royal Bank of Canada president David McKay has repeatedly warned that "Canada is at risk of squandering its energy advantage if it does not come together to tap the potential of its energy sector."[xxviii] New energy investments could add an additional 1 per cent of GDP, which is the equivalent of putting a new auto sector in place in Canada. It would also generate $200 billion in additional tax revenue over a ten-year period.

Geopolitical risks: international trade tensions sideswipe Alberta

Alberta's trade and investment opportunities with the rest of the world, especially with emerging markets in Asia, are also affected by rising geopolitical tensions that hit Alberta farmers hard recently. The collateral damage that Alberta and Canada suffered when China blocked canola and pork and beef imports and incarcerated two Canadians in retaliation for the arrest of Huawei executive Meng Wanzhou at the request of American law enforcement officials is a telling example of the direct costs that were inflicted on Alberta and the Canadian economy more generally from deteriorating relations between China and the United States. China's restrictions on Canadian canola and meat imports were a major blow to Alberta's producers. Forty percent of Alberta's canola exports normally go to China. Fortunately, a major drought in Europe allowed Canadian producers to partially make up for the shortfall in Chinese sales and the restrictions were eventually relaxed, but the situation underscored the political risks of doing business with China.

The risks of China-U.S. trade wars are also accompanied by the risks of a nascent "trade truce" as China and the United States look to patch their growing rift with new "managed" trade deals. Phase 1 of the agreement between the United States and China signed on January 16, 2020, includes formal pledges to tighten rules on intellectual property protection, pirated goods and the theft of commercial property, to avoid currency manipulation, and open China's financial services sector to U.S. companies.[xxix] More importantly, the pact commits China to buy an additional $200 billion (U.S.) in American goods over the next two years, including $40 (U.S.) billion to $50 (U.S.) billion in agricultural products such as soybeans, canola, fresh and frozen pork, beef, wheat, corn, barley and a range of machinery, all on preferential terms unavailable to Canadian producers. China's other purchase commitments under the deal include $54 billion in additional energy purchases, $78 billion in additional manufacturing purchases, $32 billion more in farm products, and $38 billion in services. As the *Globe & Mail*'s Barrie McKenna reported, the deal is bad news for Canada's farmers: "Whatever China commits to buying from the U.S. will inevitably come at the expense of other exporting countries. In farm products, Canada is among the countries most at risk of losing market share, along with Australia, New Zealand, Brazil, and Argentina. For Canada, some of the exports that could suffer include frozen pork, beef, soybeans, canola oil, lentils, beans, wheat, coal, and seafood."[xxx].

Although some analysts have suggested that the agreement may be in violation of Article XXIV on free trade agreements in the World Trade Organization (WTO), this is cold comfort. Both China and the U.S. have defied previous WTO rulings and the U.S. is now depriving the world's trade court of new judges in a move that is crippling the institution.[xxxi] As trade lawyer Jacob Kronby notes, although "China has cast itself as the defender of the multilateral trading system.... Agreeing to legally questionable purchases smacks of hypocrisy."[xxxii]

The increasingly aggressive actions and ambitions of China are also a major source of global instability. China's track record on COVID-19 should be an eye opener for even those with a rose-tinted view of the Asian behemoth. For more than two months, China concealed the outbreak from the world and seriously handicapped a timely response. Chinese authorities also claimed falsely that human to human transmission was not possible, a position initially endorsed by the WHO, and then lamely pointed the finger at the U.S. as the culprit. Some have even suggested that the virus may have been caused, not by bats in a wet market, but by a leak from the government's research facility in Wuhan.

No country or province, including Alberta, can ignore the power and potential of China. At the same time, as Canadians we cannot blithely accept the threat China poses to basic human rights and to the fundamental principles of global trade. It would be prudent to adopt some social distancing with China on several fronts. As the adage suggests, "When you sup with the devil, bring a long spoon."

We could be moving more to a law of the jungle trade world as the two largest economies joust between themselves for mercantilist advantage, leaving small and medium sized countries to fend for themselves as best they can. That should conceivably spark a move to complete free trade within Canada but that would require leadership and tenacity from Ottawa which is not assured.

However, by virtually any measure, the opportunities in the burgeoning

Chinese market, especially when it begins to recover in a post-COVID-19 world as it surely will, are unprecedented and cannot be ignored. Many suggest that, within a decade, the Chinese economy will surpass that of the United States in size. This growth and a corresponding increase in the middle class of the Middle Kingdom will stimulate demand for commodities and skills that constitute Canadian strengths: agricultural products like canola oil, pork, and wheat as well as energy resources like liquefied natural gas, oil, and uranium. According to the International Monetary Fund, China accounted for 33 per cent of global growth in 2017 (up from only 4 per cent in 2000), outstripping the rest of Asia (28.8 per cent), Europe (15.2 per cent), and the Western hemisphere, including the United States (12.8 per cent). Although China is Canada's second largest export market, half of the G20 countries sell more in absolute terms to China than does Canada, including South Africa, Brazil, Saudi Arabia, and Indonesia. This situation illustrates what is being missed for Canada as a whole, and Alberta, in particular.

The lack of U.S. global leadership on trade combined with China's aggressive ambitions for global dominance simply makes a bad situation worse for Canada and Alberta. India is also an important market for Alberta notably for LNG exports. The mini-TPP agreement offers preferential access to Japan, Malaysia, Vietnam and other key markets in South East Asia When it comes to Alberta's strategic trade and investment options, the fundamental question is whether the province's objectives can best be met by pursuing a much more comprehensive interprovincial free trade in Canada and deriving access benefits from Canada's preferential trade agreements (USMCA, CETA, Canada Korea, etc.) or by a more independent approach by Alberta with the rest of Canada and with the world.

Promoting free trade within Canada

Alberta has been in the vanguard of efforts to establish genuine free trade within Canada but has been unable to overcome resistance from Quebec and Ontario, which jealously protect their own markets. To cite one example,

Canada's system of supply management for dairy products discriminates in favour of Quebec and Ontario and against Alberta. Quebec exported $445 million of milk and cheese to Alberta in 2015 while Alberta's dairy farmers sold only $275 million in their own province because of the disparity of quota allocations. Alberta consumers are also denied access to U.S. dairy products because of supply management restrictions. Similarly, Alberta's objectives, especially on agriculture, in international negotiations are often constrained by persistent support in Ottawa, Quebec, and Ontario for supply management programs for dairy and poultry, which inevitably reduce Alberta's and Canada's leverage in seeking more open access for its globally competitive grains and meat exports.

In December 2014, federal, provincial, and territorial governments launched discussions to strengthen and modernize the Agreement on Internal Trade (AIT) with the goal of securing "an ambitious, balanced and equitable agreement that would level the playing field for trade and investment in Canada."[xxxiii] Negotiations eventually produced the Canadian Free Trade Agreement (CFTA) which went into effect on July 1, 2017, committing Canada's provinces to "a comprehensive set of rules that will help achieve a modern and competitive economic union for all Canadians" and lead to the eventual elimination of barriers to interprovincial trade in "goods and services, investment and labour mobility" while also expanding procurement coverage and promoting regulatory cooperation within Canada.

However, the CFTA continues to meet with resistance, primarily from Quebec and Ontario, and even with its new protocol is more aspirational than real (the original agreement contains 130 pages of "exclusions"). Thus, when Alberta's newly installed Premier Jason Kenney announced at the July 2019 meeting of provincial premiers that his province would unilaterally "eliminate 80 per cent of its restrictions on interprovincial trade" and later called "on all other provinces and territories to meet Alberta's ambition to end the economic balkanization of our country, and become the true economic union envisaged by the fathers of confederation," there was widespread approbation.[xxxiv] But without tangible commitments from Quebec and Ontario approbation is meaningless. Under Kenney, Alberta has eliminated a total of 21 internal-trade restrictions. Manitoba has followed suit by removing six of its own barriers to interprovincial trade. These parallel initiatives, along with recent moves involving all four Western provinces under the New West Partnership Agreement's third protocol to further eliminate trade barriers,[xxxv] demonstrate convincingly that broader moves to trade liberalization within Canada are necessary.

The International Monetary Fund predicts that the result would stimulate much greater GDP growth (roughly 4 per cent growth in Canada's GDP) than Canada's recently concluded trade agreements, including the USMCA.[xxxvi] They would also strengthen Canada's competitive edge and bargaining leverage in global trade. As Martha Hall Findlay explains, "Internal trade barriers cost the Canadian economy between $50 billion and $130 billion annually. They keep Canadian businesses from expanding effectively to other Canadian customers beyond their own provincial borders. They create inefficiencies that cost businesses, consumers and taxpayers, and limit overall economic activity and growth. This means fewer international export opportunities. And all of these factors make Canada less attractive for foreign investment. These trade barriers between provinces and regions also impede greater pan-Canadian social and political cohesion."[xxxvii]

While the federal government's immediate responsibility is to restore the health of the Canadian economy and jobs as restrictions ease on the pandemic, it also must focus on Canada's distinctive strengths in energy, agriculture, forestry, fisheries, telecommunications and financial services, etc. with policies that enhance Canadian interests and reduce Canada's vulnerability to further economic shocks going forward. The $1.7 billion bail-out package announced by federal government in April 2020 to clean up abandoned oil and gas wells was derided for not providing much-needed liquidity to Canada's oil companies and catering to the government's environmental priorities.[xxxviii] The fact that the cabinet committee overseeing the COVID-19 recovery plan is chaired by the current and former environment ministers is not auspicious for Alberta's energy development.

A key priority should be to displace non-North American imports of oil with more competitive and secure domestic sources of supply, and to promote the development of a national strategic petroleum reserve where the federal and/or Alberta government purchases the oil, taking advantage of low prices to build such a reserve to insulate the Canadian economy against future supply disruptions and price shocks as well as giving the country (and Alberta) greater leverage vis-à-vis other major oil producers.[xxxix] Pipelines to Canada's West and East coasts are essential to self-reliance on energy. We should abandon the ostrich-like mentality that assumes the age of fossil fuels is over. Far from it. Furthermore, exports of natural gas to reduce coal production and promote the development of transitional energy sources in major polluters like China and India will do more for climate change goals than a national carbon tax. It is illusory to think otherwise.

The government must also act to bolster, not hamper, a sector that contributes 10 per cent of our GDP. Tax credits can be introduced to induce Canadian firms, including energy companies, to reduce their carbon footprint, a proposition that would be far more balanced and effective, promote jobs and innovation, and be less disruptive economically than punitive carbon taxes that stifle productivity and economic growth. Carbon capture, for example, is a promising technological innovation if it can be brought to scale. There are currently forty-three major carbon-capture projects operational or under development worldwide. In the United States nearly 160 million tonnes of carbon dioxide have been captured and stored. Most of the captured carbon goes into enhanced oil recovery (using carbon to extract more oil from a producing well). The International Energy Agency projects that carbon-capture incentives of $40 per tonne could support storage of 450 million tonnes of carbon dioxide per year.[xl]

Tax credits could be tied to direct reductions in carbon emissions by the energy sector with a goal of being carbon neutral by 2050. If a major oil producer like British Petroleum (BP) can commit itself to becoming carbon neutral by 2050, so can Canada's energy sector if the right market incentives are put in place. A system of phased tax credits for meeting specific carbon reduction targets is a much smarter approach to encouraging innovative change and meeting Canada's climate change goals than taxes— which invariably cease to be "revenue neutral" or equitable over time because governments will divert those revenues to other uses, instead of returning a full tax credit to consumers, while also imposing other taxes.[xli]

Another idea worthy of consideration is to promote major sales of Quebec's hydroelectricity, which is in surplus, to markets west of the Ottawa River where electricity rates have gone through the roof as a result of years of poor political stewardship. In exchange for access to new markets in eastern Canada, notably in Ontario, and the construction of a new electricity grid that runs East-West, Quebec, in turn, would agree to the construction of a new oil East-West pipeline and refinery capacity in its own province. A new "grand bargain" for energy based on the principles of affordability and national self-sufficiency will likely have greater appeal in a post-COVID 19 environment because of the impact that major infrastructure projects will have on jobs and the economy. It could readily be struck by the premiers of Quebec, Ontario and Alberta, but it will also require the easing of what is now a federal regulatory stranglehold on new energy projects of any kind.

Yet another option would be to subsidize the Laurentian LNG project in Quebec abandoned by Warren Buffet because of political uncertainties. Because of its potential for exports to heavy coal-producing countries like China and India, this project would have a beneficial dimension both for concerns about climate change as well as essential post-COVID-19 economic recovery. Continuing federal and provincial government incentives to further develop Canada's petrochemical feedstock and manufacturing facilities should also be part of this strategy because even in a low-carbon future most projections forecast strong and growing demand for petrochemicals in a market where Canadian producers are highly competitive. Low-cost supplies of natural-gas-based feedstocks such as methane, ethane and propane, which can be transformed into methanol, ammonia, ethylene and propylene, are projected to be a major driver of economic growth in North America. In the U.S. alone, some 333 new U.S. chemical industry projects using shale gas had been announced as of September 2018, accounting for an estimated $202 (U.S.) billion in new capital investment and 431,000 direct and indirect jobs by 2025—a figure that dwarfs Canada's petrochemical expansion plans.[xlii]

Alberta should also demand that the federal government exercise its constitutional power for interprovincial pipelines and approve Energy East while dismissing Quebec's right to duplicate regulatory review. Recent court decisions on the Trans Mountain pipeline endorse this approach.

Failing that, Alberta (along with Saskatchewan, Manitoba and Ontario) could strike their own deal to expand pipeline capacity to Ontario and then transport oil via a combination of barge and/or tanker from Sarnia to refineries in Atlantic Canada, which have the infrastructure to process sour (heavy) crude.[xliii] (Another option would be to transport oil via pipeline to Superior, Wisconsin, where it could be shipped eastwards.) This would be far safer than shipping crude by rail as the Lac-Mégantic rail disaster attests, and the volumes would also be much greater.[xliv] Quebec could hardly object because the Line 9 reversal of 2015 already provides Valero's Quebec City refinery with access to lower cost Canadian crude via the transportation of crude oil by ship from Montreal to Quebec City.[xlv]

Canadian refineries in Atlantic Canada continue to import sour crude from as far away as Nigeria and Azerbaijan and find that it is competitive to do so because they have already made the investment in heavy oil upgrading equipment and desulfurization. (That Irving oil secured approval to bring oil from British Columbia via the Panama Canal to its St. John's refinery speaks volumes about the competitiveness of Canadian crude.[xlvi]) Irving's refinery, which is the country's biggest, also has a decided competitive advantage when it comes to supplying refined oil products to the U.S. east coast's largest market, Boston, because transportation by tanker takes only two to five days as compared to a minimum of 10 days from U.S. ports on the Gulf of Mexico.

Under any of the above scenarios, Alberta should press for a more open regulatory and policy environment that attracts, rather than repels, investment in Canada and facilitate exports. Unlocking the internal blockages for investments and for exports of Alberta's key oil and gas resources will be the most critical aspect of any assessment. These have been severely hampered in recent years by constipated federal regulations, by blanket opposition to pipelines by provinces like Quebec and British Columbia, and by limp support from Ottawa other than the expensive purchase of the Trans Mountain pipeline. Both foreign and Canadian investment in the energy sector have sagged significantly. Virtually all foreign energy companies have decamped and some Canadian companies, e.g. Encana, have moved their head office outside Canada.

Alberta's third option

Many Albertans believe political independence may not be a viable option for a landlocked province.[xlvii] However, if they continue to feel shut out by Ottawa, the Alberta economy continues to deteriorate, and job losses rise to stratospheric levels, there is a viable third option. That is for Albertans and their leaders to embark on a path leading to some form of quasi political union with the United States that starts with common market arrangements between Alberta and the United States and a break from the rest of Canada.[xlviii] Although the constitutional and political obstacles should not be underestimated, they would not be insurmountable.

The first step would be to commission a MacDonald Royal Commission-style six-month study of the pros and cons of a Common Market arrangement with the United States and a break from Canada.[xlix] The second step would be to take a high-level informal sounding with the U.S. Administration and Congress. Assuming interest in the U.S. and a positive recommendation from the study, the third step would be to subject the study result to a referendum. A positive referendum result would trigger formal negotiations with the United States.

A study by itself would be wrenching for the federation but, in democracies, the moment of real crisis is often the stimulus needed for bold action. Besides, it might prompt a more enlightened response to Alberta's needs within Canada. Ottawa needs to understand that, if it pushes Alberta to the wall, Alberta may have no choice but to exercise the most radical option of all.

Should negotiations be successful while recognizing the time needed for ratification, Alberta would then negotiate the terms of secession from Canada in accordance with the provisions set out in the Clarity Act that the federal government introduced following the 1995 Quebec referendum. Albertans should be under no illusion that this would be easy, especially because the federal government and Canadian courts would throw up roadblock after roadblock to prevent secession. As Britain's experience with Brexit shows, the practicalities are that, if you try to negotiate the terms of your divorce before you leave the matrimonial home, negotiations will be endless, and you will not secure a favorable agreement. (Boris Johnson clearly understood this and cut the Gordian knot.) Accordingly, negotiations with the rest of Canada would have to occur after the conclusion of an agreement-in-principle with the Americans on a new economic and political partnership. This would give Alberta the leverage it would need for negotiations with the rest of Canada about future economic ties other than trade.

Many Americans would applaud the deal, given that Alberta's vast natural resources, especially in hydrocarbons, would catapult the United States' own total proven reserves to levels rivaling those of Saudi Arabia. Whatever lingering feelings of nostalgia Albertans might have about cutting loose from Canada would almost certainly be counterbalanced by the prospect of a well-paying job and a secure economic future in the world's biggest economy. Alberta's dried-up stream of foreign investment in its energy sector would suddenly be flooded by American investors moving northwards as Alberta shed itself of Ottawa's carbon tax and regulatory restrictions. Albertans would also likely reap higher prices for their oil from refiners in the southern United States after the border was removed. Calgary would soon come to rival Houston as the center of North America's oil and gas business.

Alberta's farmers would also be the beneficiaries of such an arrangement as they would have preferential access to Chinese markets for their produce, meat, and cereals under the new deal that Trump has stuck with China.

Admittedly, this third scenario is radical, but it is not one that should be dismissed out of hand given the volatile political environment, frayed federal-provincial relations, and the dire circumstances that Alberta (and other Western provinces) now face. Above all, it is doable. Ottawa and the rest of Canada must recognize this before it is too late. They also must understand that the only way Alberta can grow and prosper economically is through the continued development of its energy and related industries; and if cannot do it under the Canadian federal system, Albertans will be obliged to look an alternative political regime, which ineluctably leads southwards.

Crafting a new negotiating strategy

As a negotiating strategy, Alberta's first priority on trade should be to take advantage of the crisis caused by a global pandemic to demand more complete internal trade in Canada, including on energy, within a specific time frame and ideally in tandem with Canada's other provinces. Alberta should also demand that the federal government use its constitutional powers for "trade and commerce" to mandate full internal free trade.

Alberta's leverage on federal transfers should be used to try to reverse the trend in the past decade during which actions or simply inertia by Ottawa and certain provinces have hobbled Alberta's most promising avenue for growth. But if attempts to strengthen Alberta's position in the federation are ignored, the bolder option for a common market, a break from Canada and closer association with the United States, will become the only credible course of action.

Frustration over the status quo is not a prescription for vision or bold challenge. Solid analysis and unflinching determination are the best remedy. There is no guarantee of success in negotiations but there is minimal risk in trying. The status quo is not a viable option for either Alberta or Ottawa.

The Future of the Alberta resource sector

Kelly J. Ogle

RESOURCE DEVELOPMENT has been the source of great economic strength in Alberta, and by extension, the rest of the country.[i] When discussing resource capture and sale, those Albertans who believe that Alberta should declare itself an independent political entity need to consider the infrastructure challenges and requirements (past, present and future) of an independent Alberta.

Alberta, as owner of its resources, has benefited greatly from the economic activity and revenues generated by the resource industry and so has Canada, as persuasively laid out by Emery and Fellows in this volume. However, climate change has raised legitimate concerns at the international level that will eventually require some form of transition to a new energy system depending on technological development. An overarching problem facing Alberta is that Canada has not yet developed a clear, sustainable path forward for responsible energy development of which infrastructure is a critical component.

For more than a decade, resource developers and utilities have struggled with all levels of government and non-governmental organizations (NGOs) to build critical infrastructure, more specifically pipelines. Although an independent Alberta would be a land-locked country, the 1982 United Nations Convention on the Law of the Sea provides access rights for land-locked states on the sea. More importantly, the convention provides "the right of access to and from the seas and freedom of transit."[ii] However, this may be easier said than done and may be subject to the vagaries of policy development and implementation by others that may not have the new republic's best interests in mind. Is there a solution to the transit and sale of Alberta resource products? For Alberta to remain in the federation a new approach to the construction of critical long-term infrastructure projects in needed. And that raise several questions. Why is this necessary and what are the current system's failings? Is there a solution, and most importantly, how does it happen?

Canada's federal structure, on the surface, seems to be the at the core of this current system failing. Yet, it has not always been that way. Despite its complexities, Canadian federalism worked quite well for over a hundred years. However, federalism is at a crossroads. Indeed, in a recent poll citing the inability of legislators to deal with recent railroad blockades, two-thirds agreed with the statement, "Canada is broken."[iii] Policy changes at both the federal and provincial levels have dampened, and some say stifled, the resource sector.

Piled on tenuous federal/provincial relations is all-encompassing federal climate and environmental policy. Contrary to what some may believe, carbon policies and more rigid stewardship of the environment are an integral part of an increasingly environmental, social, and governance-centric public policy playbook. Therefore we need to ask if there are transitional carbon policies that better accommodate resource development. Are there bigger, all-encompassing solutions to this problem? Unless more aggressive "outside-the-box" solutions such as those suggested below are implemented, the resource sector will face significant headwinds to sustained growth. That would be a missed opportunity. Regardless of these challenges, the global demand for resources will increase in the coming decades.

This chapter will discuss a bold and dynamic approach to infrastructure that is critical to efficient Alberta resource development, and which may keep Alberta in Canada. Towards the end, it will also discuss another option—one best avoided, but one Alberta may be forced to consider if other efforts fail.

Alberta's fiscal benefits from energy development

Canada is unique among western countries in the degree to which the consumption and production of energy polarizes governments and regions. Prior to Alberta and Saskatchewan becoming provinces in 1905, the federal minister of the interior governed petroleum exploration and the federal government sold exploration leases.[iv] For the next two decades, most oil and gas exploration and development occurred in southern Alberta and "waste" became a legitimate concern. When abundant supplies of oil and natural gas were discovered, natural gas was flared into the atmosphere due to a lack of transport capability. To counter this practice, in 1926 the Alberta government, under the leadership of Premier John Brownlee, enacted the Oil and Gas Wells Act, to establish regulations governing every phase of oil and gas development.[v] The legislation was underpinned by consultative interaction with industry, setting precedent for future legislative development, a trend that, although not perfect, has generally proven successful to the present day. However, Ottawa still controlled resource development until, finally, in 1930 the Western provinces were granted ownership of natural resources.[vi]

From that date forward, the crown interest in all lands, mines, minerals (precious and base), and royalties, and all sums due or payable for such lands, mines, minerals, or royalties, belonged to the provinces. For the past ninety years, resource royalties have provided immeasurable benefit to the citizens of Alberta. The current inability to build the infrastructure that delivers the resources to global markets is stifling this revenue source.

Albertan's reap the benefits of the oil and gas wealth in their province through a number of institutional mechanisms. The value of Alberta's oil and gas resources is shared between Albertans, as owners, and the companies developing these resources. A royalty is assessed by the resource owner to be paid by developers.[vii] As the resource manager, the Alberta government sets conditions and royalties for development. Each producing oil or gas well, or oil sands project, has its own variable royalty rate, determined by the price the resource garners; the volume produced; an industry average of capital costs for each individual oil and gas well; and capital costs to begin production for oil sands projects. Oil sands projects are based on a cash flow approach with capital and current costs deductible from revenues (but not interest expense). This is quite different from conventional royalties. Resource revenues also come from: land sale bonuses (payments to government for the right to develop the resource); jobs and economic activity generated by the sector; and taxes paid by companies and people working in the sector. Corporate and personal income taxes relevant to the oil and gas sector are complex. Provisions for deductibility (corporate royalties are deductible from income) and costs associated with "exploration" versus "development" vary by province.[viii] Suffice for this discussion is the fact that corporate and personal tax revenues associated with resource development are significant.

Alberta's royalty system is complex because the province produces conventional oil, natural gas, oilsands bitumen, and other products. Created in 2016, the Modernized Royalty Framework (MRF), applies to oil and gas wells drilled after December 31, 2016, and partially emulates a revenue minus cost royalty structure across all hydrocarbons.[i] The framework is consistent with global standards for the pre-payout/post-payout models of risk and profit sharing, without introducing costly process burdens for the thousands of wells drilled every year. Additionally, it encourages industry to innovate and reduce drilling and completion costs, which will increase revenues shared by Albertans regardless of commodity prices. Harmonization of the royalty structures reduces exploration risk, enabling producers to assess the highest value development opportunities based on market forces without worrying as much about how the well's products or productivity will be characterized by the royalty framework.

In the past several years, West Texas Intermediate (WTI), the benchmark for the North American price of oil, has decreased by 80 per cent from its June 2014 high of $105.15 (U.S.) per barrel. Moreover, in the past ten years North American natural gas prices have dropped from $5.03 (U.S.) to $1.78 (U.S.), largely because the growing shale gas supply more than meets the strong demand in industrial, chemical, and power generation.[ii]

How do Alberta royalty rates compare to other jurisdictions? When the Alberta price of oil is low, so are royalties. Currently, many Alberta oil wells are not paying any royalties as the province's royalty regime is structured to insulate producers during a crash in oil prices. The oil sands royalty framework reflects the enormous front-end capital investments required. The framework, which originally was developed in 1997, and employs a "revenue minus cost" approach, meaning a flat royalty rate will apply until a mine's or well's allowable costs have been covered (pre-payout). The rate goes up as oil prices increase. It is hard to gauge how much Alberta's oil and gas royalties have been negatively affected by falling energy prices brought on by international oil supply demand destruction. Suffice to say, it is dramatic. Moreover, production cutbacks in late 2018 and 2019 due to the lack of takeaway capacity drove oil prices dramatically lower, further accentuating substantially lower royalty capture for the citizens of Alberta.

In addition to the discussion of low prices and consequently lower royalty capture, much debate has occurred in Canada about energy industry subsidies. Moreover, while the world grapples with an economic downturn, anti-energy activists have spotted an opportunity, making three claims to that end: that the oil and gas industry is massively subsidized (some claim the figure is over $3 billion annually); that fossil fuel extraction should not continue in Canada, given carbon emissions from oil and gas; and that the sector is destined to die.

In a 2011 paper from the University of Calgary School of Public Policy, economists Ken McKenzie and Jack Mintz suggest the assumptions behind the claim the industry received billions in subsidies is false.[iii] McKenzie and Mintz found four flaws, including using a subsidy definition designed for a different purpose and inappropriately adding individual tax expenditures and royalty relief items, without accounting for critical interactions. McKenzie and Mintz also argued there are negative subsidies in that the write-off was insufficient. For example, royalties should be based on rents but instead they discourage exploration even for marginal projects without rents since the costs are not deductible. Another study from the Montreal

Economic Institute found actual energy sector subsidies amounted to just $71 million.[iv] Furthermore, a 2017 study discovered that most subsidies to energy companies were for green energy projects.[v]

Conversely, there are those such as the Geneva Switzerland based International Institute for Sustainable Development (IISD), who believe "fossil fuel subsidies at the federal level are largely directed to fossil fuel producers, as opposed to consumers…[and]… subsidies have shifted from an emphasis on exploration to one on the development of infrastructure for fossil fuel production and exports.[vi] This continued negative interpretation of Canada's resource sector is the continuation of a much larger, and more existential problem. NGOs such as the IISD have free rein to provide dictates to jurisdictions such as Alberta without referencing other international jurisdictions such as Middle East/OPEC countries. Many of these NGOs consistently and without fail suggest that fossil fuels is a twilight industry, destined to be replaced with 100 per cent green sources of energy. Perhaps, but many others, including the International Energy Agency (IEA) predict several decades of expanded fossil fuel usage, including oil.

This expansion of fossil fuel usage is borne out in the numbers. At the turn of the century production from Canada's oilsands was 610,000 bbl/day, roughly 1 per cent of global oil production at the time. By 2018 total production form the oilsands exceeded 2.9 million bbl/day, more than tripling Canada's pro rata share of global production.[vii] Furthermore, in 2014, capital spending in the oil and gas sector exceeded $80 billion. In 2019, that number plunged to $35 billion and will fall again in 2020. Much of the decline can be attributed to the plunge in oil prices in the last several years; however, in the same period U.S. capital spending increased markedly.[viii] Why? The U.S. has streamlined its regulatory system, while Canada's has become more complex and uncertain, and Canada's inability to advance infrastructure projects has driven investment to other jurisdictions. Moreover, the ad infinitum browbeating by those that believe climate Armageddon is around the next corner have completely captured reasonable debate about climate change and by extension carbon policy.

Carbon policy

One can only hope that at some point later in 2020, the global economic crisis will have substantially run its course and a process of genuine recovery will begin. When the world returns to what will be a new normality (however chastened as to what was truly an immediate existential crisis) climate change will again grab national attention. Canadians must be made aware that this country's Paris climate commitments are solely aspirations, not an explicit binding obligation on the country. The cost of compliance for Canada requires levels of carbon pricing exceeding what the world has heretofore shown any capacity to impose on itself. These aspirational compliance goals would require a price on carbon exceeding $200/tonne when most of the developed world has not exceeded even the current Canadian carbon tax level of $30/tonne.[ix] This concession to reality has never been made by the current federal government. The Trudeau government has never been transparent with Canadians on how much the cost of compliance would be, in absolute or relative terms, or whether incurring those costs will have any material impact on global net emissions. Neither has it been made clear to Canadians that having Canada forego value from increased hydrocarbon exports will not have any negative impact on global demand for hydrocarbons, and in turn future emissions. An economic sacrifice to what end?

Will any growth in Canadian hydrocarbon production over the short-term and medium-term or worse be sacrificed for the current federal government to believe it can more credibly achieve its 2030 emission reduction commitments from the 2015 Paris climate process? Many are of the view that any re-invention of existing national climate policy that would preserve Canada's hydrocarbon growth potential, let alone enable it, is beyond the capacity of existing Canadian political leadership. Overwhelmingly, most of the culpability lies with the existing Trudeau government, even acknowledging unconstructive resistance by Alberta to carbon pricing as Canada's pre-eminent carbon policy instrument.

Hydrocarbon production and achieving emission reduction commitments were never intended to be dichotomous. In October 2018, William

Nordhaus[x] was the co-recipient of the Nobel Prize in economics for his pioneering work on the economics of climate change. That same day, the United Nations' Intergovernmental Panel on Climate Change (UN IPCC) released a special report advising the governments of the world of various steps necessary to limit cumulative global warming to 1.5 degrees Celsius. The major media coverage treated the two events as complementary, when in fact, they are incompatible. Nordhaus favors a carbon tax to slow climate change; however, his model shows that the U.N.'s target would make humanity poorer *than doing nothing at all* about climate change.

In a more perfect world, global climate policy would be collectively coordinated and enforced to ensure that the net cost of climate change, appropriately risk adjusted, was reflected in fundamental economic decisions on energy consumption, while balancing the short-term and medium-term capacity of modern economies to cope with such additional cost. Sadly, since the early 1990s that has never been the direction of the United Nations process. Rather it has allocated physical reduction targets to specific developed economies, not progressive carbon pricing. Canada has consistently acquiesced, regardless of how uniquely unfair and onerous actual compliance would be to achieve these goals relative to other countries. Furthermore, from an emissions accounting perspective, Canada made various low-carbon decisions in its economy long before it got credit for them, such as electric generation systems based substantially on hydro and nuclear power and enormous forestry carbon sinks. One should hope that economics will trump draconian carbon policies in the future. Canada should be advocating the basic terms set out in the Nordhaus theoretical model.[xii] However, that would require more inspired, economically realistic policy in Ottawa that truly supports responsible energy development, not no new energy development.

Infrastructure and regulatory challenges and struggles

Infrastructure is the keystone to Alberta's continued resource development. For purposes here, infrastructure is physical. Railroads, pipelines, electrical power grids, irrigation systems, waterworks and sewage systems, roads and bridges, fiber optic networks, are necessary for the smooth functioning of a modern society.

Despite infrastructure's critical nature, as of recent, it has been all but non-existent. Since the beginning of the new millennium one of this country's greatest failings has been an inability to build infrastructure and get its resources to market and pipelines have dominated the transportation infrastructure narrative and debate. However, today, all jurisdictions face extensive, laborious, and clock-robbing consultation processes to build *any-thing*. Regulatory burden is a problem in effectiveness and inhibits efficiency across Canada. According to the 2020 World Bank Ease of Doing Business Index, Canada ranks thirtieth out of thirty-four OECD countries in the time required to get a permit for a construction project.[xiii] Furthermore, according to the Business Council of Canada, "inefficient regulation [i]s the single greatest obstacle of competitiveness and economic growth."[xiv] The basis for Canada's creation, in fact the fundamental premise of confederation, was the elimination of barriers to interprovincial trade. Unfortunately, 150 years later, regulatory burden and inter-provincial impediments continue to constrain productivity.

As pointed out, much of Canada's existing infrastructure is inadequate, including road and rail networks, ports, airports, and the interprovincial electricity grid. In the past, solutions have been ad hoc, reinforced by a lack of public consensus for the social acceptability of resource exploitation and transportation. Unfortunately, pipelines are only a small part of much larger national concerns.

Sadly, at a time of historically low capital cost, Canada has created a deteriorating investment climate for resource development. Compounding these difficulties is an overarching focus on environmental priorities, most notably emissions reductions in line with Canada's United Nations Paris Accord commitment. Canada's environmental track record is not the fundamental problem. The problem is the rigid focus on the environment at the expense of other essential priorities, more specifically investment and economic growth.

Some startling facts:

- Since 2014, Canadian GDP growth per capita was the worst of all G7 countries and less than half that of the United States (4 per cent versus 8.7 per cent)[xv]
- Business investment is about 20 per cent below peak levels of 2014. Although the resource extraction sector accounts for much of this, most other sectors remain below 2014 levels[xvi]
- Since 2015 Foreign Direct Investment in Canada has grown at half the global rate (10 per cent versus 21 per cent globally)[xvii]
- The World Bank places Canada 20th on the 2018 Logistics Performance Index, which ranks countries on certain key dimensions of trade, including transport infrastructure and logistics service[xviii]
- 2019 per-worker investment ranks Canada fifteenth among the seventeen OECD countries. In Switzerland, businesses invest twice as much per worker as Canadian businesses. This is critical to competitiveness and higher productivity[xix]
- Canada's productivity has significantly lagged the U.S., in 2018 Canada generated $55.00 (U.S.) GDP per hour of labour compared to $76.50 (U.S) in the U.S.[xx]

These data uncover a disturbing reality. For decades Canada was recognized as a global leader in responsible resource development. The Canadian polity, albeit small in population, is highly educated. Furthermore, Canadians possess world-class technical skills and have custody of vast natural and intellectual resources. The development of these resources under our environmental and governance oversight was a natural advantage. This advantage is now gone, and many leading resource companies have pulled up stakes. Since 2014 at least fifteen major companies have shifted their focus to the U.S. or elsewhere.[xxi] This is partly because of market reasons and sagging commodity prices; however, many left because they did not feel welcome in Canada and did not feel that they were stewarding their investors' capital well by investing in Canada. Regulatory complexity, delay, inefficiency, and uncertainty, often compounded by obstructionism and intensely politicized in-fighting, were also cited by investors.[xxii]

Much debate has occurred in Canada about the effectiveness of the various regulatory reviews of energy projects, large and small. The debate illustrates a tension between those stakeholders wanting a concerted stewardship of our natural environment with those that seek to create private and public benefits from energy project investments. Recently, the Canadian Energy Research Institute (CERI) conducted a study providing impartial facts and evidence so that stakeholders can move forward with individual oil and gas project reviews and conversations regarding improvements in the process.[xxiii] This study compares the competitiveness of Canada's regulatory frameworks at the federal and provincial levels with the United States. It also intended to show how regulatory matters compare with other investment factors such as market conditions and project economics. The study found that for typical day-to-day approvals of routine small-scale onshore oil and gas wells, Canada and the U.S. have similar requirements and similar processes. For those projects, there is no significant difference in the competitiveness of Canadian and U.S. project approvals. However, CERI confirmed that Canada has a competitive disadvantage when comparing liquified natural gas (LNG) projects and interprovincial oil and natural gas pipelines. Canada's approvals period average thirteen to nineteen months longer and dramatically adds to project costs. Moreover, increased uncertainty, and risk-based cost assessments, if higher, add to profitability hurdle rate for investors. Perhaps looking to the past offers a solution to these contemporary regulatory issues.

Northern Corridor

The concept of multi-modal right of way corridors has been raised as a potential solution for decades. However, given today's challenges perhaps the idea is worth revisiting. A central Canadian resource and transportation corridor is not a new idea. During the 1960s, decorated Canadian war hero Richard Rohmer posited that the Canada of 2016 could be home to as many as 70 million people.[xxiv] Plans included a diagonal trans-continental railroad connecting Labrador ports to the Yukon, a highway to the Arctic, and large new or expanded cities including Flin Flon, Whitehorse, Labrador City, Thunder Bay and High Level. However, according to historian Ken Coates, "The North almost always disappoints its promoters."[xxv] From the Klondike gold rush to Northwest Territories diamond mines, the promise of the North is never quite what it seems, and Rohmer's dream died on the vine.

Although Rohmer's dream failed to be actualized, the thought in general presents a swath of question and potential opportunities. Does the current circumstance offer an opportunity to usher in a new era of Canadian public/private infrastructure development? Perhaps in the shorter term, should important infrastructure projects be fast tracked? What about an enormous, multi-decade make-work project such as the northern corridor?

Canadians have done this before. The transcontinental railway, the TransCanada Highway and the St. Lawrence Seaway all started with a national commitment. The St. Lawrence Seaway turned Sault Ste. Marie and Thunder Bay into Atlantic ports. Why can't Churchill, Manitoba, be the same? As a recent example, the federal government purchasing the Trans Mountain pipeline is not the first time a federal Liberal government has purchased a pipeline.[xxvi] Furthermore, the Alberta investment in the Keystone XL project most likely is the primary reason TC Energy is continuing with the project, which is currently facing new existential challenges.[xxvii] Mark Twain said history may not repeat itself but it rhymes. In certain circumstances government can provide a catalyst for industry.

In the spring of 2016, Kent Fellows and Andrei Sulzenko of the University of Calgary School of Public Policy published a paper in collaboration with the Center for Interuniversity Research and Analysis of Organizations (CIRANO).[xxviii] Fellows and Sulzenko clarify some of the numerous potential benefits: a significantly more efficient and reliable transportation system; re-establishing our competitiveness in global markets; a major positive impact on growth and jobs at the local, regional and national level; the rationalization of Canada's overall transportation system and easing congestion in the southern portion; diversifying export markets; enhance Canada's negotiating leverage in international trade and commercial relations; and promote Canada's Arctic sovereignty. The northern corridor would be a major public-private, nation-building initiative, with governments exercising their authorities to set policy frameworks and related legislative/regulatory regimes, tax/expenditure programs, and Aboriginal engagement.

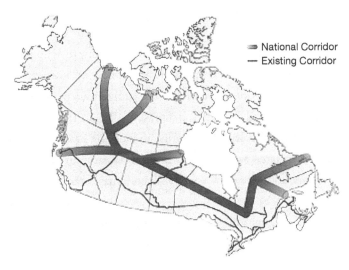

The School of Public Policy, University of Calgary

A northern corridor approach would need multi-level discussion as to how to implement it in a federal system. A cross-Canada electric transmission network has been pushed by some, especially Manitoba but there are significant physical limitations.[xxix] As discussed previously, the elephant in the room is coordination of sustainable environmental policies and economically feasible development. How could this be implemented?

The Fellows and Sulzenko paper got the attention of the Standing Senate Committee on Banking, Trade, and Commerce as a visionary, future-oriented infrastructure initiative and in June 2017 the committee recommended that "the federal government provide up to $5 million to the University of Calgary's School of Public Policy and CIRANO for their research program on a corridor in Canada's North and... the federal government should establish a task force to conduct consultations across Canada... to determine how the proposed northern corridor should be developed."ˣˣˣ The Senate committee called several expert witnesses to provide commentary and advance ideas about the corridor:

> The committee's witnesses identified a number of benefits that would result from the development of the proposed northern corridor. Specifically, they said that such a corridor would facilitate Canada's efforts to diversify its markets, improve approval processes for infrastructure projects, enhance economic growth and job creation, provide benefits for Indigenous peoples and residents of Canada's North, decrease traffic on the country's southern transportation networks, reduce the environmental impacts associated with transportation infrastructure in northern regions, and support Canada's sovereignty in the Arctic.ˣˣˣⁱ

From an Alberta perspective, it is important to note that the purposefulness of the corridor would be about much more than oil, providing market access for forestry and agriculture products, and perhaps most importantly, less dependence on trade with the United States. Recent trade agreements with far east nations and the European Union demonstrate the need for better transportation infrastructure to serve these markets. During committee testimony, Mr. Sulzenko stated that the Port of Churchill's closure was unfortunate because it is the shortest route to Europe for several of Canada's exported commodities.

Sulzenko and Fellows suggested that the capital cost of the proposed *Canadian Northern Corridor* could be as much as $100 billion and would be funded by the private sector, as well as by the federal and provincial/territorial governments. Potential sources of private financing could include corporations, private equity funds, pension funds and sovereign wealth funds. The Committee also discussed several risk-sharing models, including public-private partnerships. Mr. Sulzenko also spoke about a segment that would connect with Hudson Bay through the Port of Churchill and Dr. Jack Mintz noted that perhaps the Manitoba sector be pursued as a pilot project.

Climate change experts advise that Arctic ocean sea ice is rapidly melting. Does this mean that the Manitoba port of Churchill could operate year-round? Is not the north (broadly defined) the place to start? Optionality is a fundamental key to unlocking value for resources. For decades, the Churchill transportation and port corridor has existed but is significantly underused. Agricultural products, especially grains and pulse crops, timber, minerals, and oil could all exit Canada from Churchill. Existing rail line right of ways could be expanded to include pipelines, roads, and related energy systems.

Is re-invigorating the construction of the Energy East pipeline also wishful thinking? The Energy East pipeline proposed the extension of the Trans Canada mainline from Ontario to New Brunswick. Why not turn the line north in Manitoba and build an oil export terminal in Churchill? Connecting mining, oil and gas, agricultural, and forestry activities from across the West, the Arctic and northern Ontario and Quebec to an outlet port with rapid access to the European Union is worthy of consideration. Moreover, joint participation of Canada's Indigenous peoples in and around the project becomes actual rather than aspirational.

Security considerations, including modernization of NORAD are also important. Churchill is central to logistics, procurement, and transportation of all materiel and personnel necessary to the Arctic portion of North American defence modernization. Furthermore, even if a free-flowing Arctic is years away, an academic study noted the successful rise of Russian icebreakers shipping through Arctic regions.[xxxii] Year-round shipping capability from the Port of Churchill could be realized with these new icebreaking technologies, including LNG carriers. However, Canada has not engaged, despite having the capability to become a world leader in Arctic transportation.

Could a mega-project like the *Canadian Northern Corridor* provide a bold, new approach to unlock the potential of our renewable and non-renewable resource base? Creating multi-modal road, rail, pipeline, electricity generation and transmission lines, airports and seaports, and linking Canada's existing and potential resource base to the rest of the globe? What has happened since the committee's recommendation?

According to Dr. Jennifer Winter, Director of the Canadian Northern Corridor Research Program at the University of Calgary's School of Public Policy, there has been substantial activity following the Senate Standing Committee's dictate. A new website was created in 2019 which contains completed research papers (including the original 2016 concept paper), and information on partners and outreach. She added that Fellows and other co-authors are working on a revised and updated scoping paper to better situate the corridor concept in the current environment. They are also constructing several framing studies to establish a foundational knowledge base for further theme-specific inquiry, including other corridors around the world, existing constraints and pinch-points in Canada's trade infrastructure, defining meaningful and respectful consultation with Indigenous peoples in the context of corridor development, and climate change considerations important to exploration of a corridor system.[xxxiii]

Although the scope of such a project is daunting, the work being conducted at the policy school stands as clear evidence that further study of a *Canadian Northern Corridor* is warranted. Can the study and development of the northern corridor lead to a multi-decade twenty-first century nation building exercise? Perhaps this valuable work could lead to a royal commission to study its development?

Remember, the Canada-U.S. Free Trade Agreement succeeded only after a series of smaller, sectoral negotiations failed. The push for free trade originated with the MacDonald Royal Commission (1982) and was championed by the business community before being taken up by government.[xxxiv] The ambitious pursuit of a pathway to a northern corridor has a substantial potential to benefit all Canadians. The recently announced federal/provincial memorandum of understanding (MOU) to discuss the feasibility of a new Calgary to Banff rail link could provide a catalyst and serve as a first step to long-term federal provincial cooperation in the infrastructure space.[xxxv] If completed, the project would create a critical airport-rail link to downtown Calgary and Banff National Park, increasing tourism opportunities and labour mobility, and reducing vehicle greenhouse gas emissions and congestion in the travel corridor.

Unlocking Alberta in another way

In March 2019, the Canadian Global Affairs Institute held a sold-out dinner event where Peter Zeihan provided a controversial but prescient keynote address. Zeihan is a prominent American geopolitical strategist and author. His 2014 book, *The Accidental Superpower*, discusses the past, present, and future of American hegemony. Zeihan devotes a section in the book to "The Alberta Question" wherein he discusses the "Unlikelihood of Canada" and "The American Option." Zeihan believes that Alberta separation is inevitable. After his provocative presentation, Colin Robertson, former diplomat and vice-president at the institute, interviewed Zeihan. Robertson then held an informal and unscientific straw poll of the more than 300 who attended asking how they saw the political future of Alberta: the status quo, independence from Canada, or annexation by the United States. A show of hands indicated a plurality for the American option.

There is a definite affinity between the United States and Alberta. The United States played a major role in the development of Alberta's oil and gas sector. Throughout the 1930s and during the Second World War, the prairie provinces were mired in debt, did not have access to capital, and subsequently had difficulty exploiting their resources. Alberta Premier Ernest Manning finally turned to American oil companies, "which were not only willing to invest in Alberta but also promised to bring their expertise… something the central Canadian and British investors could not do."[xxxvi] Therefore, from the outset, American multinational corporations (MNCs) largely controlled the oil and gas industry. American companies were familiar with the geography, leasehold and pro-rationing systems, and had the expertise, and access to capital that Canadian companies lacked.[xxxvii]

Could Alberta become the fifty-first state? If so, America would gain a wealthy state nearly as big as Texas and would replace Canada as the second largest country on the planet. Furthermore, the U.S. would gain the world's third largest oil reserves and Alberta production of 3.9 million barrels per day[xxxviii] would ensure that for a long time, the U.S. would be the largest oil producer in the world. Future energy security issues, at least from an oil supply perspective, would fall by the wayside. From Canada's perspective, 90 per cent of oil reserves would be lost, as well as 37 per cent of refining capacity,[xxxix] and Canada would become a large net importer of crude oil, gasoline, diesel fuel and jet fuel, much of it from Alberta. Furthermore, according to a recent survey from polling firm Abacus Data, more than 40 per cent of Americans polled were in favour of trying to buy Alberta.[xl]

According to Zeihan, "Alberta as a U.S. state would have a vibrantly well-financed and diverse economy that would put its former (and a lot of its newfound) countrymen to shame."[xli] Zeihan also argues that demographics are a major reason why Alberta should jump ship. "Alberta produces more energy than the rest of Canada put together, their primary export market is the United States and a merger would eliminate everything from tax liabilities to foreign currency fluctuations."[xlii] Albertans' federal taxes would decrease, and the GST would disappear, along with carbon taxes. Although lagging the big populous states of New York and California, U.S. dollar purchasing power would add prosperity to Albertans, the most prosperous polity in Canada.[xliii] Much of this prosperity has been created by energy and resource development.

If Alberta is unfortunately landlocked getting its energy transported to international markets through Canada, it could look at an alternative approach, which would be deepening its relationship with the United States. Although, joining the United States, as Zeihan suggests, might be one approach, it raises a host of issues that cannot be explored here. Alternatively, Alberta could benefit from a North American energy strategy where the United States would have a more secure source of oil and gas for its future needs. This could be sought for as a new Republic of Alberta, or, far better, the federal government could seek an agreement with the United States that would benefit Alberta, Saskatchewan and Newfoundland & Labrador. The key is Canada working through an arrangement for responsible resource development.

Conclusions

Canadian federalism requires a reset. In 2018, government revenues from Canada's energy sector were $14.1 billion, responsible for more than 10 per cent of Canada's nominal GDP, employing 282,000 people directly while supporting 550,500 jobs indirectly. Pre the COVID-19 pandemic, Canada was the fourth largest producer and fourth largest exporter of oil in the world. In 2018, oil and gas extraction alone accounted for more than 7 per cent of Canada's total gross domestic GDP and is this country's largest export and economically underpins the Canadian national interest. But things must change, and hard choices must be made.

Other authors in this volume have discussed the social, economic, fiscal and tax, and security facets of the future of Alberta and confederation. Fiscal levers such as pensions, transfers and income tax must better represent Alberta's contribution to the national interest. Moreover, the resource-rich provinces of Western Canada must have greater say in the solutions needed to clearly define and underpin the national interest.

More specifically, Canadians must recognize that the world's third largest oil reserves are not the problem. This requires leadership and political will at all levels, federal, provincial municipal, and institutional, coupled with collaboration and inclusivity. Perhaps stated more clearly: the energy producing sectors are part of the solution. Policy choices, made strategically for the long term, need to transcend political and environmental ideologies, and move Canada's resource sector back to a prominent position in the global commons. The long-term global ramifications of the COVID 19 crisis will be dramatic and all nations must pull together to return to prosperity and safety. To suggest that being swallowed up by the United States would be beneficial to Albertans is fraught with concern, accentuated by current racial and societal pressures, not to mention the economic ramifications of the current crisis. However, attitudinal change, beginning at the federal level is required and aggressive use of the resource sector as leverage for more effective and fair federalism is a must or prophesies such as those proposed by Zeihan may become reality.

Secession and Constitution in Alberta

Richard Albert

Introduction: A tragic choice

I T WOULD be a tragedy if Alberta were to secede from Canada. It would rip apart our country, it would divide east from west, and it would reduce our strength and diversity. Much as Quebec's departure from Canada would weaken the federation, Alberta's exit would severely diminish Canada both internally and abroad. No longer would our admirers around the world consider us a model for how successfully to manage deep differences in a complex multinational state. We would instead become the prime example of a federation that failed to find a way to stay together.

But as wrong and regrettable as Alberta's secession would be, the choice should nevertheless be open to Albertans. Democracy demands nothing less than the free, fair, and informed power of choice. The fundamental promise of democracy is that the people should have the power to chart their own path, whether that means how to restructure their government, what powers should be delegated to their representatives, and when their Constitution should be revised to reflect new values. No democracy should ever deny the people the right to make a properly considered decision about self-government. All options should be available, even the choice to make a wrong turn.

The trail to independence is not an easy one, nor should it be. There are legal and political hurdles to overcome, not to mention the powerful sociological ties that bind Albertans to Canada, and Canadians themselves to Alberta. The entire process of secession would take an extraordinarily long time from initiation to completion—and with good reason because Alberta's decision to leave Canada, if indeed it is ever made, would likely be irreversible. Once a province makes the choice to exit the federation and that choice is properly ratified in law by a constitutional amendment, the doors to re-entry will be shut for all practical purposes.

In this chapter, I outline the legal steps Alberta must take ultimately to secede from Canada. In my personal view, I hope Albertans never go down this road. But I have nonetheless sought to ensure that I explain the steps both fairly and objectively. After tracing the path to secession, I offer what I regard as a preferable alternative that could give Albertans some real measure of independence without ever leaving Canada: Albertans should give themselves a written constitution to codify their legal and political institutions, to honour their cultural and social commitments, and to express their distinct values, all while remaining proud partners in a strong and united Canada.

A legal framework for a political process

Secession is a political decision often accompanied by force of arms. In Canada, however, there exists a legal infrastructure for its peaceful execution. The supreme court has outlined the principles that must guide any effort to secede from the country.[i] The court was pulled into the political thicket of secession when Quebec threatened to make a unilateral declaration of independence. The court's resolution of the matter appears in the Reference re Secession of Quebec, a judgment that applies today not only to Quebec but to all provinces that may have a valid claim to secession, a process the court has defined as "a legal act as much as a political one" spurred by "the effort of a group or section of a state to withdraw itself from the political and constitutional authority of that state, with a view to achieving statehood for a new territorial unit on the international plane."[ii] Parliament has drawn on the principles articulated by the court to build a legal framework of discrete rules that apply when any province seeks to secede from the country. These rules are intended to bind both federal and provincial governments alike.[iii]

There are six major steps in the secession sequence to authorize a province to secede from Canada: (1) initiation; (2) pre-referendum evaluation; (3) provincial vote; (4) post-referendum evaluation; (5) negotiation; and (6) constitutional amendment. This secession sequence is rooted in the expectation that a province will make an unambiguous expression of its intent to exit confederation. The likely (but not only) vehicle to simultaneously register and broadcast this expression of intent is a provincial referendum initiated through the legislative assembly. Yet whether a province deploys a referendum or some other tool to aggregate the preferences of its voting residents, the key is to devise a means that reveals the will of the many peoples in a province to determine whether a sufficient proportion wants the province to become an independent state. The court has correctly observed that the Constitution makes no mention of the use of referendums, nor does the Constitution recognize the "legal effect" of a referendum result.[iv] And yet, as the court rightly concluded, "a referendum undoubtedly may provide a democratic method of ascertaining the views of the electorate on important political questions on a particular occasion."[v] Although holding a referendum entails enormous challenges, if it is well designed a referendum offers an effective and efficient way to record voter preferences across the province.

Initiation. The first step in the secession sequence begins in the legislative assembly of a province. If it were to initiate the secession sequence, the government of Alberta would have to reveal publicly its plans for a secession referendum, likely by tabling in the legislative assembly a bill containing the precise language of the referendum question on which it plans to hold a secession vote.[vi] There are good reasons to require a provincial government to release the terms of the question well before the vote is held, namely to compel the provincial government to give serious advance thought to the wording of the question as well as to give provincial voters and the rest of the country notice of the government's intent to hold a secession referendum.

Pre-Referendum Evaluation. An additional purpose for releasing the referendum question doubles as the second step in the secession sequence: the House of Commons must evaluate the question Alberta proposes to ask voters in the referendum. Within thirty days of Alberta's official release of the referendum question, the House of Commons must "consider the question and, by resolution, set out its determination on whether the question is clear."[vii] As part of its evaluation whether Alberta's question is clear, the House of Commons must consider a multiplicity of views including those of all political parties represented in the legislative assembly, governments or assemblies outside of Alberta, and representatives of the Aboriginal peoples in Canada.[viii] In the end, the House of Commons must determine "whether the question would result in a clear expression of the will of the population of a province on whether the province should cease to be part of Canada and become an independent state."[ix] It would be inadequate for Alberta's secession referendum to ask voters for a mandate to negotiate the terms of secession without asking Albertans to express their will on whether the province should exit Canada.[x] Nor would be it appropriate for the referendum question to include alternatives to outright independence, for instance economic or political arrangements with Canada. The reason why neither of these referendum questions would be appropriate goes to the heart of the question whether the referendum is clear: the question must ask voters directly whether they wish Alberta to terminate its membership in confederation.

The clarity of the question is a necessary condition for the secession sequence to proceed under law. The clarity standard comes from the court's Secession Reference, which insists that the question inviting residents to vote on whether to remain or leave "must be free of ambiguity."[xi]

Provincial Vote. When the House of Commons has determined that the question is clear, Alberta may proceed to hold its referendum with confidence that the House of Commons will not later seek to stifle the province's plans on the basis of the wording of the question. This is the third step in the secession sequence: holding the referendum.

But not all referendums are equal. Imagine a referendum is announced on day one and held on day 180. Imagine further that in the northern half of the jurisdiction there are no official activities organized in that time, while in the southern half there are public debates between the yes and no camps on whether the jurisdiction should ultimately remain or leave, there are open forums hosted by an independent body to inform residents of the costs and consequences of a vote in either direction, and the yes and no camps are afforded an equal amount of money to mount their campaigns to persuade voters. Voters in the northern half of the province would be at a severe disadvantage in relation to voters in the southern half; the latter group would be better equipped to cast an educated ballot in this momentous vote.

The court missed an opportunity in the Secession Reference to insist on these finer points of referendum design. But that should not prevent leaders in any legislative assembly from giving serious thought to how best to prepare its residents to make this enormous decision. Only an educated vote can reflect the considered judgment of residents and in turn possess the durability to survive the pressures of the long secession sequence. A well-designed referendum should be concerned with more than asking a clear question. It must be open to the whole population, it must be scheduled to give sufficient time to learn about the issues and implications of the choice, and it must be funded to allow official sides to make their case to the people, whether through public debates or arrangements for equal air time and advertisements. A well-designed referendum may also require a confirmatory second vote some reasonable period of time after a cooling off period following the initial vote. These are essential considerations when designing a modern referendum.

Were Alberta to hold an unarguably deliberative, fair, and informed referendum on secession, it would be difficult to deny the validity of the outcome of the vote. As the court has recognized, "an expression of the democratic will of the people of a province carries weight, in that it would confer legitimacy on the efforts of the government of [Alberta] to initiate the Constitution's amendment process in order to secede by constitutional means."[xii] It is therefore in the interest of all parties to design a referendum process that ensures the result reflects the durable will of provincial residents.

Post-Referendum Evaluation. Step four in the secession sequence brings us back to the House of Commons. Just as the House of Commons must first evaluate the clarity of the referendum question prior to the actual vote, the House of Commons must again evaluate the clarity of the referendum result after the vote. The test, this time, is whether there is a "clear" majority vote in favour of the "clear" referendum question on secession. As the court has explained, the clarity of the result is essential to trigger subsequent steps in the secession sequence because "the clear repudiation by the people [of a province] of the existing constitutional order would confer legitimacy on demands for secession, and place an obligation on the other provinces and the federal government to acknowledge and respect that expression of democratic will … ."[xiii] But what are the standards the House of Commons must apply to determine whether the result is clear?

The Clarity Act outlines the criteria that must guide the House of Commons in evaluating whether the result is clear. The first builds on the House of Commons' evaluation of the question in the pre-referendum phase. Only if the House of Commons has earlier determined that the referendum question is clear may it proceed to evaluate the referendum result. That evaluation requires the House of Commons to examine whether "there has been a clear expression of a will by a clear majority of the population of that province that the province cease to be part of Canada."[xiv] The House of Commons must take into account the size of the majority in favour of secession, the rate of voter turnout, and other factors it considers relevant to determine whether a clear majority does indeed wish to leave the country. In addition, the House of Commons must consider the views of other parties represented in the legislative assembly of the province where the referendum has been held, the views of governments and legislative assemblies across the rest of Canada, any expressed views of the Senate, and the views of representatives of the Aboriginal peoples, among those of other relevant interested persons.[xv]

Negotiation. The two evaluative periods in the pre- and post-referendum stages of the secession sequence are crucial tests. If the House of Commons concludes that the referendum has failed both tests—meaning that neither the question nor the result is clear—the House of Commons must reject the referendum as invalid.[xvi] However, if the House of Commons determines that both the question and the result are clear, the province then accedes to the next step in the secession sequence: negotiations on the terms of secession. The right to enter into negotiations must therefore be earned in the design and outcome of the referendum.

A province earns the right to negotiate by satisfying the pre- and post-referendum tests, specifically by designing an approved referendum question and by achieving a favourable referendum outcome. When these conditions are met, the other partners in confederation become bound by a corresponding obligation to negotiate. The court explained that Canada's federalist and democratic foundations remove all discretion from federal and provincial governments to refuse to negotiate where the people of a province have properly asserted their wish for independence. In the court's own words:

> The federalism principle, in conjunction with the democratic principle, dictates that the clear repudiation of the existing constitutional order and the clear expression of the desire to pursue secession by the population of a province would give rise to a reciprocal obligation on all parties to confederation to negotiate constitutional changes to respond to that desire.[xvii]

The court qualified this right and its corresponding obligation to negotiate in several ways. For one, negotiations must respect what the court identified as foundational principles of Canadian constitutionalism, namely federalism, democracy, constitutionalism, the rule of law, and the protection of minorities.[xviii] Second, the right to negotiate does not entail a legal obligation on the federal and provincial governments to agree to the secession of the province.[xix] The court envisions a genuine negotiation, carried out in good faith, but one that might not yield an eventual agreement on the terms of secession. Third, when faced with a "clear expression of a clear majority" in a province to exit Canada, the federal and provincial governments must recognize and credit as valid the popular will for provincial self-determination.[xx] The obligation on the federal and provincial governments to negotiate therefore requires authentic engagement with the seceding province.

Negotiation, the court conceded, "would undoubtedly be difficult."[xxi] A Quebec secession, for instance, would require a total reconfiguration of national institutions, including of Parliament, where a certain number of seats are reserved for the province in both the House of Commons and Senate,[xxii] and of the supreme court, whose nine-judge bench must include three justices from Quebec.[xxiii] Negotiations would presumably also touch on a multiplicity of other issues, including how functionally to dismantle or at least formally to disentangle the economic, political, and social infrastructure that connect the province to Canada, how to safeguard national interests, and how to protect the linguistic, cultural, and other rights of affected populations.[xxiv] Other issues that would likely arise during secession negotiations would include matters of citizenship, borders, mobility, migration, and currency, as well as the national debt, armed forces, environment, and political relations between Canada and the seceding province.[xxv] In addition, Indigenous rights and representation would be central subjects for negotiation. Arriving at agreement on each of these items would be no easy task. But, as the Court insisted, secession terms "would have to be resolved within the overall framework of the rule of law, therefore assuring Canadians resident in [the seceding province] and elsewhere a measure of stability in what would likely be a period of considerable upheaval and uncertainty."[xxvi]

Constitutional Amendment. The final step in the secession sequence requires a constitutional amendment to implement the negotiated terms of provincial exit from Canada.[xxvii] This last stage is the legal culmination of the complex and quite likely very long political process of negotiating the province's secession from Canada. By the time the amendment process is initiated, the seceding province and the rest of the partners in confederation should have agreed to a detailed resolution spelling out the particulars of the provincial secession. By that stage, much of the hard part will have been done, and at this point all that would remain is to make the secession official by amending the Constitution to reflect the secession of a former partner in confederation. Ratifying the secession amendment could pose serious challenges of its own if the negotiating parties had not properly prepared the ground for the ratification votes required in the legislative assemblies of the country.

The Clarity Act specifies some of the preconditions for how the amendment must be made. For one, the amendment to approve a provincial secession must involve "at least the governments of all of the provinces and the Government of Canada," a formulation that invites the claim that others may have a valid claim to participate in either the consultations leading up to the amendment or the approval of the amendment itself, or indeed both. An additional rule applies to the federal government: no minister may propose an amendment to make secession official unless the government has agreed in prior negotiations to secession details on "the division of assets and liabilities, any changes to the borders of the province, the rights, interests and territorial claims of the Aboriginal peoples of Canada, and the protection of minority rights."[xxviii] The Clarity Act therefore sets conditions precedent for a secession amendment, namely that an amendment cannot lawfully be proposed without first securing the necessary agreements from the relevant partners in confederation and without the House of Commons having initially validated the referendum question and its results.

But there remains an open question about precisely how the amendment must be ratified. Must it proceed through one of the Constitution's five codified amendment procedures or must an altogether new one be designed especially for a provincial secession? In the Secession Reference, the Court did not specify how the secession amendment must be approved. One theory as to why speaks to the court's sensitivity to the historical and political context surrounding the Secession Reference: perhaps the court believed it was inappropriate to require conformity with the constitutional amendment rules codified in the very Constitution whose legitimacy those seeking Quebec's secession have long rejected.[xxix]

We can quite readily eliminate some of the five amendment procedures as viable options for formalizing a provincial secession amendment. For instance, a province cannot, nor should it, use the Constitution's unilateral provincial procedure to secede from the country, not least because amending whatever is identified as a provincial constitution entails a continuing membership in the larger union whose federal Constitution retains superiority over the provincial constitution.[xxx]

It likewise seems clear that a provincial secession cannot be authorized using the unilateral parliamentary amendment procedure, which authorizes the Parliament of Canada to amend the Constitution of Canada "in relation to the executive government of Canada or the Senate and House of Commons."[xxxi] Parliament may deploy this narrow amendment power only to formally amend matters within its own internal constitution, for instance parliamentary privilege, legislative procedure, and the number of members of Parliament.[xxxii]

We can also exclude the regional amendment procedure, which requires the approval of the House of Commons, the Senate, and the assemblies of the affected provinces.[xxxiii] This procedure applies, at a minimum, to constitutional changes that have provincial-federal scope in respect of a single province and, at most, to those changes that have a regional, though not national scope. A provincial secession would have national scope, affecting national institutions and structures, not to mention the transformation it would exact on confederation. One could of course construct an argument that we could use this regional procedure for a secession amendment but it would be an unreasonable view that is outcome-oriented—in order to make secession more feasible—and not grounded in first principles.

Each of the two remaining procedures raises problems of its own, yet each could be justified as the one that must be used to formalize a provincial secession. The most stringent amendment procedure requires approval resolutions from both houses of the federal Parliament and from each of the provincial assemblies.[xxxiv] There are five specifically designated subjects for which use of this unanimity amendment rule is required: the monarchy, the established ratio of provincial representation in the House of Commons and the Senate, Canada's official languages beyond their provincial or regional use, the composition of the Supreme Court of Canada, and Canada's formal amendment rules themselves. Since a provincial secession would reverberate across the entire country and would impact all of Canada's most important institutions, it could make good sense to give a voice in the terms of secession to every partner in confederation. But one could justifiably object to this procedure because it grants a veto to everyone. Imagine all partners in confederation agreed to the terms of secession except for one province that continued to hold out in an effort to extract concessions wholly unrelated to the matter of self-determination for the seceding province. Surely that would be an inappropriate exercise of the veto power, but it would not be precluded by this unanimity procedure, which requires no justification from a province choosing whether to give or withhold its assent to the constitutional amendment.

The fifth and final possible amendment procedure to formalize a provincial secession requires approval resolutions from the House of Commons and the Senate in the federal Parliament as well as approval resolutions from the provincial assemblies of at least two-thirds of the provinces whose aggregate population is at least half of the total.[xxxv] This procedure is known colloquially as the 7/50 procedure. It applies exclusively to a specially designated class of subjects, including proportional representation in the House of Commons, the powers and membership of the Senate as well as the method of senator selection, the Supreme Court of Canada for all items except its composition, the creation of new provinces, and the boundaries between provinces and territories.[xxxvi] One could argue that a provincial secession falls into this class of constitutional changes just as compellingly as one might claim it falls into the class of changes contemplated by the unanimity procedure.

There is a strong though not conclusive argument why this 7/50 procedure is the one that ought to be used to formalize a provincial secession: it is also Canada's default amendment procedure. By its very text, it must be used for all amendments not otherwise assigned to a specific amendment procedure. And since none of the amendment procedures expressly provides for secession, a long-standing canon of constitutional construction points to the 7/50 procedure as the answer. *Expressio unius est exclusio alterius*, meaning that when a text enumerates a list, anything not enumerated must be taken to be have been consciously excluded. The theory, then, is that the choice not to enumerate secession under any of the procedures for amending the Constitution means that it must be assigned to the default amendment rule.

The challenge of constitutional amendment

Let us assume that we agree on which of these five amendment procedures must be used to formalize a provincial secession. Many questions would nonetheless remain unanswered. The most important involves the voice of Indigenous peoples in Canada: what would be their role in a provincial secession amendment? It is clear from the secession sequence that Indigenous peoples are necessary actors in the pre-referendum and post-referendum evaluations conducted by the House of Commons. But surely there should be some involvement in the subsequent steps of the secession sequence, specifically in the stages of negotiation and constitutional amendment. Yet at present, the Constitution contemplates only that "the Prime Minister will invite representatives of the aboriginal peoples of Canada to participate in the discussions" at a constitutional conference convened on a specific list of types of amendments.[xxxvii] Our present reality has outrun this constitutional rule, which does not go far enough to recognize the place of Indigenous peoples in any provincial secession. This will be a serious challenge confronting both the province wishing to secede as well as all other partners in confederation.

Another open question is worth highlighting: will a national referendum be required? Scholars have argued that the use of a referendum in the process to ratify the 1992 Charlottetown Accord has created a precedent—one that rises to the level of a constitutional convention—that today binds first ministers and provincial assemblies (as well as territorial assemblies) to hold a referendum before any major amendment may be made to the Constitution of Canada.[xxxviii] Some provinces and territories have adopted laws requiring or allowing their assemblies to hold a referendum before their respective legislative assemblies vote to ratify a proposed amendment. But we do not yet have an answer whether provinces and territories without such referendum laws would also have to hold a referendum. The Constitution offers no guidance on this point, and it is possible even to argue that these provincial and territorial laws are unconstitutional insofar as they have amended the Constitution's amendment rules without proceeding through the unanimity procedure, which is expressly designated as the procedure for amending the rules of constitutional amendment.

As is by now evident, the entire secession sequence from initiation to amendment is likely to take years, if it happens at all. The Constitution does not make secession easy, nor should it, though the Constitution does not does it make it impossible either. The Constitution is instead designed as a partnership of many parts whose members may seek to exercise their right to withdraw from confederation when they believe their interests require it. It follows, then, that the Constitution of Canada does not recognize a unilateral right to secede precisely because Canada is a union that cannot be dissolved at the instigation of a single partner.

But surely the Constitution cannot be a straitjacket if a partner in confederation follows the requirements of the secession sequence in good faith and with integrity only to be impeded in the final stages. Imagine, for instance, that Alberta successfully holds a referendum that has been recognized as valid by the House of Commons—in other words that the province has fulfilled all expectations in the stages of initiation, pre-referendum evaluation, provincial vote, and post-referendum evaluation. If Alberta were then to meet sustained and hostile resistance from one or more partners in confederation at the stages of negotiation or constitutional amendment such that a reasonable observer would conclude that Albertans were unjustifiably being denied their constitutional right to exit, a controversial option could perhaps present itself at that point: the right to make a unilateral declaration of independence.

A unilateral declaration of independence is a divisive form of self-help on which there is much debate as to its legality and legitimacy. On the one hand, one could well doubt that a people or sub-state should have the right declare independence from the larger state. But what if that people or sub-state is the victim, at the hands of the larger state, of abuse, oppression, and the denial of self-government? Similarly, one could look to any given constitution and find that only relatively few expressly codify the right to secede, presumably making a unilateral declaration of independence not only illegal but also illegitimate. On the other hand, what can be more deeply anchored in moral and sociological legitimacy than a collective act of a people or a sub-state to vindicate the natural right to self-determination in the face of tyrannical body intent on suppressing the voices and views of that people or sub-state? Conditions like these may provide the predicate for remedial secession, a right that may or may not exist under the international law of self-determination. But the right to remedial secession is not relevant in the case of a self-governing Alberta because Canada has not imposed any of these awful conditions of oppression on Albertans.

It is worth turning to international law to inquire into the status of a unilateral declaration of independence. In an important advisory opinion in 2010, the International Court of Justice concluded that "general international law contains no applicable prohibition of declarations of independence." [xxxix] International law, then, raises no barrier in the way of a unilateral declaration of independence. But, here, law may be less important than politics. A unilateral declaration of independence is insufficient on its own to achieve much of anything beyond echoing the preferences of the people represented by those making the declaration and exclaiming to the world an expression of discontent. In order to have real bite as a practical reality, a unilateral declaration of independence must be recognized by existing sovereign states as a justified expression of grievance and more importantly as announcing the entry of a new member into the international community of sovereign states. The Supreme Court of Canada recognized this point in its Secession Reference when it conceded that "the ultimate success of such a secession would be dependent on recognition by the international community.... "[xl] In other words, the efficacy of a unilateral declaration of independence is not unlike admission to a private club: the current membership decides whom to admit or reject. The countries of the world therefore serve as gatekeepers for any people or sub-state wishing to rise to the status of an independent state.

The Canadian model of secession

The Canadian model of secession differs from others in the world. There are three distinctions worth noting: (1) the constitution's codified rules on secession; (2) the judicial construction of secession rules; and (3) the duration of secession negotiations. A word on each of these three differences follows.

The codified portions of the Canadian Constitution are silent on whether a province has the right to secede. There is no express recognition that the right exists. But nor is there any explicit declaration that the provinces must forever remain within confederation. On the contrary, the silence of the codified rules in the Constitution of Canada leaves open the possibility of the constitutionality of secession. In contrast, the Spanish Constitution states in definitive terms that secession is impermissible when it speaks in its text of "the indissoluble unity of the Spanish Nation" and of "the common and indivisible homeland of all Spaniards," two phrases that shut the door to a legal secession.[xli] As an indissoluble and indivisible country, Spain leaves no doubt in its Constitution about whether there exists a constitutional right to secede—the answer is no.

The role of the Supreme Court of Canada in secession has differed from the role of courts in some other countries. Consider for example the United States. The Supreme Court of the United States has bolted the door to secession in its interpretation of the Constitution, insisting that the union of states that joined forces to create the United States was intended to be "indissoluble" and "perpetual" with "no place for reconsideration or revocation, except through revolution or through consent of the States."[xlii] This American case sprang from a unilateral declaration of independence issued by Texas—a declaration that had been adopted by an extraordinary constitutional convention and subsequently ratified by a majority of Texans. The court held that the declaration was inoperative and without legal force since Texas had all along remained a state in the union and each Texan had remained a citizen of the United States—because the Constitution does not contemplate the legal possibility of secession. In Canada, the supreme court has helped to construct a detailed sequence of secession rules despite there being no indication in the codified portions of the Constitution that secession is permissible.

The rules and expectations for secession negotiations under the Canadian model also differ from some others. For instance, the rules for withdrawal from the European Union specify that a member state has the unilateral right to exit.[xliii] Withdrawal is initiated according to the member state's own constitutional rules but once the member state notifies the European Council of its intention to exit, a period of negotiation follows to arrive at the terms of withdrawal and any future relationship between the member state and the European Union.[xliv] If the negotiations do not yield an agreement within two years of the date of notification, the exit of the member state becomes official without any official terms of separation or any rules to govern future relationships; the result is quite simply that the treaties of the European Union completely cease to apply.[xlv] In Canada, by contrast, the Constitution and the Clarity Act make clear by their silence that secession negotiations are not subject to a time limitation and may endure for a significant period of time. The Canadian model accordingly does not impose a date certain end to the multilateral negotiations on post-secession political and economic agreements between the seceding province and the country. This "open-ended" model gives political actors time and flexibility to negotiate the terms of a province's exit from the country. But this model offers no guarantee against obstructionist tactics, which in turn could provoke a unilateral exit and all the risks it entails.

Secessionist sentiment in Alberta

Today the centre of secessionist pressure in Canada is not Quebec but rather Alberta. Wexit Alberta intends to run candidates in federal elections and provincial contests in Alberta, British Colombia, Manitoba, and Saskatchewan with the goal of eventually making Alberta its own state. The party has organized itself around three major objectives: economic liberty, social stability, and sovereignty for Alberta.[xlvi] On economic liberty, the party aims to set a personal income tax rate no higher than 19 percent, to reduce corporate tax rates to 7 percent, to promote jobs and business relocation in Alberta, and to ensure that regulations do not hinder Alberta's environmentally-oriented energy development. On social stability, the party intends to prioritize individual rights and public order by investing in health, education and welfare programs for youth, the elderly, and homeless and at-risk populations. The party also intends to refine the rules of immigration and courtroom procedure, to harden the penalties for certain categories of crimes, and to work toward resolving the compensation claims of Indigenous peoples against the federal government. These objectives suggest that Wexit Alberta has a plan for far more than independence alone.

But it is primarily independence that is motivating Wexit Alberta. The party asserts that it "will ensure that Alberta remains sovereign, and no way subordinate to the Government of Canada, British Crown, or the United Nations...." It will issue a declaration of independence from Canada, create an infrastructure for a new national government that includes an elected head of state as well as an elected Senate. The party plans to withdraw from any multilateral or supranational agreements that "erode Alberta Sovereignty, including but not limited to the UN Compact on Migration, the Paris Climate Accord, and Agenda 2030." Other plans include the establishment of a defence force, a police corps, a national currency, as well as agreements with allied partners.

The Alberta premier has rejected calls for secession, taking an uncompromising position on Alberta secession, signalling that he believes Alberta will be at its strongest if it remains in Canada:

> "I am and always will be a Canadian patriot. I believe that in their heart of hearts the vast majority of Albertans are Canadian patriots," he said. "My own view is I cannot conceive how we would be better off by cutting ourselves off and landlocking ourselves from the rest of the continent."[xlvii]

And yet the government has prudently taken note of these secessionist sentiments in the province. The premier announced, in November 2019, the

creation of a Fair Deal panel to consult Albertans "on how best to define
and to secure a fair deal for Alberta" and moreover to "look at how best to
advance the province's vital economic interests, such as the construction of
energy pipelines."[xlviii] The purpose of the Fair Deal panel was simultaneously
to acknowledge the deep dissatisfaction in Alberta with the province's treatment in confederation and to examine how to assert Alberta's rights more
fulsomely. Even if in the end the Fair Deal panel is no more than a public
relations effort, the Alberta premier will have achieved what he had hoped:
a reduction in the secessionist anger directed at him and the government he
leads, and some useful data on the views of Albertans on many of the controversial subjects that currently dominate headlines in the province.

The Fair Deal panel submitted its report to the Government of Alberta
on May 5, 2020.[xlix] The report was made public on June 17, 2020.[l] The panel
made a series of twenty-five recommendations, including one set that could
be implemented in the near term by the Government of Alberta alone and
another set that requires collaboration with, or the agreement of, other
partners in confederation.[li] The first category of recommendations includes
creating an Alberta Police Service to replace the RCMP, opting out of new
federal cost-shared programs subject to full compensation, appointing a Chief
Firearms Officer for the province and, among others, holding a referendum
on withdrawing from the Canada Pension Plan and creating an Alberta
Pension Plan. The second category of recommendations includes reducing
interprovincial trade barriers, democratizing senator selection, asserting greater control over immigration, and pressing Ottawa for increased civil service
offices and jobs in Western Canada. The panel moreover choose to highlight
two recommendations in particular, setting them out from the others in
their own category: (1) the government should "press strenuously for the
removal of the current constraints on the Fiscal Stabilization Program, which
prevent Albertans from receiving a $2.4 billion equalization rebate"; and
(2) the government should also "proceed with the proposed referendum on
equalization, asking a clear question along the lines of: 'Do you support the
removal of Section 36, which deals with the principle of equalization, from
the Constitution Act, 1982?'"[lii]

A constitution for Alberta

The Fair Deal panel should be commended for its report. Written by Albertans for Albertans, the report is rooted in and informed by the views expressed by Albertans across the province in live town halls, consultations with experts and representative groups, as well as written and oral surveys conducted between December 2019 and March 2020.[liii] This is an excellent model for robust engagement with the people of the province in a compressed period of time.

Yet the report has simultaneously gone too far and not far enough. Some of its recommendations would risk great harm to the country if implemented, and this might well result in isolating Alberta from the other partners in confederation. Yet the reality that Canada would see its resources and capacity severely diminished if Alberta implemented certain recommendations—for instance, withdrawing from the Canada Pension Plan—reinforces the very point that many Albertans have been making for years: that their province gives more to Canada than it receives in return. On the other hand, the Fair Deal panel has missed a perfect opportunity to make one recommendation in particular that could go quite far toward alleviating secessionist sentiment in the province and giving Albertans greater voice in confederation: creating a constitution for Alberta.[liv] The Fair Deal panel announced that its members "were unable to unanimously agree if we should recommend a formal constitution for Alberta."

Codifying a provincial constitution would be an unprecedented event of high moment in Canada. No province currently possesses a codified constitution nor has any province ever enacted one. This makes Canada stand out among many of the roughly twenty federations of the world. The equivalent of provinces—for instance, states or *Länder*—have codified their constitutions in federations as varied as Australia, Austria, Brazil, Germany, and the United States. This should come as no surprise, since an overwhelming majority of federal constitutions either permit or require their subnational states to enact a constitution.[lv] The Constitution of Canada is no different: it recognizes that provinces may, if they wish, codify and in turn amend their own constitutions.[lvi]

The purpose of codifying a provincial constitution in Canada is rooted less in law than politics. The Constitution of Canada remains supreme over all other laws, and this subordinates any provincial constitution to the federal constitution. The Canadian Constitution, moreover, imposes limitations on what a province can do in any constitution it creates for itself and its peoples. For example, a provincial constitution may not violate certain democratic or language rights, nor may it make changes to specified institutions, namely the monarchy.[lvii] It is also possible that the federal government could exercise its power either to disallow an enacted provincial constitution or to reserve a bill on its enactment, though these two powers have sat unused for generations and are unlikely to be revived in our present day in light of the new norms and expectations of federalism.[lviii]

But within these parameters, Alberta could enact its own provincial constitution to great political effect. Writing down the rules governing the province's basic institutions of democracy could serve the functions of preservation, entrenchment, and legitimation. First, preservation: the social fact of the writtenness of rules that had in the past been unwritten could give those codified rules a special status that would make them seem less fleeting or susceptible to misapplication or violation. Second, entrenchment: the procedure by which the provincial constitution were adopted could entrench the text against future repeal by an ordinary legislative majority, assuming the text had been adopted by a special supermajority and therefore protected against repeal or amendment by the same threshold. And, third, legitimation: the acts of proposing, designing, debating, and then of enacting the constitution could clothe the constitution in an unassailable sociological legitimacy reflecting the considered will of the people, assuming the constitution-making process had engaged the people directly in the project.

The process of designing a constitution for Alberta could take many different forms. It could be a strictly legislative process, a largely people-driven process, or a combination of the two. As a legislative process, a new Albertan Constitution could be created by a government bill or a cross-party bill following inter-party consultations. As a people-driven process, the new constitution could engage Albertans directly in province-wide riding-level or even regional public hearings where persons could make submissions or comments about what they wish to see in a new constitution for their province. Alternatively or in addition, a constituent assembly of trusted persons specially chosen for the purpose of deliberating on and eventually proposing a constitution could gather over a period of weeks to engage in the work of designing the new Albertan Constitution. An additional or alternative dimension of a people-driven process could include a province-wide referendum to approve the new constitution proposed by its authors. There are many possible paths in the process for creating a constitution for Alberta.

The best strategy would merge legislative and popular procedures to fashion a process that blends the knowledge and experience of legislators with direct input from Albertans themselves. The combination of legislative debate and design along with many opportunities for popular input throughout the process culminating with popular ratification as a condition of enactment offers the best outcome for legal efficacy, political palatability, and popular legitimation.

Perhaps most importantly, the project of codifying a provincial constitution would give Albertans an outlet to express how they wish to define themselves and their values. The symbolic function of a provincial constitution is powerful in a federation defined by differing provincial interests. A constitution, in this case, gives a province a vehicle to communicate to the rest of the country and indeed the world how and why it is distinct in its culture, history, and aspirations. Albertans could accomplish this project of self-definition in any combination of ways, as long as the constitution remained legally compatible with the Constitution of Canada. For instance, a new Albertan constitution could include a declaration of values specific to the province. Alternatively or in addition, the new constitution could incorporate an Alberta-specific constitutional Charter of Rights that includes rights not currently protected in the Canadian Charter of Rights and Freedoms. It would be permissible to give a broader interpretation to these rights than applies to those in the Charter. Alberta might also choose to instruct the interpreters of those rights to afford deference to executive and legislative decision-making where possible. And this provincial Charter of Rights could include protections that are not presently enumerated in the

Charter, for example private property rights. Another way for Albertans to define themselves in their new constitution could be to adopt a made-in-Alberta preamble that speaks to the unique values of the province. Here, for example, is a draft preamble that could prove effective as the opening lines to a new Albertan Constitution—a draft preamble that shows in both concrete terms and evocative imagery the many possibilities for expressing distinct Albertan values within a strong and united Canada:

> We, the united People of Alberta, in everlasting awe of our clear blue skies and our abundance of riches across our land, grateful to our ancestors for instilling their pioneering spirit and frontier values, recognizing that we must remember our heritage and safeguard our institutions, and affirming that Canada is at its strongest when we, the united People of Alberta, are thriving in all aspects of our lives, do ordain and establish this Constitution of Alberta, keeping faith with our motto—*Fortis et Liber*—strong and free.

The overriding purpose for codifying a Constitution for Alberta would be to give Albertans an overtly public and prominent forum to declare what makes them different from the rest of Canada and also why Canada is at its strongest when Alberta is a collaborative and prosperous partner in confederation.

Conclusion—the challenge of confederation

Confederation was not easy to create, nor will it be easy to keep. The possibility remains ever present that the Canada we know today may not be the Canada we have tomorrow. We have in the past confronted moments of deep division in the country and this may be the direction in which we are once again heading given the existing and perhaps intensifying secessionist sentiment in Alberta. Fortunately, the Constitution of Canada anticipates these challenges and equips us with tools to respond. Our Constitution recognizes the right to provincial self-determination within a legal framework, making it possible for a province to exit confederation where the circumstances justify it.

The Constitution is as much a legal framework as it is an aspirational ideal. As higher law, the Canadian Constitution divides powers between two levels of government, each authorized to act within its separate spheres of authority with mutual respect for the powers and prerogatives of the other. And yet the Constitution of Canada also requires that we find ways to affirm the cultural, linguistic, and regional differences that distinguish the many peoples across the country.

Secession need not be the only answer to Alberta's grievances within confederation. Codifying a constitution for the province and its peoples could help assuage some of Alberta's misgivings with confederation. It could also ultimately strengthen confederation by giving voice to Albertans to express their unique priorities and values within a Canada united around the strength of its diversity. In the end, codifying an Albertan Constitution could go a long way to giving the province some real measure of agency and independence without ever leaving country. This option should at least be considered before making the tragic choice to secede from Canada.

Challenges for western independence
Barry Cooper

B EFORE DISCUSSING the challenges for western independence, it is important to consider the context within which these
obstacles have emerged. Some are as recent as the 2019 election;
others are a simple reflection of the geopolitics of Canada and the self-un-
derstanding of Canadians in different parts of the country. These latter
considerations were in existence long before confederation.

The significance of the 2019 election

The 2019 election was like the elections of the 1980s insofar as the results
emphasized the regional divisions of Canada. The west is more or less
Conservative; Quebec is a mixture of Liberals and nationalists; Ontario
and the lower mainland of British Columbia are Liberal and NDP. As might
be expected with such a combination, nothing decisive emerged from this
trip to the polls. Indeed, it simply postponed some serious decisions and
guaranteed that the circumstances under which several well-known and
long-standing problems must eventually be faced will make a moderate
compromise much more difficult. The most significant consequence of 2019
was that the Liberals returned to office with the smallest share of the vote
of any government in Canadian history. Previous and precarious minorities
all had greater popular support.

The result was deeply disappointing to westerners. Worse, the manner of the Liberal victory was especially insulting. Rather than attempting to defend an indefensible record, the Liberals attacked Conservative Leader Andrew Scheer as a continuation of the Liberally-detested Stephen Harper. They claimed Scheer and the Ontario premier, Doug Ford, were northern Trumpians, neither of which charges was remotely plausible to normal people. The Liberals added to their sanctimonious virtue-signalling by claiming they would ensure that Canada remain a "progressive" northern bastion against nativism, polarization, authoritarianism and the demonization of enemies, all evils they attributed to the Trump Administration. That is why they expended so much energy to lobby Barack Obama to endorse Justin Trudeau. That kind of election interference by foreigners is perfectly acceptable to the progressive left.

The data summarizing the October 21 results are clear, even eloquent. The Conservatives won 68 per cent of 104 seats in the West. The Liberals won 60 per cent of 234 seats in the non-West. According to an old adage, Canadian elections have become opportunities for Ontario to decide how much money the West will send to Quebec. Several commentators recalled the advice of the Liberal campaign manager of the 1980s, Keith "The Rainmaker" Davey: "Screw the West; we'll take the rest." It worked for the first Trudeau and now it has worked for his son, who then had the temerity to accuse Alberta premier Jason Kenney of fomenting national division, disunity, and Alberta independence. As Trudeau's environment minister, Catherine McKenna, famously tweeted from a St. John's bar: "If you say it loud enough and often enough, people will believe you. For sure." Thank you, Dr. Goebbels.

Looking back, the 2019 minority is quite unlike, for example, the Conservative minority of 2006. Following the 2004 Liberal minority, the Harper conservatives tailored their policy to appeal to Quebecers—cancelling the plan to cancel corporate subsidies to Bombardier, for example. When westerners have endured Liberal minorities, as in the present, there is no pressure for the government to appeal to westerners. On the contrary, we can look for the Liberal Laurentians to double down on the damage they have imposed on the West. Westerners know this, which is why there has been a spike in media chatter reflecting increased support for western independence.

About a year ago an Angus Reid poll found that nearly three out of four westerners thought that Ottawa doesn't treat them fairly. Shachi Kurl, executive director of the Angus Reid Institute, told Global News that the West "does not see itself reflected or represented in our so-called national institutions" and suggested that the data reflected the position of the Reform Party in the late 1980s and cited their slogan: "The West Wants In."[i] Westerners are still not represented in our so-called national institutions. The difference this time is that increasingly the West wants out.

The response of the Laurentian media, particularly in Toronto's national newspaper, was entirely predictable. On October 24, 2019 in the *Globe and Mail*, Eric Reguly said westerners and especially Albertans were punishing themselves. They should have been "sophisticated" like the admittedly "cynical," which is to say, corrupt electorate of Quebec, and voted strategically to "keep the federal favour-train running." Instead, masochistic fools that we are, Alberta "rendered itself totally defenceless in Ottawa" and now must "prepare itself to take a few lashings."[ii]

The next day, Reguly's colleague, Marcus Gee, revealed to an expectant nation that "Toronto and the dynamic communities in its orbit have become the key to winning elections in the country." This, of course, is a good thing. "Whether Canada succeeds depends on whether its biggest city succeeds." Accordingly, "Toronto deserves every bit of its growing influence. Sensible Canadians will cheer it on." For those miscreants suffering from some kind of false consciousness who see no reason to cheer, his advice was brutally clear: "Get used to it."[iii]

Even Andrew Coyne, writing in the *National Post* on October 26, 2019, half-endorsed Reguly's notion that the Government of Canada is really a "national protection racket." Evoking *The Sound of Music*, he begins: "How do you solve a problem like Alberta?" He asks with indignation rather than irony: what can they be complaining about now? The Liberals just bought them a pipeline. They have "one of the highest standards of living on earth" and the highest of all the provinces. And yet, the fools, they claim the federation "does not work for them." Ottawa, which passed Bills C-69 and C-48, is not to blame for the destruction of the Alberta economy (low world oil prices are, he says; but then why is the American oil and gas sector doing well?).[iv] The carbon tax, Coyne avers, is "good policy in the national interest." The courts and activist groups, not the Government of Canada, are responsible for the absence of pipe. But who other than the Liberal Government of Canada has encouraged them both with poisoned rhetoric about social licence? Coyne did, however, condescend to observe: "But for goodness sake, it is hardly unreasonable for Albertans to feel themselves besieged." Thank-you, Andrew. But for goodness sake, stop the silliness. Albertans do not *feel* themselves besieged, they *are* besieged. Indeed, they have been under attack for the past four years. Have you not noticed? Probably not. It is so hard to see past Mississauga. Nor have you noticed that the only significant question discussed nowadays in this province is: how deliberate, how calculated has the attack on Alberta been? And what is the malign motive of the Laurentians?[v] Coyne has since departed for the presumably more congenial *Globe and Mail*.

A few weeks later, Gary Mason, based in Vancouver and Toronto's eye on the West, weighed in with his own interpretation of the post-election political landscape. He was indignant that Jason Kenney "would like to see Alberta carve out almost the same level of independence as Quebec." *Quoi? Quel scandale!* "For students of history" such as Mason, it is all redolent of the notorious firewall Letter of a couple of decades ago. "And so here we are today," Mason opines, "with conservatives in the province once again upset about the outcome of a federal election, once again stoking divisions because they don't have a government in Ottawa that reflects their ideological leanings." All the talk about pipeline expansion, Bills C-48 and C-69 and so forth, is "tedious to the point of being irrelevant." And he ended by quoting Rachel Notley, clearly an unbiased observer of Alberta politics, who uttered the old canard that Kenney was "intentionally stoking the fires of western alienation."[vi] A few weeks later, as talk of independence increased in Alberta, Mason observed that such talk was "hurting Alberta." The whole thing, evidently, was "backward... patently ridiculous" and "just dumb."[vii]

The Laurentian journalistic consensus is that Alberta and Saskatchewan have only themselves to blame for whatever adverse policies—Marcus

Gee's figurative "lashings"—Laurentian Canada imposes on them because they were stupid enough not to vote Liberal. Who knows why, but they just refuse to go along to get along. Trying to change things by asserting provincial powers and provincial jurisdiction is a dangerous threat to the Laurentian bugaboo, "national unity." In order to avoid having to specify what the danger might be, these deep thinkers quickly invoke the spectre of "western alienation."

That term has been around since at least the 1980s. The great problem with it is that is forestalls further thought and categorizes the injustices of confederation in a way that serves both the interests and the moral certainty of Laurentian Canada. Alas, it is entirely bogus. Ask yourself: what would it take not to be alienated in the eyes of Laurentian Canada? What policies would westerners embrace to show the rest of Canada they had overcome their alienation and now were normal and healthy? At the very least they would have to acknowledge that Quebec and Ontario are the real Canada. Our job in the boonies is to support the real Canada, the old colony Canada, by providing whatever they want, no questions asked. To show our good faith we will become enthusiastic supporters of the CBC and especially of Radio-Canada. We will also petition—nay beg—for a local edition of the *Toronto Star* to keep us properly informed.

Of course, we will heartily cheer on the growing influence of Toronto. Torontonians deserve nothing less. Indeed, they deserve much, much more. We will also gratefully support the shutting down of the oil and gas industry on the prairies, particularly the filthy tar sands. Why? Because we must save the planet by reducing to zero our nearly 1 per cent contribution of global CO_2 production, which (unquestionably) causes apocalyptic climate change. Here we show our good faith by applauding in unison the tanker ban on the north coast of B.C., and the shutting down of any expansion of Trans-Mountain pipeline that would have released a shocking additional 0.6 per cent of oil production into the global market. Of course, westerners will embrace joyfully the wisdom of Bill C-69 to ensure no other pipelines get built, ever. Also, we will support our prime minister come what may. Here our non-alienation will be reflected in the public approval we accord the dear leader for his great and wise actions on behalf of all Canadians, especially middle-class Canadians and those who are working so hard to join the middle class. As he so often reminds us.

Ted Morton provided a western appraisal of the significance of the election in the *Calgary Herald* on October 26, 2019. The spike in support for independence has moved a long way past anger, to say nothing of alienation, he said. The difference between the response of westerners, particularly in Alberta and Saskatchewan, in 2019 and the response, say, to the National Energy Program of Pierre Trudeau a generation ago is that many westerners see a pattern even if they don't remember first-hand the devastation caused by the NEP. As Morton observed, "our vulnerability to federal politics and policies is structural not temporary." Very simply, "the Liberal party doesn't need any votes from the West to form a government." This "demographic vulnerability," as he calls it, is not episodic but historical and virtually permanent. Moreover, the political consequences are "compounded by our very different regional economies," namely that efficient resource extraction has made the West a major element in the Canadian economy, contributing nearly a third of Canada's GDP with around a quarter of the population. The result, as Morton also pointed out, is a net fiscal transfer from Alberta in particular of $611 billion since 1961. Since 2010 Alberta has provided Ottawa with over $20 billion a year, even when the province was running budgetary deficits. In contrast, Quebec, which contributes under 20 per cent of Canada's GDP now receives two-thirds of every equalization dollar. "The electoral math is that simple," Morton concluded.[viii]

A few weeks after the election an exchange took place between Premier Kenney and Yves-François Blanchet, leader of the Bloc Québécois. After a pleasant meeting with the prime minister, Blanchet announced there was no national unity problem because of the election. Coming from the leader of a party that advocates Quebec sovereignty, at least as a vague future desideratum, he was indicating quite clearly that the sovereigntists of the Bloc are not serious. In fact, they never have been. The current crop of separatists are just a contemporary version of Robert Bourassa's *fédéralisme rentable*, profitable federalism. Westerners have known this for years.[ix]

In a speech in Calgary a couple of days later Kenney said: "If you are so 'opposed to' the energy that we produce in Alberta then why are you so keen in taking the money generated by the oilfield workers of this province and across Western Canada? You cannot have your cake and eat it. Pick a lane." To which Blanchet replied: "You know what? I like my cake and I will do what I like about it." The miraculous option of having your cake and eating it too, the absence of any need to "pick a lane," was made possible, as Blanchet perfectly well knew, because next year more cake is on its way from Alberta.[x] Blanchet's condescending remarks, to say nothing of Trudeau's comments on how fortunate we are to have so many Quebec francophones in cabinet, indicate the main contextual problem: the never-serious threat of Quebec sovereignty excuses every insulting remark from the mouths of Quebec politicians. Any criticism, especially from Alberta, is met with serious and sombre admonitions to pipe down and quit endangering "national unity."

Shortly after the exchange between Kenney and Blanchet, Campbell Clark, writing in the *Globe and Mail*, reminded his readers that Blanchet "is not trying to promote national unity." Just in case we didn't know: "He is a separatist. When it comes to the parts of Canada getting along, he's not here to help." Once again, a sophisticated Laurentian journalist seeks to instruct the Western rubes who clearly were unaware of how dangerous Blanchet truly is. "And when he shoots off his mouth, Mr. Kenney should not treat the Bloc leader as he does. Because he's not rooting for Canadian unity."[xi] Across the West we are enjoined only to root for Canadian unity and to do so with the same enthusiasm we need to show for the "growing influence" of Toronto. Really?

The centrality of Quebec in Canada, which constitutes the foundational myth of Laurentian Canada, was reiterated in the pages of the *Calgary Herald*. Don Braid, who really ought to know better, advised Kenney to "brush off Blanchet as a separatist crank who's poking a stick into Canadian divisions. That's only the truth."[xii] The "truth," it seems to me, is that there are and always have been "divisions" in Canada but that Quebec and Ontario, and their government in Ottawa, are on one side and the West is on the other. This brings us to the perennial problem of Canadian geopolitics.

Canadian geopolitics

Historically, the largest resource deposits have always been in the West—apart from cod and white pine—while population has been centred in the St. Lawrence valley. Fur, especially beaver, was replaced by grain, mainly wheat, then potash, uranium, oil and gas, but the resources are still chiefly in the West. Federalism was supposed to reconcile population and resource wealth, and for many years westerners believed it. That is why, as David Smith observed, westerners initially worked within the dominant parties to get their interests acknowledged. Then they tried third parties—Social Credit, the CCF, the Progressives, Reform. Westerners have engaged with every party under the sun and deployed strategies from balance-of-power to disruption. None of them worked.[xiii]

The reason is simple: Laurentian Canada has never seen the West as part of a federation. The Canadian federation, so far as they are concerned, is made up (as was implied by all the Laurentian journalists cited in the previous section) of Ontario and Quebec. The Maritime provinces were sidelined during the nineteenth century within a generation of confederation. Newfoundland managed to hold out until 1949. The important thing to notice is that the West was never considered part of the deal. So what were we?

Consider first the Latin motto on the Canadian coat of arms: *a mari usque ad mare*. The text is from the Latin Vulgate translation of Psalm 72:8. It does not include the rest of the verse: *et a flumine usque ad terminos terrae*, nor does it contain the opening words, *et dominabitur*. The King James Version translates the entire verse: "He shall have dominion also from sea to sea, and from the river unto the ends of the earth." The Latin *dominium* referred to a territory that was mastered; it was used in its English form by the British to refer to their colonies and possessions. Before the American Revolution the colonies were often referred to as the Dominion of New England. When, out of fear of offending the United States, the British Foreign Office objected to the name Kingdom of Canada, which the Canadian colonials preferred, Sir Leonard Tilley of New Brunswick suggested the term dominion. It has remained the formal title of the country ever since, though it is hardly used today.

More interesting for present purposes are the additional implications: the Canadian dominion shall extend from the river to the ends of the earth. There is no question that the river is the St. Lawrence and the contemporary west is their *termini terrae*, the ends of the earth, excluded from confederation in order to be dominated by it. Hence the expression "out" west.

When the ends of the earth were transferred from the Imperial Crown to the Crown in right of Canada, they were to be administered from Ottawa "for the purposes of the Dominion." It is important for understanding the current relations between the West and Laurentian Canada to recall that 150 years ago Canadians were oblivious of the fact that the inhabitants of Rupert's Land and the northwest constituted a distinct society.

Contemporary historians of Rupert's Land and of the "distinctive regional way of life" achieved by the fur-trade society that lived there have recalled for contemporary westerners as well as Laurentian Canadians that a sense of distinctiveness was central to the inhabitants of the contemporary west, whatever their nineteenth-century ethnic composition was.[xiv] For a generation after the 1821 amalgamation of the Hudson's Bay Company of London and the Northwest Company of Montreal, Canada showed no interest in Rupert's Land. As with the New England settlements a century before, this neglect enabled something like a political self-awareness to develop at the Red River Settlement. When Red River looked towards Canada at all, it was in order to find political allies, not because the inhabitants sought to become Canadians. "For their part, Canadians—that is, the inhabitants of the old colony of Canada—seem never to have understood this."[xv]

Meanwhile, the inhabitants of Rupert's Land and the settlement underwent the more or less futile experience of petitioning imperial parliaments for redress of such familiar imperial abuses as taxation without representation or consent. In 1845-6 the inhabitants of Red River even petitioned the U.S. Congress for help. In 1861, following yet another unanswered petition to Parliament, the inhabitants raised the possibility of forming a crown colony at the Settlement. "To state only the most obvious and significant consequence: by its failure to attain the status of Crown colony, Red River and the whole of the North-West could never join confederation." The inhabitants of the settlement "saw themselves as distinct, but could only be annexed. And in the event, annexed by force of arms. The consequences of the failures of the 1860s constitute an important structural feature of Canadian federalism to this day."[xvi]

Thus, when Red River was transferred to Canada, neither the imperial government nor the Canadian government saw any reason to consult the inhabitants of the settlement. When, in 1869-70 the rebellion, resistance, or insurrection erupted, this showed, in the understated words of W.L. Morton, that "there was... little active sentiment for union with Canada."[xvii] As Ted Morton (no relation to W.L. Morton) has often said, it is unlikely in the extreme that Alberta and Saskatchewan today would join Canada under existing circumstances or conditions. In this respect contemporary critics of the relationship between the West and Laurentian Canada echoed Isbister: the pretentions of Canada to Rupert's Land and the northwest degraded their homeland into being "a colony of a colony." The inhabitants of Rupert's Land and of Red River were, in contrast, determined to enter Canada, if at all, on their own terms, as did British Columbia.

So far as the understanding of Laurentian Canada is concerned, where better to look than the founder of the Laurentian School of Canadian historians, Donald Creighton? The opening words of his first book are worth recalling: "When in the course of a September day in 1759, the British made themselves the real masters of the rock of Quebec, an event of apparently unique importance occurred in the history of Canada."[xviii] French power in North America collapsed and the basis to achieve the reality indicated by the title of his book was established. As he remarked a few pages later, "The whole west, with all its riches, was the dominion of the river.... The dream of the commercial empire of the St. Lawrence runs like an obsession through the whole of Canadian history and men followed each other through life, planning and toiling to achieve it."[xix] The great problem with empires, whether commercial or political, particularly in the context of British political culture, is that the inhabitants tend to look upon themselves as citizens rather than as subjects. The British first discovered this with respect to their North American colonies in 1776. Laurentian Canada seems to be discovering the same reality today.[xx]

As a final contextual citation, consider the words of James R. Mallory, a distinguished political scientist of an earlier generation.[xxi] In his contribution to the multi-volume deployment of (mostly Laurentian) intellectual power to the study of Social Credit in Alberta and other untoward western eruptions such as the Progressive movement, he wrote a balanced and fair appraisal entitled *Social Credit and the Federal Power in Canada*.[xxii] Mallory described the new provinces of Alberta and Saskatchewan thus: They "were provinces not in the sense as were Ontario and Quebec, but in the Roman sense." The Latin word *provincia* carries with it the implication of rule on behalf of (*pro*) the vanquished or conquered (*vincia*). A Roman province was a territory where *imperium*, administrative power, was exercised by an agent of Rome, a governor. In addition, unlike the Roman inhabitants of Italy, those of the "provinces" paid tribute—taxes—to the imperial capital. Mallory's meaning was clear: the West was ruled by the new Rome on the Rideau as conquered territory; in return for such a favour, the West was granted the right to pay taxes to Ottawa. Such a deal!

The context of the 2019 election, as interpreted and understood by the Laurentian media is continuous with the historical understanding of Canada's (and Britain's) involvement in the West, which long antedated 1867. The problem for westerners is that we see ourselves as part of a federation, not the vanquished members of a Laurentian empire; we see ourselves as provinces like Ontario and Quebec, not Roman provinces. We have forgotten that from the start Sir John A. Macdonald referred to the West as a crown colony, the nineteenth-century British version of a Roman province, and also forgotten Isbister's warning that the West would soon become "a colony of a colony." Stupid us.

Challenges to western independence

The American Declaration of Independence acknowledges that "all experience hath shown that mankind are more disposed to suffer, which evils are sufferable, than to right themselves by abolishing the forms to which they are accustomed." Such is certainly the position of contemporary western politicians. On October 26, 2019, former Saskatchewan Premier Brad Wall wrote an op-ed in the *National Post* setting out his views for a "new federal deal with the prairies." That is, a new deal between Laurentian Canada and the West. He drew attention to Justin Trudeau's words, which he characterized as "nice." Wall suggested it would be a good idea to have western representatives in cabinet, but he also pointed out that when there actually were western cabinet ministers, such as the "formidable" Ralph Goodale, they were part of a government that brought us to the present situation of endlessly sufferable evils: no Northern Gateway, no KXL, no TMX, and the disastrous attacks embodied in C-69 and C-48. Wall concluded by suggesting that this time, Canada might be serious in its desire for "reconciliation." He gave no reason why Canada might desire reconciliation nor any evidence that Canada had entertained such a notion, not recently, not ever.

A second example of a politician endorsing sufferable evil is Alberta Premier Jason Kenney. In response to a letter from Peter Downing, founder of Wexit Canada, which urged the premier to introduce legislation to hold a referendum on independence from Canada, Kenney said, "We should not let Justin Trudeau and his policies make us feel unwelcome in our own country... I'm not going to let Trudeau push me out of my country."[xxiii] Like Brad Wall, Premier Kenney apparently believes Canada will eventually be persuaded to give Alberta a "Fair Deal." That at least is the premise of the Fair Deal panel tasked with "consulting Albertans on strategies to secure a fair deal in the Canadian federation,"[xxiv] and the rest of the Fair Deal delegation to Ottawa in mid-December 2019. As with Wall's op-ed, Kenney gave no arguments as to why Canada would be interested in a genuine fair deal nor did he provide evidence that such a notion had ever crossed the minds of Canadian politicians and bureaucrats.

A third example is Scott Moe, current premier of Saskatchewan. Despite a meeting with Justin Trudeau where the prime minister provided, in Moe's words, "more of the same" on the carbon tax, equalization restructuring, and market access for western resources, Moe declared that independence is not "the way forward."[xxv]

With all due respect to former premier Wall, his is nought but wishful thinking. There is zero possibility of a new deal with Canada. As for Premiers Kenney and Moe, they are cautious politicians. Ralph Klein used to joke that politicians like to see which way the parade is going so as to take up a position at the head of the line—and look over their shoulders to see if they are still being followed. This may not be an edifying spectacle, but it does mean that if the parade gets large enough the two premiers will seek the front rows and pretend to lead. Nevertheless, the first obstacle to independence is that, to use the language of the declaration, the "long train of abuses and usurpations, pursuing invariably the same object" has not yet persuaded these two political individuals to abolish the evidently adverse political forms to which they are accustomed. To Laurentian Canada and Alberta alike, the Fair Deal panel looks like a timid effort at postponing action.

The real question facing western politicians is actually quite plain and simple: how much more abuse will it take to persuade westerners that serious action is required? How many times must polite petitions be answered with repeated injuries? As in eighteenth-century America, so in twenty-first century Canada, these are not theoretical issues but practical ones. Westerners will determine in practice what the outcome will be.

If the major obstacle to independence is clearly political, there are also a number of minor and merely legal ones that can be discussed in a more summary fashion. I will endeavour to show that these so-called legal problems and obstacles are really political as well.

There has been considerable discussion of resurrecting the policies outlined in the "Firewall Letter" or "Alberta Agenda" first articulated in early 2001.[xxvi] At the United Conservative Party convention in late November, 2019, a series of straw votes endorsed several of these proposals, and Premier Kenney has indicated he was interested particularly in withdrawing from the Canada Pension Plan. Withdrawing from CPP was a no-brainer in 2001 and it remains so today. In 1966, under S.94A of the Constitution Act, 1867, Quebec established its own pension plan. With a relatively young population, higher than average wages, and greater participation in the work force than the Canadian average, Alberta could provide the same benefits to pensioners with lower premiums to contributors. And it would hurt the rest of the country. And to be clear, that is precisely the idea: to inflict a little pain on Canada, and especially on Ottawa.[xxvii] The same effect would follow from leaving the Employment Insurance scheme. Leaving the dairy supply-management plan would target Quebec, which supplies Alberta and Saskatchewan with expensive and inefficiently produced milk and milk products. Alberta and Saskatchewan could also immediately give notice to the RCMP that their contracts would expire in two years and announce to Canada that they would be replaced with a new Northwest Mounted Police.

More serious changes would involve court challenges and perhaps even constitutional amendments. These are obviously significant obstacles, but they are ultimately political. And always in the background is the real possibility of independence. It goes (almost) without saying that for westerners independence is *not* a bargaining position. As with the Thirteen Colonies, the serious consideration of independence entails some controversial and even dangerous political measures, as we shall see below.

Several groups have urged Premier Kenney, perhaps in conjunction with Premier Moe, to hold a referendum on the need to amend s.36.2 of the Constitution Act, 1982, which governs equalization payments. There are several constituent elements to this particular move that need to be distinguished. Referenda are not unknown in Canada but they, like another populist measure, the Initiative, are rare and the language involved must be crafted with care.

In the first place, however, s.36 is about as far from the black-letter law of the Constitution as one can get. It is a statement of commitment by the several governments to promote "equal opportunities," to further "economic development," to reduce "disparities in opportunities" and to provide public services "of reasonable quality to all Canadians." On the basis of such desiderata, Parliament is committed "to the principle of making equalization payments to ensure that provincial governments have sufficient revenues to provide reasonably comparable levels of public services at reasonably comparable levels of taxation" (Constitution Act, 1982, s.36). Section 36.1 speaks of the well-being of Canadians, which seems to imply individual citizens, the promotion of opportunities, and so on; section 36.2, however, speaks of recipient provincial governments getting revenue to provide public services. The connection between individual opportunities and government-to-government transfers is never discussed or accounted for. Accordingly, several analysts have observed that it may easily happen that income may be taxed from poor citizens in wealthy provinces such as Alberta and Saskatchewan to pay for services in poor provinces such as Quebec to benefit the rich citizens of that province.[xxviii] Finn Poschmann found in 1997, for example, that an Alberta family making between $30K and $40K contributed 9 per cent to federal programs but a family in Newfoundland making over $100K received benefits equal to 1.2 per cent of their income.[xxix]

Section 36.2 on its own is a tissue of ambiguities. The several governments are committed to the "principle" of equalization payments but nothing is said about the actual practice. Nor is the meaning of a "reasonable" or "comparable" level of public services or taxation discussed. If Alberta has a lower level of taxation than other provinces, does this imply that Alberta should have higher taxes or the other provinces should have lower ones? The question practically answers itself, which is why equalization has been called a welfare trap for provinces.[xxx] For these reasons alone legal scholars have reached a rare consensus that s.36 is non-justiciable. That is, in the view of these experts, no court can legitimately determine that s. 36 imposes any obligations on any of the governments that have pledged their "commitments."[xxxi] In other words, the actual working out of equalization is entirely political. In the language of the Declaration of Independence, how can this be anything other than a usurpation? In this instance, it is a usurpation of the foundational principle of what we now call responsible government. Since the days of the first British Empire and the representative institutions of 1619 Virginia, the goal always involved limiting executive power and especially instituting financial controls over the executive.

The issue of responsible government introduces another question of principle: from where did the central government gain the constitutional authority to collect federal revenues and give them to the provinces? Of course, under s.91 of the Constitution Act, 1867, the central government can *raise* "money by any mode or system of taxation," but whether Ottawa can *spend* money as it sees fit is a different question. In the Unemployment Insurance Reference of 1937, the Judicial Committee of the Privy Council observed that "it by no means follows" from the power to raise money by any mode or taxation "that any legislation which disposes of it [money] is necessarily within Dominion competence." Accordingly federal expenditures made in areas of provincial jurisdiction under s.92 of the Constitution Act, 1867 were prohibited.[xxxii]

Apart from the now repealed s. 118 of the Constitution Act, 1867, authorizing special grants to New Brunswick, what has come to be called the federal spending power was clearly circumscribed. Nothing was changed by the amendment to s. 118 in the Constitution Act, 1907. The point, very simply, is this: given that the expression "spending power" does not occur in any judicial decision or statute,[xxxiv] and given that the only jurisprudence in defence of the spending power is the very odd view of Frank Scott that the royal prerogative under the common law does not prohibit "generosity" nor the giving of gifts to persons, including provinces,[xxxv] the fact that the legality of the equalization clause depends for its constitutional validity on the legality of the spending power makes it seem imperative to litigate the legality of *that* power. It is practically self-evident to the taxpayers of Alberta and Saskatchewan that the equalization program is unjust. Indeed, equalization is one element of the long train of abuses that sustains the current support for independence. If the current equalization program is also beyond the jurisdiction of Ottawa, its inclusion in the Constitution Act, 1982 was invalid. Unless the anomalous status of s.36 of the Constitution Act, 1982 is acknowledged, its questionable continuation in force and effect will simply make independence more attractive. Once again, therefore, we are dealing with questions of politics and political leadership, not constitutional law. The whole problem is political, all the way down.

The argument has occasionally been made that the Clarity Act might be enlisted on behalf of Alberta and Saskatchewan to challenge s.36 of the Constitution Act, 1982. The theory is that, under the terms of the Clarity Act, a clear majority on a clear question would oblige the Government of Canada to engage in good faith negotiations regarding amendments to the Constitution. However, the Clarity Act was passed as a specific response to the 1998 secession reference to the Supreme Court of Canada, and the content of the Act was based on the question of the secession of Quebec, which would require a constitutional amendment. It did not address amendments to other parts of the constitution. There does not seem to be any way for Alberta and Saskatchewan, even after putting to a referendum vote their desire to amend s.36, to oblige the other provinces and Ottawa to negotiate. Moreover, since the actual terms of the formula used to calculate payments have changed over the years, the argument would be made that no constitutional issues would be involved anyhow.

On the other hand, if a referendum on s.36 were limited to a referendum on secession in the (likely) event that initial negotiations regarding the equalization formula went nowhere, we can easily anticipate further political complications. Let us make a couple of simplifying assumptions: if there were no meaningful negotiations to change s.36 within, say, three months, a second referendum, on secession, might be held. Such a constitutional two-step would be rather complex, but the threat of secession might be sufficient to inspire some serious negotiation for changes in the funding formula. Again, much would depend on the political leadership of Alberta and Saskatchewan; and, while modifying the formula or amending or repealing s.36 might go some distance to restoring a sense of justice in the West, it would obviously not meet the requirement of independence.

Even if a referendum on independence were held, either in connection with an equalization referendum or not, there are further obstacles to consider. The first is that the House of Commons, not the province or provinces holding the referendum, decides *before* the referendum whether the question is clear. The House of Commons also decides, *after* the vote on a clear question has been held, whether there was a clear majority in favour of secession. Whatever the role and whatever the question, and however clear the question and the vote may be to common-sense or to the voters, the House can always "deem" things to be otherwise. Moreover, the Government of Canada can disallow or reserve *any* provincial legislation. That disallowance and reservation have not been used since 1943 and 1961 respectively suggests only that it is only by *habitual practice* that these provisions of the Constitution are no longer in force. It may be politically unwise for the Government of Canada to disallow a referendum on equalization, particularly if it were coupled to another referendum on secession, but that would be a political choice, not a question of legal capacity. What then?

Then all bets are off because it would be clear that the legal path to independence is a fraud. If Alberta and Saskatchewan and, for the sake of the argument, Manitoba as well, held referenda anyway, they would be illegal and Canada would have no duty to negotiate. Such an impasse reinforces the contention made several times already that the problem of western independence is political, not legal. So let us propose the following hypothetical: following an intensive and effective educational campaign detailing the long train of abuses suffered by the West, Alberta and Saskatchewan vote overwhelmingly (say, 95 per cent) in favour of a straightforward question: do you wish Alberta and Saskatchewan (and perhaps other parts of the existing country of Canada) to be independent of Canada? Then what?

Then we must consult Niccolò Machiavelli, the greatest modern political philosopher. One of his still pertinent observations, which was echoed in the Declaration of Independence, is that the experience of lengthy injustices by necessity leads to political action. More to the present point, in chapter 12 of *The Prince* he argued that good arms make for good laws. But where are our arms? Not in the Edmonton Garrison or the Alberta Sheriffs. In the absence of any agreement on how to divide the Canadian Forces along the lines contemplated with regard to Quebec secession, it is evident that the great weakness of the West is its lack of an army. This is the danger mentioned above because it means that if westerners are serious about independence we must have American assistance for the same reason that the Thirteen Colonies required the assistance of France. The implications of this Machiavellian necessity are significant. From the oil sands as a strategic North American petroleum reserve to the use of the third largest air base in the world at Cold Lake, Alberta, westerners certainly have military bargaining chips to offer the Americans.

The penultimate paragraph of the Declaration of Independence recalls how often the Colonies had warned their "British brethren" against their extension of unwarrantable jurisdiction by Parliament. The colonists had often appealed to the "native justice and magnanimity" no less than the pain of disrupting the connections across the North Atlantic, but to no avail. Since before the confederation of Canada, westerners have done the same regarding their imperial masters in London and in Ottawa. Westerners may yet await their own Thomas Jefferson and there can be no guarantee that one such will arrive. On the other hand, as the alternatives to independence are successively forestalled by Laurentian Canada, the likelihood increases that westerners will not long wait in vain. The windows of opportunity to counteract sentiments in favour of independence are shutting, one by one.

Security considerations for an independent Alberta

David J. Bercuson

A LBERTANS WHO now believe it is time for the province to declare itself an independent political entity need to consider the security requirements of independence. What would a security policy for an independent Alberta entail? The possible implications are set out here, and would apply to an independent Alberta or an Alberta that achieves independence together with the province of Saskatchewan. They would also apply whether the newly independent Alberta would seek to be a constitutional monarchy (as Canada is now) or become an independent republic.

We will take it as given that an independent Alberta would have friendly relations with Canada and the United States and would apply to be part of the United States/Mexico/Canada continental trade agreement, and a part of both NATO and NORAD. Alberta's economy will be closely integrated with that of both the U.S. and Canada, and Albertans have a long history of supporting free trade. Alberta would have little to contribute to NATO and NORAD, but symbolically it would be important to signal to Alberta's allies that it is in tune with their North America air and space defence policies and the collective defence of NATO.

The fundamental question that Albertans must come to grips with is: what is "security"? The simple answer is that security can be applied to almost every human endeavor. From security of the state to security of an individual, the concept entails keeping people, their institutions, their property, their structures and infrastructures, safe from harm. Abraham Maslow, an

American psychologist, constructed a pyramidal hierarchy of needs in a 1943 paper entitled "A Theory of Human Motivation," published in *Psychological Review*. His ideas were more fully explored in his 1954 book, *Motivation and Personality*.[i] His pyramid placed human security or human safety at the top of human needs. In other words, a society has to put the physical safety of persons as its highest priority. This, of course would apply to a separate or independent Alberta. There is no use discussing independence unless the new entity can provide for the safety and security of its citizens.

Before discussing the means by which an independent Alberta will provide for the safety and security of its population, there must be a discussion of the political and structural framework of this independent Alberta. If it can be assumed that Alberta's departure from the Canadian confederation would be peaceful, if not amicable, it can also be assumed that an independent Alberta would adopt the The Constitution Act, 1867 and The Constitution Act, 1982 as a basic framework for the operation of its government and politics.

Section 91 of The Constitution Act, 1867 bestows on Parliament, the "central government," the responsibility "to make laws for the peace, order and good government" of the nation. This responsibility would pass to the new government of Alberta (GOA) in the event of Alberta secession. It is likely that the constitution of an independent Alberta would resemble that of Canada in that Alberta would be a parliamentary democracy with a Charter or bill of rights. Alberta would be a unitary state and not a federation. Thus responsibility for the maintenance of "peace, order and good government" would fall solely upon the Government of Alberta. An independent Alberta would have a population of roughly 4.4 million people; Saskatchewan has a population of 1.2 million people. If Saskatchewan joins a secessionist Alberta, the new political entity would have a population of 5.6 million people. The small size of the new political entity will make the preservation of security far more expensive than it is now because the measures which will be necessary to maintain a full spectrum of security (as outlined below) will be costly and will be borne by a much smaller population base than the 37 million Canadians who bear those responsibilities now.

"Security" today involves many more issues than would have been the case two or three decades ago. To begin with, security for Alberta must include the safeguarding of Alberta's borders; maintaining the security of all national infrastructure; underpinning criminal law within Alberta; securing Alberta, including its citizens and its corporate entities and private organizations, against the theft of intellectual property; providing oversight of all police and judicial operations; developing or coordinating a capacity for special police operations throughout Alberta when necessary; the establishing of penitentiaries; the safeguarding of cyber space within Alberta; and the protecting of businesses and industries in Alberta from any type of illegal interference in the operation of those enterprises.

The current Alberta Security & Strategic Intelligence Support team (ASSIST) is a small unit within the Department of the Solicitor General. It works with Canadian authorities to safeguard Alberta, but the overall responsibility for security in Alberta today lies with the federal government. That will no longer be the case after independence, so ASSIST must be the basis for a greatly expanded Alberta security apparatus.

In a recent study, ASSIST defined "security of Alberta" as security against acts of sabotage or espionage committed inside or outside Alberta but directly affecting the well-being of Alberta citizens; activities that are influenced by any foreign organization or person designed to influence the policy choices of the Alberta government in ways that are detrimental to the economy and society of Alberta; threats of, or use of, violence within Alberta designed to achieve a political, religious or ideological objective that is inimical to the interests and well-being of Alberta or Alberta institutions; any attempt to overthrow the Government of Alberta or to limit the constitutional authority of the GOA within the boundaries of Alberta; efforts attempting to encourage radicalization and violence in Alberta.

ASSIST also defines security of Alberta as the prevention of interference with the lawful activities of the government of Alberta; interference with the critical infrastructure of Alberta; the promotion of violence in Alberta; the prevention of the use of Alberta territory for illicit purposes including the use of Alberta territory for the promotion of hate and bias crimes within

Alberta or outside of Alberta; espionage or sabotage directed against the security of Alberta or any part of Canada or the United States; interference with Alberta's public safety mechanisms or institutions; the identification of risks within or relating to Alberta especially when those risks threaten the economic well-being of Alberta; identification of risks to the government of Alberta or any of its institutions; attacks (kinetic or otherwise) against private institutions such as water works or the electrical power grid; the safety of individuals or institutions in the private sector which have a direct impact on public health and safety.[ii]

The primary job of protecting Alberta should come from a new department or ministry of public safety (Safety Alberta). This ministry would be home to both the new nation's armed forces and to its intelligence services. The head of the department would be the minister of public safety who would hold a seat on Alberta's executive council. Ultimately all military and quasi-military services within the province would fall under the authority of this minister. All police services would continue to fall under the authority of the minister of justice or its equivalent (the solicitor general or the attorney general). The department of public safety's most important job would be to integrate all communications and intelligence services and to ensure that the different security agencies under its jurisdiction have open communication with all other branches of Safety Alberta. Safety Alberta would fully coordinate its activities and intelligence with the minister of justice. A second key function would be to evaluate intelligence from a variety of agencies or departments so as to present the GOA as complete a picture as possible of daily shifts in the security picture. Intelligence failures are almost always failures of imagination to discern the "signal" from the "noise"—not so much intelligence gathering as the interpretation of the intelligence being gathered.

We live in an age where power and influence are wielded in many non-traditional ways. National boundaries are meaningless in an increasingly globalized society. The internet has not only tied widely disparate companies, corporations, governments, and industries together in a global network (a positive development), but it has also exposed citizens, corporations, and governments to mass interference from remote locations. The challenge to modern nation states is to safeguard society from malign interference while also keeping channels of communication as open as possible.

As an independent entity within the heart of western Canada, Alberta would have no "traditional" enemies on any of its borders. Thus a minimal armed force would be maintained to demonstrate a token capability to respond to any incursions of the border by armed groups. The likelihood of such incursions is very low, thus "guarding" the borders would be a token responsibility. The Alberta military would no more guard the land boundaries and skies of Alberta than the Canadian or even the United States military guards the borders of Canada or the United States. Put another way, Alberta would not face any "kinetic" threats.

Why then have any military at all? Because an independent Alberta would wish to add its minimal military capability, when necessary, to either Canadian or United States military expeditions, coalitions of the willing, or responsibilities under NATO or NORAD, which Alberta would adhere to. Again, an independent Alberta would aspire to membership in both NORAD and NATO and thus ought to be willing to share in shouldering the burden for mounting expeditionary operations abroad. And although Alberta would not need an air force, it would need air assets for policing, rural patrols, airlift for paramilitary forces, search and rescue, and disaster relief. The aviation component would be placed under the authority of Alberta's small armed forces and under the overall administration of the ministry of public safety.[iii]

Alberta would allow open skies for North American air defence purposes. It ought to be willing to participate in any aerial or space defence schemes that might be proposed by Canada or the United States. Alberta must ensure that Alberta's neighbours would never see Alberta independence as creating a "hole" in North American defence architecture; it should never be a launching pad for nefarious activities directed against either Canada or the United States. It is also important that Alberta, although small in population compared to Canada or the United States, is still ready, willing, and able to do its part to ensure the collective defence of North America or of NATO partners everywhere.

The actual requirements for defence capabilities for an independent Alberta would likely unfold along the following lines. The four large bases in Alberta (Cold Lake, Suffield, CFB Edmonton and CFB Wainwright) should be leased to the United States, Canada, or the United Kingdom in the case of Suffield. Arrangements should be made with the new landlord of Wainwright to allow Alberta's small military forces to train there. Alberta's "army" would be a combination of full-time regular force soldiers and reservists. The regular force would consist of a battle group of three companies of mechanized infantry including engineers, medical personnel, and other specialized military occupations. There ought also to be three battalions (roughly 1,800 personnel) of reservists. One reserve battalion would be located in Calgary, one in Edmonton and the third would operate (as companies or even as platoons) in other urban areas throughout Alberta. All should be equipped with the most updated kit. All should exercise alongside Canadian and/or U.S. military units. Both branches of the army, regular force and reserve, would operate under a single chain of command, and the prime responsibility for training the reserve forces would fall to the regular army.

An independent Alberta ought to consider the establishment of a small paramilitary force to act as a first line of defence in case of civil disorder that could not be handled by Alberta's civil police departments or should not be handled by the Alberta armed forces. This force could be based either in Edmonton or Calgary and equipped with a small contingent of transport helicopters (such as the Ch-47 Chinook) so that it could deploy to any part of the province within hours. This paramilitary force would also be responsible for reacting to kinetic threats to infrastructure within Alberta and acting as a Special Weapons and Tactics (SWAT) force in Alberta's rural areas. Municipal police already have well-prepared SWAT units and would continue to maintain them. Under the Ministry of Public Safety, Alberta's armed forces would be considered an integral part of the new nation's overall defences, coordinated with the Alberta Sheriffs (which would be the successor of the Royal Canadian Mounted Police for all rural and highway policing) and Alberta's several municipal or tribal (First Nations) police services.

Alberta Sheriffs would become a true armed police service for rural policing, including policing of small municipalities. The Alberta Sheriffs will
need to be able to bring to bear in its crime-fighting activities and its small
urban space policing all the modern requirements of a major police force.
Its members would have to be recruited first from among former members
of the RCMP living in Alberta and then from any Albertan who aspires
to a career in police work. The Alberta Sheriffs will have to be equipped
with a wide variety of equipment including modern radio and internet systems, patrol cars, aircraft and helicopters, detachment buildings, and an
Alberta-wide communication system tied in to those of municipal police
services in the larger cities and tied in also with state or provincial police
to the north, south, east, and west of Alberta. Alberta Sheriffs will have to
assume responsibility for border law enforcement, counterfeiting, customs
and excise, immigration and passports, crime of all sorts and general public
safety.[iv] So, once again, Alberta security will be, in part, dependent on close
cooperation with both Canadian and American first responders.

The new Alberta will need significant intelligence resources. Threats
to Alberta will not be kinetic, in other words, there will be no threats to
Alberta's borders or Alberta's society by an external enemy using traditional
military-style tactics to gain a traditional military victory. Threats to Alberta
will come in the form of foreign interference in Alberta's management
of its own affairs, thefts of Alberta intellectual property, efforts to attack
Alberta's infrastructure, and efforts to undermine the faith of Albertans
in the integrity of systems such as water, electric and natural gas supplies,
open public discourse, the ongoing activities of Alberta's commercial and
industrial sectors etc. In other words the current challenges that Canada
faces daily from both governmental and private sources to the integrity of
systems, will continue.

When we think of threats to an independent Alberta, we need to consider the threats that any nation faces today. It is no longer the case that
threats to democracy and civil institutions in modern democratic nations
come primarily from military-type threats from outside actors. Nations
such as Russia, China, North Korea, or Iran (to name just the largest) have

large cyber capabilities and maintain large armed forces but do not pose significant kinetic threats. Such threats are less and less viable in a world where teams of cyber security experts embedded in the militaries of foreign countries can do immense damage to their rivals by computer attacks against major infrastructure components of their protagonists. Why launch actual wars, risking tremendous losses, when cyber-attacks can wreak havoc on enemies by targeting government agencies, the military and defence establishment, political parties, financial institutions, the media, private corporations including credit card companies and banks, as well as private individuals. Attacks of this nature can undermine the confidence of the public in its institutions, manipulate elections, shift public opinion, destroy morale, disrupt a nation's economy and trade.

The first line of defence against such attacks is a robust cyber-security regime.[v] Cyber security has become a catch all phrase to refer to the threats posed by the extreme vulnerability of internet systems in governmental agencies and ministries, security services including first responders, industry, infrastructure and any other form of information repository whether commercially or privately held. The cyber security challenge today is a simple one: the growth of the internet, whether the "internet of things" or the internet proper, has created a global network that connects almost anything with almost everything else. Many government agencies, private businesses, and institutions take great measures to secure their entrance portals to this global network. From companies such as Norton, to give one example, to the internal bureaus in government agencies and corporations which devote themselves to 24/7 protection against intrusion, the challenge is the same: to mitigate or even avoid damage from so-called "hackers." The government of an independent Alberta will have to face these challenges in order for Alberta's private citizens, corporations, and government entities to operate smoothly in a cyber-space environment resembling a wild frontier.

Although many private citizens and corporations are today well aware of the cyber threats that can bring businesses to a grinding halt, expose the vulnerabilities of different parts of Alberta's infrastructure, and do great harm to the good names or reputations of both private citizens and public corporations, few have either the resources or the overall picture of cyber threats to deal adequately with them. That is why governments around the world have established or are establishing, cyber security agencies, or expanding the mandate of signals intelligence agencies to include cyber security.

The role of any government, and it would be the role of an independent Alberta, is to provide basic cyber-security for national infrastructure. There is virtually no part of the infrastructure—water services, the electrical grid, pipelines, municipal traffic control, sewage plants, irrigation systems—that is not connected to the internet. The safeguarding of these systems is primarily the job of the national government because the national government is responsible both for controlling access to the physical body of the nation (guarding the borders) but also, in this day and age, controlling access to the cyber space inside Alberta. How can this be done?

At the macro level, Alberta will have to establish a national office to coordinate cyber security. The office will function under the ministry of public safety and will work with Alberta's armed forces and municipal and national police. The office will reach out to similar offices in Canada and the United States to coordinate anti-hacking activities in such a way that there will be a seamless web between Alberta's cyber self-defence and that of the rest of North America. The office will maintain leading edge cyber-security capabilities to guard all governmental agencies in Alberta, work with private industry to coordinate cyber security activities, and work with the department of education to keep Alberta citizens informed of best practices in guarding private internet accounts. For example, Albertans would be taught to purchase private internet protection, to safe-guard their own private networks by not clicking on embedded links from unknown sources, and other best practices.

The best way to inoculate Alberta's many websites and networks is to make it very difficult for bad actors to penetrate those sites and networks. One way this is currently done is to remind users to continually refresh their passwords. Another is to establish an Alberta-wide warning network to contact internet users in Alberta whenever there is a massive break into major international organizations or corporations in which large numbers of passwords are stolen along with other private information. Thus users in Alberta would immediately be warned to change passwords. The cyber security office would also be responsible for safeguarding communications within Alberta and between Alberta and North America and indeed the rest of the world.

The government of Alberta would have to decide whether or not to attempt to join up with the "five eyes community." This community shares signals intelligence across five states (the United States, Canada, the United Kingdom, Australia, and New Zealand). Currently, the community is also considering adding Japan. The result is global coverage of signals-intercept and code-breaking activity. In one sense Alberta would not have to join the community because Alberta would probably not have a robust signals intelligence capacity. But some sort of arrangement would have to be made either with the Communications Security Establishment in Ottawa or the National Security Agency in Washington to warn Alberta of possible penetrations of Alberta signals communication.

Alberta's economy is heavily reliant on resource extraction.[vi] Resource extraction is heavily dependent on a well-maintained infrastructure. Oil and gas pipelines, the electrical power grid, irrigation systems, waterworks and sewage systems, roads and bridges, fiber optic networks, and the like are necessary for the smooth functioning of a modern society. Threats to the Alberta infrastructure are no longer primarily physical. In the weeks after 9/11, much attention was given to keeping the infrastructure safe from actual kinetic attack. Such attacks never materialized but the threat is nevertheless real. It is impossible to maintain actual human guardianship over large infrastructure projects. Some safety can be assured by contracting with private security firms to patrol pipelines and other infrastructure components, but the real threat to infrastructure today is cyberattack. For example, oil and gas pipelines must have pumping stations to keep product flowing. Pumping stations today are all networked so that the transmission companies can monitor the smooth flow of oil and gas through the pipelines. The networking allows constant monitoring so that breakdowns in equipment, leaks, etc., can be dealt with as quickly as possible. These networks are vulnerable to cyber-attacks. Thus cyber defences are crucial to maintain public safety and to guaranty the smooth operation of the system. While it is true that a transmission corporation would have to be responsible for maintaining the cyber safety of its monitoring networks, the government of Alberta would have to establish and monitor standards of cyber-security operations. Again, these types of safeguards would have to meet minimum specifications for operational safety laid down by a special branch of the ministry of public safety which would also be responsible for ensuring that private corporations adhere to public standards.

As we have seen from the global pandemic of the Covid-19 virus, a major security concern in this globalized world is protection against future pandemics. The speed with which the Covid-19 virus spread from a wildlife market in Wuhan China to virtually all corners of the world, bringing its high death rate and severely damaging to the global economy, resulted from the close connections of trade, travel, and tourism that join all corners of the globe. It is impossible to foresee when the next pandemic will strike, although it is inevitable that it will strike. How can Alberta protect itself?

Initially, Public Safety Alberta, working with the province's two medical schools and with the medical research centres established with Heritage Fund research dollars, must draw up plans for steps the government would take in the event of the onset of a new pandemic. Such plans should be coordinated with municipal governments, rural districts, counties, and first responders. Stockpiles of medical equipment that would be needed should be built up and kept ready near major centres of population. Exercises should be held annually to simulate the onset of a pandemic and public education programs should be initiated to train Albertans how to conduct themselves in the event of a medical emergency. The main lesson to learn from the pandemic of late 2019 through 2020 is to prepare, no matter how small the odds may seem of a similar occurrence. Another pandemic is simply a matter of when, not if.

One of the most vulnerable components of Alberta infrastructure is its power grid, and power grids have been shown to be especially vulnerable with attacks shutting down major urban power systems in Ukraine.[vii] Here again, safety will not come from physically guarding a power grid, which would be almost impossible in any case, but in maintaining adequate cyber defences against attacks. Here too, the main responsibility for attempting to ensure safety of the system will lie with the corporation that owns the grid, but Alberta-wide standards would have to be established and monitored by the ministry of public safety.

One type of security that will be absolutely vital for the future prosperity and well-being of Alberta is economic security. With a small economy, Alberta must ensure that its economy is safe from espionage. Espionage comes in many forms but in general there are two: theft of intellectual property, and commercial espionage designed to cripple the economy of commercial rivals. In early December 2019, the director of the Canadian Security Intelligence Service, David Vigneault, told the Economic Club of Toronto that while terrorism remains the number one national security related danger in Canada, commercial espionage is "the greatest threat to our prosperity and national interest." Vigneault said that state sponsored commercial espionage was already emerging in fields such as artificial intelligence, quantum technology, 5G wireless technology, biopharmaceuticals and low quantum energy. Vigneault warned that the information that their businesses store (customer data, intellectual property, prototypes, and financial figures) is invaluable to international competitors who want to give themselves any advantage in the global competition for markets.[viii]

What is true for Canada would be equally true for an independent Alberta, except that the resources that Canada can devote to security of commerce are far greater than the resources that an independent Alberta could devote to such a pursuit. Once again, Alberta would have to pursue agreements with both Canada and the United States to share information and take concerted action to safeguard Alberta commerce. There is also the possibility, however remote, that Canadian and American corporate entities would prey upon Alberta businesses especially in the oil and gas sector but also in the growing cyber-security field. An independent Alberta would have to consider whether its small economy would be victimized by Canadian and American competitors.

As part of its overall security challenges, Alberta would have to develop mechanisms to review foreign acquisitions of Alberta-based businesses. Alberta will be a free enterprise society in a mixed economy. But in a free enterprise society, business pursues profit disconnected to any political considerations.

An independent Alberta would have to provide for its own immigration policies and protection of its borders. It can be assumed that Alberta would have a tightly-controlled immigration policy not aimed at restricting immigration on an ethnic, religious, or national basis, but aimed at controlling the number of people who might enter Alberta in any given year. Like Canadian immigration policy, Alberta's immigration policy should be based on attracting new citizens who would add to Alberta's pool of skilled and educated citizens. Allowance would have to be made for Alberta to take in a certain number of refugees each year, commensurate with its population, but immigration should be based upon a keen consideration of what each immigrant can bring to Alberta—education, skill, investment funds, etc.—to grow the Alberta economy.

Alberta's infrastructure, like that of Canada, is especially vulnerable to individuals or groups who aim to use "direct action" to make their political points about various social issues especially their opposition to fossil fuels and resource extraction. Efforts by the RCMP to clear demonstrators from a natural gas pipeline construction site (Coastal Gas Link) in early 2020 were met by blockades of rail lines at sites thousands of kilometres from the Coastal Gas Link construction location. For several weeks, those demonstrations froze rail transport at key locations around the country. The most damaging to the Canadian economy was the blockade of Canadian National Railway tracks connecting Toronto and Montreal. There was major damage to the Canadian economy. Infrastructure in Alberta is no less vulnerable to these types of direct action. The Alberta government under Premier Jason Kenny passed a bill early in the 2020 legislative session to make such efforts to stop road or rail traffic illegal, with heavy fines and possible imprisonment for violators.[ix] An independent Alberta would face the same challenges to public order. It is important that democracies safeguard the right of their citizens to protest government policy but such demonstrations must be peaceful and not harm businesses or private citizens going about their peaceful way.

The main challenge to security comes from public ignorance of people or events that would do harm to Alberta, but which are not readily recognized by the public or security agencies in Alberta. Here the new government has a responsibility to educate Alberta citizens as to what sort of action they should take in the event their systems have been compromised. This would be a new area for a North American government. The aim of these public-education programs is to teach citizens how hackers penetrate their systems and how to keep those systems safe. Few Albertans will have the expertise to recognize how "phishing" expeditions allow hackers to penetrate even the most sophisticated systems. The education program should start at the earliest feasible grade in Alberta's schools. Through its control of the curriculum the government of an independent Alberta should ensure that Alberta's students have a broad-based knowledge of computer systems and the threats to those systems. Ultimately, this education should considerably reduce hacking, ransomware, and other means of bad actors penetrating computer and internet systems.

The most important impediment to the maintenance of a secure Alberta is the size of the population. A separate Alberta will consist of about 4.4 million people. Add in Saskatchewan and that number increases to 5.6 million people. That is a low number to sustain the sort of security envisioned here. In large nations, costs for security are born by large populations allowing considerable economy of scale. A good example is Canada's medicare program. In medicare, a population of 37 million people spreads the cost of full health services among a pool of 37 million people. The same applies to the various measures necessary to secure an independent Alberta. The measures outlined here will be expensive but the small population of Alberta will limit Alberta's ability to spread the costs of security widely. It is too early to fully cost out the program outlined here, but it is a certainty that the costs per taxpaying citizen (including corporate taxes) will be high. Nevertheless, such a system will be absolutely necessary to create defences that will allow Albertans to go about their daily lives with a sense of security. The measures outlined here are realistic suggestions for a possible situation and it is best if Albertans know and understand what it will cost to keep them secure. Today, Alberta is an integral part of Canada and the security of Alberta, like the security of any part of Canada, is largely dependent on spreading security costs among all Canadians. An independent Alberta will not have that luxury.

The conclusion is obvious: Albertans ought to know how they will be able to keep themselves safe from all the challenges that modern liberal democracies face. The main challenges are not kinetic; they come in subtler forms and in ways that are not usually thought of by the citizenry. The enemies of security are generally highly-sophisticated and use techniques that are way beyond the understanding of most citizens. The bottom line is that security for an independent Alberta is certainly plausible. None of the suggestions posited here are science fiction. But security for an independent Alberta will not be cheap.

A final word

Tom Flanagan, Jack Mintz
and Ted Morton

Introduction

A S DETAILED now in the preceding chapters, many federal policy decisions today, more so than in the 1980s, have been contrary to Alberta's interests.

- Federal encroachment on provincial resource development including Bill C-69 requirements for pipeline approvals
- Costly delays in building Trans Mountain Expansion (TMX) and Coastal Gas Link, resulting in Alberta oil and gas prices being sold at discounted values to U.S. markets
- Effective federal vetoes of Northern Gateway and Energy East, reducing access to new global markets and higher global prices
- Federal government-mandated carbon tax and regulatory policies without Alberta's consent
- $100 billion capital exodus out of Canadian energy sector
- $21 billion (in 2018 dollars) in annual net federal transfers out of Alberta from 2010-18
- Over $630 billion cumulative net transfers (in 2018 dollars) since 1961
- Making the federal income tax more progressive in 2015, affecting Alberta's competitiveness for skilled labour and resulting in a larger net fiscal transfer
- Absence of an elected Senate that would be representative of regional

interests common in other federations like Australia and the United States

- Restoration of Quebec's constitutional veto, making Senate reform virtually impossible
- Regional/political bias in bilingual federal bureaucracy
- Supreme Court Charter of Rights rulings as a disguised federal policy veto over provincial policies
- No effective checks on judicial policy-making under the Charter of Rights
- De facto Aboriginal vetoes over resource development because of judicial decisions that keep expanding the meaning of the "duty to consult"
- Ottawa's failure to stop the foreign funding of "death by delay" litigation campaigns to block new pipelines.

The political vulnerability of the West is the predictable consequence of two structural defects in Canada's political system. One is the loss of equilibrium between Canada's economy and its political institutions. The second is Canada's asymmetry between size and wealth, combined with our "rep by pop" electoral system, that invites federal political parties to try to win elections by promising policies that transfer wealth from the energy-rich, voter-poor Western provinces to the energy-poor but voter-rich central provinces.

An electoral system that invites redistribution of western wealth

The harmful policies listed above contributed directly to Alberta's five-year recession. But were these policies the causes of the recession, or symptoms of a deeper problem? Most coincide with the 2015 election of a majority Liberal government. Could Alberta's vulnerability to destructive federal policies be reversed simply by a change of government? If Andrew Scheer and the Conservative Party had won the November 2019 election, would Alberta's problems have been solved?

In the short term, perhaps some Alberta issues would have been addressed. But this would have been a temporary reprieve, not a solution to Alberta's deeper structural vulnerability. Being part of a winning national majority government—the Mulroney government in 1980s, the Harper Government in the 2000s—may bring Alberta some short-term protection, but the *status quo ante* returns.

The root cause is an electoral system that invites federal political parties to win voter majorities in Ontario and Quebec with policies that transfer wealth from Western Canada. Ontario (121) and Quebec (78) together have 199 MPs, well over the 170 seats required to form a majority government. In the absence of effective regional representation in an elected and equal Senate, the interests of the less populated provinces are always at risk of being marginalized. Historically, this has typically been the political strategy of the Liberal Party. But the same defect shapes the electoral strategies of conservative parties. Their typical base in Western Canada does not have enough MPs to form a majority government, so it too must be attentive to the central Canadian interests.

The most extreme version of this was memorably summarized by Keith Davey, Pierre Trudeau's campaign strategist for the 1980 federal election: "Screw the West. We'll take the rest." The Liberals formed a majority government without winning a single seat in the West.[i] They then implemented the now infamous National Energy Program (NEP), which, over the next four years, drained over $70 billion dollars out of Alberta, most of which went to Ontario and Quebec, the Liberals' political base.[ii]

Thirty-five years later, in 2015, Justin Trudeau and the Liberals won another majority government with virtually no representation from Alberta (4) and Saskatchewan (1). In the 2109 election, after four years of climate change policies and pipeline politics, the regional discrepancy became even greater. The Liberals again did not win a single seat in Alberta or Saskatchewan, but were kept in power by winning 72 per cent of their seats in Ontario and Quebec.[iii]

The Federal government's repeated use of Alberta's wealth for partisan political purposes is not a Canadian idiosyncrasy. As detailed by Mintz:

> Less populated but wealthier regions have limited political power to protect themselves from predatory policies supported

by national majorities. Their ability to influence central government decision-making is limited when they do not have sufficient representation in the national government to modify or block harmful policy decisions.

In just the past decade, asymmetry between size and wealth, combined with underrepresentation in national governments, has produced separatist and autonomist political movements in Spain and Italy. In Italy voters/tax-payers in the wealthier regions of Lombardy and Veneto have formed the Northern League Party, elected regional governments, and won referendums for greater fiscal autonomy.[iv] In Spain, the Catalan Independence Movement—based in the wealthier regions around Barcelona—has formed the regional government in Catalonia and won two referendums to become an independent state.[v]

The parallel experiences of Catalonia, Lombardy, and Alberta are systemic and predictable. They demonstrate a variation on the familiar theme: you win elections by promising to give a majority of the voters something for nothing—but instead of targeting wealthier individuals and families (a minority of voters), you target wealthier regions (with a minority of voters). Vote-seeking national political parties will seek to win elections by promising policies that redistribute wealth from regions with more wealth but fewer voters to regions that are less wealthy but have more voters.

Canada's political-economic disconnect

For large federal democracies to remain politically stable, there must be a rough equilibrium between the country's economy and its political institutions. In post-war Canada, this has been lost because of our electoral system's systemic underrepresentation of Western Canadian interests. Our politics have failed to keep pace with our economy.

Historically, the preferred political status enjoyed by Ontario and Quebec may have made sense. As J. R. Mallory, one of English Canada's leading constitutional scholars, wrote in 1954:

The inequalities in size and population of the provinces of Canada have been recognized tacitly in a constitution which to a large extent embraces two levels of federalism. The superior size and bargaining position of Ontario and Quebec give them a status and autonomy which are different in kind from those of the rest of the provinces.[vi]

The Western provinces, Mallory observed, were "provinces... in the Roman sense... under the sway of the predominant economic interests of the central provinces." This made sense, he said, because it "recognizes what have been so far, the economic realities of the country." That was in 1954. Today's economic reality has changed, but Canada's institutions have not.

The West's post-war self-assertion in national politics has been driven by the new economic strength of Alberta and British Columbia. At the end of the second world war, their combined population was only half that of Quebec's. Today, the combined populations of B.C. (5 million) and Alberta (4.3 million) are almost one million greater than Quebec (8.4 million). Economically, the change has been even more dramatic. As recently as 1961, the combined provincial GDPs of Alberta and British Columbia were only half that of Quebec. Today, they are almost half again greater (46 per cent) than Quebec's.

Canada's economy has changed qualitatively as well as quantitatively. Historically, most trade was on an East-West axis. But over the last three decades, the old East-West economy has been replaced by a series of north-south, cross-border regional economies. Today, every province except Manitoba exports more to the U.S. than with the rest of Canada (Emery and Fellows, chapter 7). Predictably, this change has been accompanied by declining internal immigration among provinces. And as Mintz recounts, both these trends are found in other countries that have experienced regional conflicts and separation movements.

But the West's post-war economic and demographic ascendancy has not been matched by a corresponding increase in political influence.[vii] Indeed, the opposite has been the case. For fifty of the past sixty years, the prime minister of Canada has been a Quebecer. The weaker Quebec has become economically, the more powerful it has become politically.

Alberta's fate has been the opposite of Quebec's. The more we contributed financially, the less we have received politically. To reverse this will require structural reforms that re-establish equilibrium between the country's economy and its political institutions. As Donald Savoie elaborates, "We need to rethink Canada's institutional arrangements so that we have a two-way mirror that reflects the economic interests of Western and Atlantic Canada, not just Quebec and Ontario."[viii]

To adequately protect Alberta and Western Canada's future, structural changes are required. These changes fall into three categories.

Re-confederation: more Alberta in Ottawa

One option is re-confederation: a set of reforms that would actually increase the scope and authority of the federal government by adding effective regional representation from and protection for the Western provinces. These include a national infrastructure corridor; reforms to the Supreme Court of Canada; and senate reform.

National infrastructure corridor

For Alberta, this is the first and most important reform in building a more effective national government. As documented in the preceding chapters, Canada's failure to build new oil and gas pipelines for export has driven out capital investment and crippled the economies of Alberta and Saskatchewan. Canada, however, is not just slow at regulatory approvals for pipelines. As documented by the World Bank, Canada is generally one of the slowest advanced countries in the world to approve permits.[ix]

As discussed by Ogle (chapter 9), an infrastructure corridor could be built according to several models. It could connect Canada's ports and intermodal facilities in the ten provinces, the three territories, and the three oceans in whole or in part, depending on what is economically feasible.

Depending on location, it could include highways, rail, broadband, cyber, electrical transmission and pipelines. For financing and construction, it would require multiple public-private partnerships. It must promote—and be seen to promote—sustainable social and economic growth that benefits all Canadians, including Aboriginals.

The corridor concept has several advantages. The Northern Corridor would allow commercial traffic, including the transportation of hazardous products, to shift from urban centres. It would also provide development opportunities to more northern parts of Canada, especially important to First Nations living there. As in Australia, a corridor approach could quicken and improve regulatory governance. General regulatory issues related to land usage by the corridor could be cleared first before any project is considered. Once the corridor is approved, qualifying projects could be proposed subject to their own specific regulatory requirements.

Legally, this reform is completely doable. Ottawa has the explicit constitutional powers to regulate all "trade and commerce." This authority is supplemented by its "declaratory power," which allows it to declare a "local work... extending beyond the limits of the province" to be "for the general advantage of Canada." In the nineteenth century, this meant operations such as "railways, canals or telegraphs," and was used hundreds of times as Canada's economy grew. In the twenty-first century, interprovincial pipelines clearly fall into this category. Finally, it would amplify and make explicit the federal government's existing authority under section 121 of the Constitution Act, which guarantees that "All articles of growth, produce or manufacture of any one province... shall be admitted free into each of the other provinces."

The bottom line is that if the Trudeau government had wanted to, it could have overridden the clearly unconstitutional attempts by Quebec and British Columbia to block new export pipelines. As a *Globe and Mail* editorial pointed out, "to connect the pipelines, connect the dots."[x] But the Liberals chose not to for short-term partisan advantage.

Politically, the creation of a national infrastructure corridor would be challenging but possible since it is important for all of our export industries.

It would require strong national leadership—both political and financial—from the government in Ottawa. Ideally it should be non-partisan with cross-party support. Aboriginal involvement at all levels and in all stages would be imperative.

Even though the corridor is more than just about pipelines, it quickly becomes immersed in energy politics. Opposition to pipelines themselves can be expected from those provinces, political parties, and advocacy groups that believe that continued development of Canada's oil reserves (the third largest in the world) are incompatible with our national commitment to reduce CO2 emissions. In the 2019 national election, the NDP, Bloc Québécois and Green Party all adopted some form of a no-more-pipelines policy and received 27 per cent of the popular vote. This vote was concentrated in key urban areas—Toronto, Montreal and Vancouver—all with strategic political value. So, building a national coalition to support a sea-to-sea-to-sea infrastructure corridor will not be easy. To succeed, Alberta leaders will have to make it clear to the rest of Canada that without guaranteed pipeline access to Canadian ports similar to other industries, there is little reason for Alberta (or Saskatchewan) to remain in Canada.

Supreme Court of Canada

A second reform that could increase Alberta's (and the West's) influence in Ottawa would be changes to the Supreme Court of Canada. As documented by Morton (chapter 2), all national courts of appeal have a centralizing influence. In Canada, this institutional bias has been exacerbated by the Charter of Rights. The Supreme Court's embrace of judicial activism to advance the policy goals of its "court party" constituents has made it the most policy-making court of any of the Anglo-American democracies.[xi] This trend could be curbed by changes in the composition of the Supreme Court of Canada and how its justices are appointed.

Currently by law, three of the nine judges must come from Quebec and, by convention, three from Ontario. In 2019, six months before the most recent federal election, Justin Trudeau signed an agreement with Quebec that "ensures greater participation by its government in the selection process of judges from the province."[xii] By practice, of the remaining three, two come from the Western provinces and one from Atlantic Canada. This means at any given time, five of the ten provinces will not have a judge from their province on the court.

This is another example of a nineteenth-century constitution not keeping pace with Canada's twenty-first century economic realities. A more representative model would expand the court to eleven members, leave Quebec with three, give Ontario four, and then three for the West and one for Atlantic Canada. While this may be largely symbolic, it would enhance the authority of the court, especially when it makes decisions that are politically unpopular in a given province or region. Western complaints about losing decisions involving resource management would have less bite if three of the majority judges came from those provinces. But presumably they would make losing less frequent.

A second meaningful reform would be to share the prime minister's power to appoint the justices of the Supreme Court with the ten provincial premiers. Critics would say this reform would "politicize" the court. But this assumes the court is not already politicized—hardly an informed opinion. In the age of the Charter, judges no longer just "interpret the law.... They make it and shape it; they exercise political choice." The consequence is obvious: "governments of all stripes will continue to attempt to appoint members to the high court who comport with their view of Charter justice."[xiii]

A provincial role in the appointment of Supreme Court justices would make for a more regionally representative court, and also increase the political diversity of the justices appointed. For the past century, the national Liberal and Conservative parties have enjoyed a monopoly on these appointments. With the recent exception of some of Prime Minister Harper's appointments, these justices have reflected and promoted the post-Charter "ideological consensus... of 'Official Canada', 'the Laurentian consensus', or the 'Court Party'."[xiv] Sharing the appointment power with provincial governments would open the door to a wider spectrum of political views: Parti Québécois or CAQ appointments from Quebec; Saskatchewan Party appointments from Saskatchewan; NDP or Green Party appointments from British Columbia.

Are these reforms feasible? In theory, yes. But in practice, probably not. Most provincial governments would welcome the enhanced participation and representation of their respective provinces. And up until 2014, the size and composition of the Supreme Court were defined by the Supreme Court Act, a federal statute, and so could be amended unilaterally by Parliament.[xv] While the Liberal Party may be reluctant to give up the patronage benefits of the power to unilaterally appoint the justices, one can imagine that the Conservative Party of Canada might be willing to do so as a way to accommodate regional interests and thereby win a majority government. This is one aspect of what the Mulroney government tried to do with the 1987 Meech Lake Accord.

Both of these reforms would be strongly opposed by the progressive left and the court party, groups that have benefitted from the court's new policy-making role under the Charter. The Meech Lake Accord proposed to give the power to nominate Supreme Court justices to provincial governments. Former Prime Minister Pierre Trudeau attacked this reform as a "capitulation to provincialism." It was also opposed by feminist advocacy groups, Quebec Anglophones, Aboriginals, and other beneficiaries of its new power. Any new attempt to implement these reforms would activate the same coalition of opponents. Only now, their prospects of defeating these reforms are much greater.

Why? Because in 2014, the Supreme Court ruled that despite the clear language of section 101 of the Constitution Act, 1867, the composition of the Supreme Court is now "constitutionalized" and can only be changed with the unanimous consent of all ten provinces plus the federal government.[xvi] While it can be—and has been[xvii]—argued that this is a problematic misinterpretation of the constitution, it is now the law of the land.

In effect, the Supreme Court has basically cemented in the status quo—unilateral federal appointment—exactly what its progressive left/court party supporters wanted. By "constitutionalizing" what had previously been a matter of statute, "a Meech-like formula may be impossible to achieve."[xviii]

In the same way that the Supreme Court has made Senate reform virtually impossible (see below), it has also protected itself—and the interests that it supports—from any future changes. Or more probably, those of which it does not approve.

Senate reform

Alberta is not inherently opposed to a more vigorous and effective national government in Ottawa. Alberta would have been much happier with a government in Ottawa that exercised its explicit jurisdiction over interprovincial trade and commerce to override British Columbia and Quebec's recent attempts to block the construction of new interprovincial pipelines. Rather, the problem is our historical lack of voice and votes, which makes us such an easy target. Meaningful Senate reform along the Triple E model—equal, elected and effective—could resolve this problem. Strong national leadership from the government in Ottawa would be welcomed by Alberta and other Western provinces if we believed our interests and voices were being taken into account.

Canada does not have to re-invent the wheel when it comes to Senate reform. We have three examples of large, geographically diverse federal states—the United States, Australia, and Germany—in which "rep by pop" in the lower house is counterbalanced by some form of regionally representative and equal senate. In each of these successful federations, the policy decisions of the national governments have legitimacy and authority because their decisions are a synthesis of competing regional views and interests, allowing all voices to be heard. There are winners and losers. But even the losers accept those results—at least until the next election—because they believe in the legitimacy of the process that produces them. This is what Canada does not have under the status quo.

The clearest example of this is how the United States and Canada responded so differently to the price shocks of the OPEC oil embargos of the 1970s. The price of oil and gasoline tripled—not once but twice—in a decade. An American study found that the purpose of Canada's response—Trudeau's

NEP—to keep the domestic price of oil below world prices was "to protect the new government's political base in the [oil] consuming regions of Ontario and Quebec."[xix] The Liberals' policy "of protecting the standard of living of its constituents in heavily industrialized central Canada... promised significant political returns."[xx]

In the United States, similar legislation with the same motives was introduced by representatives and senators from the heavily-populated eastern seaboard and industrial Midwestern states. As in Canada, the oil price shocks produced "ferocious behind the scenes battles along regional lines." But unlike Canada, efforts to impose domestic price controls "fell victim to committee efforts at turf protection." Translation: they were defeated by the senators from the energy-producing states who held key positions in the relevant Senate committees.[xxi] Then, as now, the Senate Committee on Energy and Natural Resources is dominated by senators from the West and south, and who are very good at "turf protection."[xxii] This American experience was not lost on Western Canadians who a decade later insisted that Senate reform be part of the Charlottetown Accord. "A central reason for western support for this institutional change is the belief that it would be better able to prevent a repeat of what westerners see as the NEP's raid on provincial resources."[xxiii]

For these same reasons, the Harper Conservative government (2006-2015) worked to advance Senate reform. Harper appointed four elected senators from Alberta, and in 2014 drafted legislation to formalize this practice for any other province that chose to hold Senate elections. But as explained by Morton (chapter 2), the Supreme Court not only ruled this legislation unconstitutional, but held that any future changes to the selection of senators could only be done by a constitutional amendment agreed to by all ten provinces. The practical effect of this ruling is to give Quebec a *de facto* veto over Senate reform.

As with appointments to the Supreme Court, the court has cemented in the status quo by "constitutionalizing" issues that could otherwise have been more easily dealt with via political negotiation and a new federal statute. As one commentator has colorfully but accurately noted, we are left with "a rigid Trudeauian constitutional edifice guarded by a judicial phalanx." By making such reforms virtually impossible, the court has in effect allowed Pierre Trudeau "to rule from the grave."[xxiv]

The challenge to future Senate reform will be Quebec's continued resistance to any reforms that weaken its privileged position in the House of Commons. The experience of the Charlottetown Accord in the 1990s demonstrates this difficulty. The Quebec government opposed the proposal for an elected and equal Senate until the proposed powers of the reformed Senate were so minimal as make it meaningless.[xxv]

Quebec opposition to the Senate reform option need not be the end of the story. If the other nine provinces were to decide that this is the direction that Canada needs to go to keep English Canada prosperous and united, Quebec could be given the option to leave. This would be unfortunate, but that does not make it unthinkable. Most of Alberta's (and Western Canada's) problems with the status quo—both electoral and fiscal—would be resolved or minimized if Quebec were to leave. Equalization payments, for example, would immediately be reduced by two-thirds. The need for bilingualism in the civil service would decline or disappear completely. Logistically and legally, it would be simpler and less expensive for Albertans to bid *au revoir* to Quebec than to say goodbye to Canada. These are all considerations that would have to be taken into account.

Autonomism: less Ottawa in Alberta

A second option for Alberta is to become more autonomous within Canada, utilizing its undoubted constitutional powers to opt out of federal programs that are disadvantageous to the province. These reforms would reduce the presence and size of the federal government in Alberta, by replacing what are currently federal programs with provincially owned and managed programs. Four such initiatives described in earlier chapters in this volume have already been undertaken by other provinces:

- Opt out of the Canada Pension Plan and replace it with an Alberta Pension Plan (Quebec)
- Create a provincial police force rather than rely on the RCMP for local policing (Quebec and Ontario)

- Collect provincial income tax in Alberta rather than relying on federal authorities for tax collection (Quebec)
- Substitute transfer of tax points from the federal government for some portion of transfer payments to the province (Quebec).

There are also possibilities that have not been tried by other provinces but would be clearly constitutional. Examples would include:

- Exiting the supply management system for dairy products and poultry
- Exiting from the constraints of the Canada Health Act, which are enforced only by the federal government's withholding of transfer payments under the spending power
- Adopting a provincial constitution.

On November 9, 2019, Premier Jason Kenney appointed the Fair Deal panel, consisting of nine Albertans, to consider these and other forms of what might be called autonomism (our term, not the premier's). Specific topics for consideration included:

- Establishing a provincial revenue agency to collect provincial taxes directly by ending the Canada-Alberta Tax Collection Agreement, while joining Quebec in seeking an agreement to collect federal taxes within the province
- Creating an Alberta pension plan by withdrawing from the Canada Pension Plan
- Establishing a provincial police force by ending the Alberta Police Service Agreement with the Government of Canada
- Emulating Quebec's practice of playing a larger role in international relations, in part by seeking Alberta representation in treaty negotiations that effect Alberta's interests
- Emulating Quebec's legal requirement that public bodies, including municipalities and school boards, obtain the approval of the provincial government before they can enter into agreements with the federal government
- Using the existing provincial power to appoint the Chief Firearms Office for Alberta
- Opting out of federal cost share programs with full compensation, such as the federal government's proposed pharmacare program

- Seeking an exchange of tax points for federal cash transfers under the Canada Health and Social Transfers
- Establishing a formalized provincial constitution.[xxvi]

After holding public meetings and engaging in other kinds of research, the panel delivered its report in May 2020. It assumed an unexpectedly harmonious and cooperative tone:

> Our initial inclination was to first list, and most heavily emphasize, those recommendations that Alberta could implement on its own. We were inclined to do this, because we anticipated that the cooperation and support of other governments would be most difficult to achieve, given some of the tensions which existed between Alberta and the federal government in particular.
>
> However, in recent months, as a result of the need for all Canadians and their governments to pull together to cope with the current health and economic crises, we have witnessed a much greater willingness on the part of the provincial and federal governments to mutually support and cooperate with each other.
>
> The imperative for interprovincial and federal-provincial cooperation has made us somewhat more optimistic that recommendations requiring the support of other governments to achieve a Fair Deal for Alberta—such as the need to reform equalization—will be received with respect, accepted at face value and handled positively.
>
> Hence, after describing what we have heard from Albertans concerning the necessity of a fair deal for the province within confederation, we begin our recommendations with those measures requiring the support of other governments—particularly the federal government. We do so in the sincere hope that the new spirit of cooperation and mutual support among Canadian governments—born out of the necessity to respond collectively to the current health and economic crises—will continue after those crises and their effects have begun to abate.[xxvii]

We would like to think the panel is correct, but we are less optimistic that the cooperative mood will last. We believe that long-term conflicts of interest and ideology generally trump the influence of short-term events. Time will tell soon enough.

The panel recommended holding an Alberta referendum in fall 2021 on the question of whether s. 36 of The Constitution Act, 1982 (equalization) should be repealed. The purpose would be to force Ottawa and the other provinces to come to the table to discuss the issue. The panel also recommended replacement of the Canada Pension Plan by an Alberta pension plan as well as transferring the RCMP's local policing functions to a new Alberta Police Service. It did not, however, support the idea of Alberta collecting its own taxes or of giving up monetary transfers in favour of tax points.[xxviii] With reference to adopting a provincial constitution, the panel was obviously divided and decided not to offer a recommendation.

The government of Alberta, in its response to the panel, accepted its high-profile recommendations with respect to equalization, an Alberta Pension Plan, and an Alberta Police Service. The government also insisted that it would continue to seek a transfer of tax points because that was a campaign commitment, and it would study Quebec's experience with collecting its own taxes before reaching a final decision.[xxix] Dozens of other policy initiatives with a less prominent profile were also mentioned in the panel's report and the government's response, with varying degrees of support and reservation. It certainly seems that the Kenney government plans to move in an autonomist direction, but the details will only become known over a period of years.

The benefits and costs of all such initiatives will have to be carefully evaluated. For example:

- An Alberta pension plan seems beneficial as long as Alberta has a younger population and a higher employment rate than other provinces. It could also help build a larger financial industry in Alberta. However, the benefits are eroded if Alberta's employment rate declines and young people leave the province, especially in light of systematic attempts by the federal government and some provinces to restrict the growth of Alberta's energy industry

- An Alberta Provincial Police Force could probably do a better job of local policing than the RCMP, but it might be more expensive for Alberta, given that Ottawa now pays a portion of costs for contract policing
- Collecting its own provincial personal income taxes enables Alberta to design the personal income tax base according to its own preferences for growth and fairness. However, a separate tax collection would increase compliance costs for Alberta taxpayers and administrative costs because Alberta would require staff that are now paid by Ottawa even if more jobs are created in Alberta
- Transfer of personal income tax points instead of taking cash grants gives Alberta greater tax policy flexibility but could be costly if the provincial economy declines.
- Supply management is a producers' cartel that creates higher prices for consumers everywhere while concentrating benefits on producers located mainly in Quebec and Ontario. It is enforced by tariffs against cheaper products from other countries. Unless tariffs could be adjusted, prices for Alberta's consumers might not be reduced
- Exiting the constraints of the Canada Health Act might result in a more efficient health care system in Alberta, but there would be a loss to the provincial treasury as federal transfer payments were reduced or eliminated
- A provincial constitution is symbolically attractive, but it does not directly address any of the economic or political difficulties identified in this volume.[xxx]

Beyond these individual policy considerations, we can identify some general considerations, both positive and negative, that apply to the autonomist option.

The Positive. There is a presumption in federal systems that public functions should be exercised by the government that is closest to the population being served. The national government needs to be involved only if there are significant spillovers outside of local boundaries, legal tender and national defence being classic examples. It makes eminent sense, therefore, that a function such as local policing should be carried out by local and provincial governments, as is done in all federal systems in the world except for Canada. Similar considerations can be extended to numerous other functions that are now entirely or largely dominated by the national government in Canada.

The autonomist option could be helpful preparation for some version of separatism if Alberta is forced to move in that direction. For example, an Alberta police force could serve as the interim nucleus of an Alberta defence force while the province was constructing a military appropriate to its needs. Likewise, the ability to directly collect provincial taxes would facilitate the transition to a national system of tax collection, as would provincial management of the health care system in its own sphere. In general, the more autonomous Alberta becomes, the easier it will be to contemplate full-fledged separation.

The autonomist option could be a significant weapon in negotiations to enhance Alberta's position within Canada. For example, the creation of an Alberta pension plan would disrupt the Canada Pension Plan and probably make it more expensive for the remaining provinces to operate. Thus, even the threat of withdrawing from the Canada Pension Plan might lead Ottawa to negotiate seriously in areas, such as equalization and the stabilization programs, that are harmful to Alberta but outside the province's constitutional jurisdiction. Similar considerations apply to a threat to the cartelized marketing arrangements that benefit dairy producers in Ontario and Quebec.

The Negative. As mentioned above, several of the autonomist options might bring increased costs as functions previously paid for by Ottawa were transferred to the provincial government. In the long run, the benefits of local administration might well outweigh the initial costs, but in the short run increases to the provincial expenditure budget might be required. This is of particular concern at the time of writing (spring 2020) because the Covid pandemic crisis has created a crisis for the Alberta budget, which was already in a serious deficit position before the pandemic struck. Temporary relief measures are increasing expenditures, while lowered prices for oil and gas will reduce royalties. Corporate and individual income taxes will also be hit by the generally lower level of economic activity. The need for deficit spending is not likely to be overcome for several years, making a move towards autonomism difficult in this period of time.

Beyond questions of cost, the pandemic has created feelings of insecurity all over the world, and Alberta is no exception. Albertans in the past have been characterized by optimism and confidence in their ability to manage their own affairs, attitudes that would help autonomism succeed. But in a time of insecurity, people may tend to look to the national government because of its greater financial resources and constitutional jurisdiction. Thus, for psychological reasons, autonomism may not receive as much support from Albertans in the near future as it otherwise would.

Most importantly, autonomism does not directly address Alberta's most important problems. As detailed at length in earlier chapters, Alberta's economy has been hammered from all sides: pipeline obstructionism by the federal government, other provincial governments, environmentalists, Indigenous organizations, and even the United States government at times. The regulatory climate for oil and gas has been made substantially more restrictive by passage of Bill C-69 and downgrading of the Calgary-based National Energy Board in favour of a more powerful Ottawa-based Canadian Energy Regulator. Equalization and other net fiscal transfers through the federal budget have pulled money out of Alberta for redistribution to people and governments in other provinces. Autonomism by itself does not do anything about these adverse trends. At best, the threat of autonomism might provoke the federal government to make some modification to the destructive policies it has pursued.

Overall, the benefits of autonomism are mixed. It might lead to improved public services in some areas, but also with the risk of increased costs for the province. Autonomism might also be a useful weapon in negotiations meant to improve Alberta's position within confederation, as it would take Alberta one step closer to separatism. The threat of separatism, which is discussed in the next section, would have to be taken more seriously if Alberta were already collecting its own taxes, doing its own policing, running its own pension plan, and in other ways managing its own affairs. And autonomism is more likely to be taken seriously if it is backed by robust threats of separation.

That has been the pattern for Quebec, whose threats of separation have led to repeated concessions of money and jurisdiction from Ottawa.

Separation

Separation is the third option that could be considered. Alberta, perhaps joined by Saskatchewan, would declare independence. The strongest argument for separation is that the province would have more ability to determine its own destiny. The billions in net fiscal transfers to the rest of country would be money kept by the province for its own affairs. Alberta would have full control over resource development and be able to negotiate its own trade and security agreements with the United States, Canada, and other countries.

Separation, though, is not at all an easy option to pursue. While a minority of Albertans already prefer separation, many Albertans are proud Canadian patriots, having fought in two world wars in the twentieth-century. Moreover, Albertans are closely connected to the rest of Canada with family and friends living in other parts of Canada. Open borders for trade and inter-provincial migration are a benefit to Albertans as well. Separation is also disruptive and risky, providing unknown benefits or costs to Alberta's prosperity depending on negotiated terms with the rest of Canada. Giving up on Canada will be very controversial for these reasons alone.

Alberta with only 4.2 million people and $250 billion in GDP would be the world's 127th-largest country in population size, about the same as Panama, and 45th-largest country in the world in GDP, slightly below Vietnam. Canada, which is currently the 38th-largest country in population size and 10th-largest in GDP would become the 42nd-largest in population size and 13th-largest in GDP without Alberta. Arguably, larger countries have more success by having greater punch in international affairs and more economic and fiscal capacity. On the other hand, many relatively small countries have prospered because they can be nimbler and operate with greater consensus amongst their less regionalized population. Ireland, slightly larger than Alberta, has had high economic performance among advanced countries in recent years. It has been able to punch above its weight in international affairs, beating out Canada for a seat at the UN security council in 2020.

The first question that would need to be asked is how Alberta could separate legally. Like the United Kingdom's Brexit vote, Albertans could have a referendum asking whether it wishes to separate from the rest of Canada. Although the Constitution Act is silent on whether a province could separate, the federal Clarity Act and Supreme Court decisions around the Quebec referendum have laid out a complicated process, as discussed by Albert. Even if Alberta voted in a referendum to separate, the province would then need to negotiate terms for separation with the federal government and the rest of Canada. If unanimity, rather than seven provinces representing 50 per cent of the population, is required for provincial approval, separation seems impossible because British Columbia would probably resist being cut off from the rest of Canada.

The legality of separation is not the same question as to the politics. Certainly, an attempt by Alberta to secede could be similar to Catalonia's failed confrontation with the Spanish government over separation (see Mintz). Alternatively, separation could be settled on peaceful terms as in the case of landlocked Czechoslovakia. So, if Alberta and Saskatchewan clearly expressed their desire to leave Canada, would the rest of Canada wish to block it so long as satisfactory terms are negotiable? If Canada blocked it, would that lead to hostilities with possible intervention by the United States, as Cooper raises. All this is quite unknown and risky.

Many political and economic issues around separation are complex. They would need to be addressed with considerable attention.

A provincial constitution. If Alberta were to separate, it would need a process to develop its own constitution laying out rights, governance, provincial and municipal powers. Would many provisions such as Charter of Rights under the Constitution Act be maintained or would something else be included? What about guarantees for education? Reaching a consensus will be challenging.

Residency and Migration. One of the most important benefits to Alberta has been the integration of its labour market with the rest of Canada. Generally, Albertans can easily study or take up jobs in other parts of Canada and Alberta employers can easily hire workers from other provinces. A separate Alberta would develop its own immigration policy, which currently is left to the federal government to operate and fund. With a declaration of independence, some Canadians will wish to return to Alberta and some Albertans may wish to move to other provinces. Dual citizenship might be provided for migrant populations. As in the case of Czechoslovakia, Alberta temporary workers from other provinces and students studying in Alberta would need to be provided some certainty about their work/study status.

First Nations. Certain indigenous rights have been provided historically including treaties, land claims and governance over ancestral lands and resources. Many First Nations in Alberta would be concerned that they would lose rights that they have gained over the years if Alberta were to separate. The First Nations have had financial support from the federal government that would need to be negotiated with a new Alberta government. Alberta would need to decide whether to honour all previous treaties and rights. It could even enhance provisions for First Nations by replacing the federal Indian Act with a new relationship that might resolve issues such as "self-determination" and "duty to consult."

Inter-provincial and international trade. A separate Alberta would lose benefits from access to Canadian markets and other countries unless parties are willing to renew agreements as they stand now or negotiate new trade agreements. Although a larger portion of Alberta's trade is with the United States than inter-provincially, higher trade costs with the rest of Canada would harm Alberta's economy. These costs could be reduced by a negotiated trade agreement with Canada, which could include a common market relationship similar to the European Union. As for international trade agreements, a separate Alberta could choose whether to seek similar arrangements with the United States and Mexico, Asia, and Europe. Alternatively, Alberta as a separate country might wish to improve on current trade agreements. For example, a U.S.-Alberta trade agreement could focus on a North American energy strategy while forgoing irritants with the U.S. such as supply management. Alberta could also seek a customs union with the United States if it fails to achieve a common market with Canada.

Access to tidewater. A separate Alberta would be landlocked so its exported products would need to move through other countries to reach tidewater. The lack of pipeline capacity to non-U.S. markets has been a problem for Alberta already. So, the question is whether separation makes it more possible to diversify its markets through newly negotiated trade agreements rather than rely on the federal government power over inter-provincial transportation that has been disappointing in recent years. Given that B.C. would itself need access to the rest of Canada and mid-West markets, it could be desirous of reciprocal relations under an agreement. Otherwise, Alberta would face new obstacles and costs in selling its oil and gas products to the rest of the world.

Banking and Alberta's Currency. One of the critical economic levers a country has is its conduct of banking and monetary policy. An independent Alberta would create its own central bank and institutions to regulate the banking sector and influence interest rates through monetary operations. Alberta would also need to decide on whether it would have a flexible exchange rate, or a currency fixed in value to the Canadian or U.S. currency. Commodity-based economies like Norway have a flexible exchange rate to manage volatility better with independent monetary policy. On the other hand, a fixed exchange rate facilitates trade transactions with important trading partners at lower cost but compromises monetary policy independence. Given that energy is the most important Canadian export at this time, an independent Alberta with a flexible currency would likely result a devaluation of the Canadian dollar relative to the U.S. and Alberta dollar.

Federal assets and debt. An Alberta separation would inevitably result in contentious arrangements to split federal assets and liabilities between the provinces and the rest of Canada. These can be shared according to the distribution of population, GDP or some other formula. A per capita rule, such as used in Czechoslovakia upon its breakup, favours the richer jurisdiction compared to a GDP-based distribution rule. Alberta might also argue that its past net contribution to the federal budget entitles it to take on a smaller share of existing federal liabilities net of assets. Federal assets in Alberta would need to be valued (book or market?). Arrangements would be needed to transfer to Alberta defence-related and other illiquid federal assets. The Canada Pension Plan, which is jointly governed by the federal and provincial governments, would need to have its assets apportioned between a new Alberta Pension Plan and the former CPP with Alberta assuming pension liabilities of Albertan citizens.

Security. A newly created Alberta would be responsible for safeguarding borders, countering terrorism, infrastructure and cyber security and criminal law and institutions (see Bercuson). The province will need not only its own police force but armed forces, paramilitary force for civil disorder, custom border agents and intelligence experts. The province will need to decide whether to participate in NATO, NORAD, and other internationally based security arrangements. These will be new costs to be borne by the province.

Separation is a giant leap of faith. It might provide significant long-run benefits to the province or weaken itself over time. The uncertainty created by separation will be costly in the short run not only for Alberta but for Canada as well. It is an option not to be taken up lightly.

Is one of these options preferable to the others? None of us favors separation as a first choice. Like most Albertans, we are also proud Canadians. And Canada has much to be proud of.

Finis

But we also agree with Derek Burney and Fen Hampson's observation that "the only way Alberta can grow and prosper economically is through the continued development of its energy and related industries and if can't do it under the Canadian federal system, Albertans will be obliged to look at an alternative political regime." Note that Burney is not an Albertan. He has had a distinguished career in both the federal civil service and the private sector, and he was Canada's former ambassador to the United States. He gets the big picture: without economically competitive access to global markets and global prices for our oil and gas, the policy-induced recession of the past five years will become permanent. For us—and we believe that for most Albertans—this is unacceptable. So what is the path forward?

Our first choice would be the reforms that would increase Alberta's voice and influence in Ottawa—reforms to the Senate and Supreme Court—plus a national infrastructure corridor. These reforms would re-align our nineteenth century political system with our twenty-first century economy, and end Alberta's systemic vulnerability. In plain speak, we would achieve the political stability and economic balance enjoyed by other federal states like Australia, the United States, and Germany.

Unfortunately, given that Quebec has been given a *de facto* veto over such reforms, the first two do not seem feasible at this point. With respect to a new sea-to-sea-to sea infrastructure corridor, it would require national leadership. Quebec's interest in the Northern Corridor would focus on its development of hydro-electricity and mining, but it has opposed an energy pipeline. For Alberta, pipelines could still be built in other parts of Canada, but Alberta oil would have to find another way to reach the Atlantic unless Quebec, which already imports Alberta oil to its own refineries, is overruled by the federal government that has constitutional control over interprovincial transportation. Regardless, pipeline approval through Quebec is dogged by politics unless there is a significant change to accommodate responsible energy development supported by Canadians including central Canada.

Accordingly, we support the second set of options: autonomism—increasing Alberta's ability to be self-governing with greater controls over its own destiny by taking over programs that are currently administered by Ottawa: policing, pensions and tax-collection. As noted above, each of these reforms has risks as well as rewards. To minimize the risks, they will have to be designed and implemented thoughtfully and thoroughly. But at this point in Alberta's history, they are our best choice. So we are encouraged by the Fair Deal panel's report, and Premier Kenney's response to develop these options over the next several years. We also support his decision that before any are legally adopted, they must first be approved by Albertans by a referendum. We anticipate a robust and informed public debate over each of these reforms. Albertans deserve no less.

To those who disagree, we would remind them of Peter Lougheed's message to Albertans in 1980, the day Pierre Trudeau announced his Liberal government's National Energy Policy:

Who will ultimately decide? It won't be Peter or Pierre—it will be you, as Albertans. You who will determine whether or not you want to see more and more of your lives directed and controlled in Ottawa, or whether you want to see a fair portion of the decision-making determined by Albertans in Alberta. If you choose the latter, I believe, over time, we will have a stronger Canada and a better Canada."[xxxi]

We think these words are as true today as they were in 1980. But as documented in this book, Alberta is much worse off, much more vulnerable to predatory and destructive policies from Ottawa than we were then. It is time for a new strategy.

We acknowledge that there is no guarantee that the "more Alberta, less Ottawa" reforms will by themselves resolve Alberta's current vulnerability. But the alternative—continuing on as we have for the past 30 years—guarantees more of the same. The reforms should create the political leverage that Alberta needs to persuade fellow Canadians that for Albertans, the status quo is no longer acceptable. The threat of separatism would have to be taken more seriously if Alberta were already collecting its own taxes, doing its own policing, and running its own pension plan.

To repeat, none of us favor separation as a first option. But we also see it as a viable last resort if all else fails. It may be that in order to stay in Canada, Alberta must be able and willing to leave it. Otherwise, our grievances—our request for a fair deal—will never be taken seriously. Asking Ottawa and the rest of Canada to be "fair" to Alberta has not worked and will never work. For political change of this scale, appeals to fairness do not work. We must make the rest of Canada see that it is in their self-interest to keep Alberta in Canada for the contributions we make.

This may be Alberta's paradox: That we need to go half-way down a road to a destination that we don't want, in order to get the policy and constitutional changes necessary to stay in a Canada we love.

Acknowledgments

The idea behind this book came from the many people who have engaged us in thoughtful discussions of Alberta's future. After five years of economic fragility, Albertans are increasingly concerned about the economic future of our province. And this was before the deep COVID-induced recession that is causing even more business closures, job losses, bankruptcies, foreclosures and suffering for tens of thousands of Alberta families. There have been many different ideas about how best to ensure that future generations of Albertans will enjoy the same opportunities and prosperity that our generation has enjoyed. So, we approached several recognized policy experts to identify and explain out the political, legal and economic issues that need to be addressed going forward. We want to thank those many Albertans who care about the future of our province and encouraged us to do this book.

As editors, we feel fortunate to have received the enthusiastic cooperation of so many well-known thinkers who understand Alberta's history, culture, and economy within confederation. We thank you all.

We are grateful for the financial support provided by the Buffalo Advisory Group and Modern Miracle Network that has helped make this publication possible.

Finally, we also thank Mr. Ken Whyte of Sutherland House for his willingness to bring this volume forward in a timely matter. It could take two or three years to develop a book of edited contributions, but our publisher worked diligently so that this volume could be done within a year.

Jack Mintz, Ted Morton, & Tom Flanagan

Notes

Chapter One: Manning

i Many of these are measures proposed to the Fair Deal Panel by Albertans for review by the panel as possible recommendations to the Alberta government and which could be pursued unilaterally by the Alberta government if it so chose. At the time of this writing (March 2020) the Fair Deal Panel was completing its report for submission to the Alberta government. Once that report has been reviewed and released, readers of this paper will be able to ascertain which of these recommendations have been accepted by the government for follow up.

ii The Report of the Fair Deal Panel includes an extensive explanation of the reasoning behind this recommendation, based primarily on the demographic fact that since the Alberta population is relatively younger than that of the rest of Canada, it could provide pensions equivalent to those of the CPP at somewhat lower contribution rates.

iii At the public meetings held by the Fair Deal Panel the proposal that Alberta cancel its contract with the RCMP and establish an Alberta Police Force was very frequently mentioned, especially by rural Albertans. In addition to addressing the practical problem of the rise in rural crime and the seeming inability of the RCMP to cope with it, many westerners still see the RCMP as a federal institution established specifically to bring law and order to the West, feel it still should be headquartered here, and resent the fact that it has become bureaucratized, eastern based, and wholly urban oriented. An Alberta Police Force would presumably not suffer from these deficiencies.

iv There are of course precedents for this approach to advancing the position of one's province by a very small group of individuals initiating a strategy to gain control of a federal political party and ultimately the federal government. In 1957, the Liberal government of Louis St. Laurent was replaced by the Western-oriented Diefenbaker government. In the eyes of the defeated Liberals, the Diefenbaker government was not sufficiently focused on Quebec, and there was a perceived need to restore Quebec to its historic position of prominence and influence in the federation. When the Diefenbaker government was replaced by the Liberal minority government of Lester Pearson in 1963, the scene was ripe for a reassertion of Quebec influence over the Liberal party and the federal government. And how did that come about? With the encouragement of Prime Minister Pearson, three Quebeckers, Jean Marchand, Gerard Pelletier, and Pierre Trudeau (later to be called "the three wise men from the east"), met together in Montreal and developed a strategy for that reassertion. It culminated in Trudeau replacing Pearson as Liberal leader, the election of a Liberal majority government in 1968, and the passage of the Constitution Act of 1982 containing the Charter of Rights and Freedoms. Nine of the Charter's thirty-four clauses, or more than 25% of its content, focus on linguistic and minority education rights of particular importance to Quebec.

v https://www.theglobeandmail.com/news/politics/ottawas-per-capita-health-transfers-a-windfall-for-alberta/article1358853/

vi https://www.nrcan.gc.ca/environmental-assessment/149

vii https://www.cbc.ca/news/canadian-oilsands-avoid-dirty-oil-label-after-eu-vote-1.2876072. This was an extensive, long-term effort in Europe and elsewhere: http://www.dominionpaper.ca/articles/3991 and https://www.reuters.com/article/canada-oil-sands/insight-canadas-oil-sand-battle-with-europe-idUSL4E-8GAAXW20120510?feedType=RSS&feedName=marketsNews&rpc=43

viii Note that the Calgary Shepherd MP and Alberta Caucus Chair, Tom Kmiec, has a draft private member's bill in progress which partially addresses these points. It is entitled *An Act to amend the Federal-Provincial Fiscal Arrangements Act (Equalization)*. Short Title: *The Equalization Accountability Act*.

Chapter Two: Morton

i Roy Romanow, John Whyte, & Howard Leeson, *Canada Notwithstanding: The Making of the Constitution 1976-1982* (Toronto: Carswell-Methuen, 1984), xvii.

ii Romanow et al. *Canada Notwithstanding*, 5.

iii Romanow et al. *Canada Notwithstanding*, 268.

iv Peter Hogg, *Constitution Act 1982 Annotated* (Toronto: Carswell, 1982), 83.

v "It'll be a 'day of mourning' for Indians," *Vancouver Sun*, April 15, 1982.

vi F.L. Morton & Rainer Knopff, *The Charter Revolution and the Court Party* (Broadview Press, 2000), 42-43.

vii Coldwater et al. v. Canada et al., Federal Court of Appeal, February 4, 2020, paragraph 53.

viii "Canada officially adopts UN declaration on rights of Indigenous Peoples," CBC News, May 10, 2016.

ix "TransCanada cancels $15.7B Energy East pipeline project," *Calgary Herald*, October 5, 2017

x Donald Savoie, "Politics killed the Energy East Pipeline, *The Globe and Mail*, October 16, 2017.

xi See Vivian Krauss, "Anti-pipeline campaign was planned, intended, and foreign-funded," *JWN*, June 27, 2019

xii http://www.cbc.ca/player/play/1100225603963

xiii "Vivian Krauss: Suzuki's Funding." *Financial Post*, April 19, 2012.

xiv "B.C. Liberals call for ban on foreign funds to pipeline protesters," *Victoria News*, Feb. 26, 2020. https://www.vicnews.com/business/b-c-liberals-call-for-ban-on-foreign-funds-to-pipeline-protesters/

xv "Defeating Harper: Reflections on the Vote Together Campaign," http://www.votetogether.ca/report

xvi "Vivian Krauss: Obama wasn't the only American interfering in the Canadian election." *Financial Post*, October 22, 2019. https://business.financialpost.com/opinion/vivian-krause-obama-wasnt-the-only-american-interfering-in-the-canadian-election

xvii Canadian Industrial Gas and Oil v. Saskatchewan, [1978] 1 S.C.R. 37. Central Canada Potash Co. Ltd. and Attorney General of Canada v. Saskatchewan, [1979] 1 S.C.R. 42.

xviii Romanow et al. *Canada Notwithstanding*, 209.

xix See Cheffins, Ronald I., "The Supreme Court of Canada: The Quiet Court in an Unquiet Country," Osgood Hall Law Journal 4.2 (1966): 259-275.

xx Benjamin Perrin, "The Supreme Court of Canada: Policy-Maker of the Year," Macdonald-Laurier Institute, 2014

xxi Emmett Macfarlane, "You Can't Always Get What You Want: Regime Politics, the Supreme Court of Canada and the Harper Government," *Canadian Journal of Political Science* 50:1, March 2018, 18.

xxii Andre Bzdera, "A Comparative Analysis of Federal High Courts: A Political Theory of Judicial Review," *Canadian Journal of Political Science* 25, no.1 (1993), pp.3-30.

xxiii Martin Shapiro, *Courts: A Comparative and Political Analysis* (Chicago: University of Chicago Press, 1981), p.24

xxiv See Ian Brodie, *Friends of the Court: The Privileging of Interest Group Litigation in Canada*, (Albany: SUNY Univesity Press, 2002).

xxv See Ian Brodie, "The Court Challenges Program Rises Once Again," *Policy Options*, April, 2016.

xxvi See F.L. Morton and David Snow, eds. *Law, Politics and the Judicial Process in Canada*, 4th edition (University of Calgary Press, 2018), pp. 222-223.

xxvii Richard Gwyn, *The Northern Magus: Pierre Trudeau and the Canadians* (Toronto: McClelland & Stewart, 1980).

xxviii See Peter Brimelow, "The Maple Leaf For Ever: A Short Guide to Canada," *Encounter*, April, 1990, V.74, Number 3, 18-24.

xxix See, Donald J. Savoie, *Democracy in Canada: The Disintegration of Our Institutions* (Montreal: McGill-Queen's University Press, 2019), 282-83.

xxx Brimelow, p.22.

xxxi Brimelow, p. 22.

xxxii 1970: https://www.budget.gc.ca/pdfarch/1970-sd-eng.pdf; 2019: https://www.budget.gc.ca/2019/docs/plan/budget-2019-en.pdf

xxxiii Library of Parliament publication number 2011, 69, E. revised 2017 .

xxxiv Donald J. Savoie, *Democracy in Canada: The Disintegration of Our Institutions* (Montreal: McGill-Queen's University Press, 2019), p. 139.

xxxv Thomas J. Courchene & Teresa M. Courchene, "Fiscal Fairness: How Equalization failed Alberta in its time of need and how to fix it," McDonald-Laurier Institute, April 2020, 13.

xxxvi "Quebec to receive $1.4-billion equalization boost while oil-producing provinces face deficits." *Globe and Mail*, December 9, 2018.

xxxvii "Quebec slams door on New Brunswick's pipeline dream at premiers' meeting," *The Canadian Press*, December 7, 2018.

xxxviii Conrad Black, "Western Canadian anger is real and fair. The proposed remedies aren't," *National Post*, April 17, 2020

xxxix Daniel Beland, Andre Lecours, Gregory P. Marchildon, Haizen Mou & M. Rose Olfert, *Fiscal Federalism and Equalization Policy in Canada: Political and Economic Dimensions* (Toronto: University of Toronto Press, 2017), p. 43. Beland, et al. *Fiscal Federalism and Equalization Policy*, 111.

xl For greater detail, see F.L. Morton, "Senate Envy: Why Canada wants what Australia Has," Parliament of

xli Australia: Papers on Parliament No. 39, December, 2002.

Ted Morton, "No Statecraft, Questionable Jurisprudence: How the Supreme Court tried to Kill Senate

xlii Reform," The University of Calgary School of Public Policy, SPP Research Papers, 2015.

xliii Savoie, "Politics Killed Energy East."

Chapter Three: Flanagan

i Actually, it was not a direct purchase, as both land title and money went through the government of the United Kingdom, but that detail is insignificant here.

ii Manitoba Act, S.C., 1870, c. 3, s. 30.

iii Ibid., s. 31.

iv George F.G. Stanley et al., *The Collected Writings of Louis Riel* (Edmonton: University of Alberta Press, 1985), vol. 3, pp. 33-36.

v Tom Flanagan & Mark Milke, "Alberta's Real Constitution: The Natural Resources Transfer Agreement," in Richard Connors and John M. Law, eds., *Forging Alberta's Constitutional Framework* (Edmonton: University of Alberta Press, 2005), 165-189.

vi Quoted in Franklin Forster, John E. Brownlee: A Biography (Lloydminster: Foster Learning, 1981), p. 162

vii James Rose, "Remember when? Alberta's economy under Trudeau (Sr.)." BOE Report, October 6, 2015.

viii 34 & 35 Vic., c. 28 (UK).

vix Thomas Flanagan, *Louis 'David' Riel: 'Prophet of the New Word,'* 2nd ed. (Toronto: University of Toronto Press, 1996).

x Tom Flanagan, *The Wealth of First Nations* (Vancouver: Fraser Institute, 2019), pp. 119-129. In the wider economy, similar problems are resolved by a legislated right of expropriation or by provisions in corporate law that allow mergers based on majority vote.

xi An Act respecting the regulation of vessels that transport crude oil or persistent oil to or from ports or marine installations located along British Columbia's north coast, S.C. 2019, c. 26. https://www.parl.ca/DocumentViewer/en/42-1/bill/C-48/royal-assent.

xii Coldwater Indian Band v. Canada, 2020 FCA 34.

xiii Vivian Krause, "Following the (primarily U.S.) money funding Canada's anti-oil movement." MPDA, February 27, 2017.

xiv Exported Natural Gas Tax, [1982] 1 S.C.R. 1004. See Ted Morton and Troy Riddell, "Government Use of Strategic Litigation: The Alberta Exported Gas Tax Reference." https://www.researchgate.net/publication/233075555.

xv Reference re Greenhouse Gas Pollution Pricing Act, 2019 SKCA 40. The Ontario Court of Appeal rendered a similar judgment, Reference re Greenhouse Gas Pollution Pricing Act, 2019 ONCA 544.

xvi Reference re Greenhouse Gas Pollution Pricing Act, 2020 ABCA 74. https://www.albertacourts.ca/docs/default-source/ca/rsn(c)-1903-0157ac.pdf?sfvrsn=d79e8480_3.

xvii On Haultain generally, see Grant MacEwan, *Frederick Haultain: Frontier Statesman of the Canadian Northwest* (Saskatoon: Western Producer Prairie Books, 1985); and Mary Janigan, *Let the Eastern Bastards Freeze in the Dark* (Toronto: Alfred A. Knopf Canada, 2012)

xviii Reference re Senate Reform, [2014] 1 SCR 704

xix Donald J. Savoie, *Democracy in Canada: The Disintegration of Our Institutions* (Montreal: McGill-Queen's University Press, 2019), p. 139.

xx Joel Dryden, "Wexit party granted eligibility for next federal election," CBC News, January 11, 2020.

xxi Justin Brake, "Let us rise with more energy': Saganash responds to Senate death of C-262 as Liberals promise, again, to legislate UNDRIP," APTN News, June 24, 2019.

xxii Jesse Snyder, "Controversial bills C-69 and C-48 to become law, one day after Senate enforces Arctic offshore oil ban," *National Post*, June 20, 2019.

xxiii Flanagan, Louis 'David' Riel, p. 151.

xxiv Michael Wagner, *Alberta Separatism Then and Now* (St. Catharines, On.: Freedom Press Canada, 2009).

xxv Reference re Secession of Quebec, [1998] 2 SCR 217.

xxvi An Act to give effect to the requirement for clarity as set out in the opinion of the Supreme Court of Canada in the Quebec Secession Reference, S.C. 2000, c. 26.

xxvii Ted Morton, "Let's stand up to Ottawa and get a better deal," *Calgary Herald*, March 20, 2017.

xxviii Rainer Knopff, "Refining Alberta's Equalization Gambit." Fraser Institute, 2020.

xxix Constitution Act, 1867, s. 94A.

xxx Jason Clemens, Joel Emes, & Neil Veldhuis, "Albertans Make Disproportionate Contributions to National Programs: The Canada Pension Plan as a Case Study," Fraser Institute, April 2019.

xxxi Alberta Investment Management Corporation, "Would Albertans Be Better Off with an Alberta Pension Plan?" file:///C:/Users/Flanagan/AppData/Local/Microsoft/Windows/INetCache/Content.Outlook/HFXBQIQ9/Would%20Alberta%20be%20better%20off%20with%20an%20APP%20(8%20September%202019)%20(002).pdf.

xxxii Martha Hall Findlay, "Supply Management: Problems, Politics—and Possibilities." University of Calgary, The School of Public Policy," June 2012. https://www.policyschool.ca/wp-content/uploads/2016/03/supply-management-hall-findlay.pdf.

xxxiii G. Bruce Doern & Glen Toner, *The Politics of Energy: The Development and Implementation of the NEP* (Toronto: Methuen, 1985), pp. 272-273, 311-312.

xxxiv http://www.assembly.ab.ca/ISYS/LADDAR_files/docs/bills/bill/legislature_29/session_4/20180308_bill-012.pdf.

xxxv https://www.cbc.ca/news/canada/british-columbia/turn-off-the-taps-legislation-bc-suspended-1.5295354.

xxxvi 2019 FC British Columbia (Attorney General) v. Alberta (Attorney General) 1195.

xxxvii Constitution Act, 1867, s. 92A (2).

xxxviii The Supreme Court of Canada recently upheld federal control over the regulation of pipelines. Adam MacVicar, "Supreme Court rejects B.C. appeal of Trans Mountain Pipeline Case," Global News, January 16, 2020. https://globalnews.ca/news/6422235/supreme-court-bc-trans-mountain-appeal-rejected. But that would not seem to trench on provincial control over production.

xxxix Coldwater First Nation v. Canada (Attorney General), 2020 FCA 34, https://decisions.fca-caf.gc.ca/fca-caf/decisions/en/item/460815/index.do.

xl Reference re Greenhouse Gas Pollution Pricing Act, 2020 ABCA 74. https://www.albertacourts.ca/docs/default-source/ca/rsn(c)-1903-0157ac.pdf?sfvrsn=d79e8480_3.

xli Sarah Rieger, "Teck Withdraws Application for $20 billion Frontier oilsands mine." CBC News, Feb. 23, 2020.

xlii Les Perreaux & Emma Graney, "Berkshire Hathaway drops out of Énergie Saguenay investment, citing 'current political context,'" *Globe and Mail*, March 5, 2020.

Chapter Four: Mintz

i Per Fuglum, Norges hisotrie, bd, 12: Norege I stopeskjeen, Cappelan, 1980.

ii Jack M. Mintz, "Two Different Conflicts in Federal Systems: An Application to Canada," SPP Research Paper, Volume 12:14, The School of Public Policy, University of Calgary, April 2019.

iii This idea is based on analysis in R. J. May *Federalism and Fiscal Adjustment*, Oxford at Clarendon Press, United Kingdom, 1969.

iv See Don Savoie's chapter in this volume that argues that few mechanisms were considered to provide regional representation in national decision-making except through geographical representation in the cabinet.

v I have not included the European Union as a case (where Brexit is closer to reality) since it is not a true federation with a sovereign central government that has the ability to make fiscal transfers amongst countries.

vi Iain McLean, "Fiscal Federalism in Australia", Australian National University, manuscript, 2002.

vii D. Heriot, "Western Australia: A State of Secession," Parliament of Australia, 2017. While the Australian constitution provides for increasing the number of states, it does not have a provision that enables secession. Like Canada, a constitutional amendment is not easy to pass, and a unilateral withdrawal is viewed by authorities as not constitutional.

viii See Commonwealth Grants Commission, 2020. https://www.cgc.gov.au/about-us.

ix Belgium's constitution recognizes three regions (Wallonia, Flanders and Brussels) and three communities (Dutch, French and German). Even though Brussels is officially bilingual, it is dominated by the French-speaking population, due to French initially being the only official language after 1830 and Dutch being viewed as less prestigious.

x W. Liebfritz, Fiscal Federalism in Belgium,: Main Challenges and Considerations for Reform", OECD Working Paper 743, 2009.

xi https://everythingexplained.today/Partition_of_Belgium/

xii Ibid., p. 14

xiii See abstract of a talk by Jiri Pehe at http://www.pehe.cz/prednasky/2004/ the-split-of-czechoslovakia-a-defeat-or-a-victory.

xiv Metta Spencer, "The Partition of Czechoslovakia", Chapter 8 of *Separatism: Democracy and Disintegration*, Maryland, Rowman and Littlefield 1998, http://www.mettaspencer.com/?Papers:Academic_papers:The_Partition_of_Czechoslovakia.

xv Ibid.

xvi Peter Baláži and Zuzana Staržcková, "Application of Fiscal Federalism Theory to the Constitutional Organisation of Czechoslovakia after the Establishment of Federalism at Different Stages of Historical Context," Bratislava, 2016.

xvii Spencer 1998.

xviii Travers Smith, "The Dissolution of Czechoslovakia – Are there any Lessons for Berxit?" 2017. https://www.traverssmith.com/knowledge/knowledge-container/the-dissolution-of-czechoslovakia-are-there-any-lessons-for-brexit/.

xix https://news.expats.cz/czech-culture/czech-slovak-relations/.

xx See Agreement concluded between the United Kingdom of Great Britain and Northern Ireland, the Federation of Malaya, North Borneo, Sarawak and Singapore, Cmnd. 2094, 1963

xxi R. J. May, 128.

xxii Singapore's per capita GDP in 2020 is $65,000 ($101,000 in purchasing power parity> http://statisticstimes.com/economy/projected-world-gdp-capita-ranking.php.

xxiii Encyclopedia Britannica, https://www.britannica.com/place/Norway/The-16th-and-17th-centuries#ref39310.

xxiv Ola Honningdal Grytten, "The Economic History of Norway," Norwegian School of Business and Economics, EH net.

xxv Norway's per capita GDP is 53 percent higher than Sweden's in 2020. Ibid.

xxvi An earlier agreement to identify Catalonia as a "nation" was challenged within the governing Socialist national party. Ibid. p. 238.

xxvii Ibid. p. 243.

xxviii "Catalonia in Contention", Harvard Political Review, http://harvardpolitics.com/world/catalonia-contention/.

xxix Spain's Sanchez says there will be no "online" independence for Catalonia, Reuters, October 2019. https://news.yahoo.com/spains-sanchez-says-no-online-121838083.html.

xxx R. J. May, 1969, p. 156.

xxxi Office of the Historian, Milestones. https://history.state.gov/milestones/1989-1992/breakup-yugoslavia.

xxxii Keystone XL, the Trans Mountain pipeline, now owned by the federal government, and Enbridge's Line 3 replacement are to be completed after years of regulatory tie-ups.

Chapter Five: Savoie

i See, for example, Vivien Lowndes & Mark Roberts, *Why Institutions Matter: The New Institutionalism in Political Science* (London: Red Globe Press, 2013) and B. Guy Peters, *Institutional Theory in Political Science* (London: Bloomsbury, 2005).

ii Ramsay Cook quoted in Northrop Frye, *The Bush Garden: Essays on the Canadian Imagination* (Toronto: Anansi, 1971), i-ii.

iii Richard Simeon, "Conflicts and Contradictions: Contemporary Strains in Canadian Federation," Conference on Social Development in a Pluralist Society, Proceedings (Ottawa: The Canadian Council on Social Development, 1977), 9.

iv See, for example, Alexander Hamilton, John Jay, & James Madison, *The Federalist Papers* (New York: McGraw-Hill, 1987).

v Ged Martin, "Faction and Fiction in Canada's Great Coalition of 1864," the Winthrop Pickard Bell Lectures (mimeo, Mount Allison University, Sackville, NB, November 1991), 3.

vi Quoted in C.M. Wallace, "Albert Smith, Confederation and Reaction in New Brunswick: 1852-1882," *The Canadian Historical Review*, 44, no.4 (December 1963): 298-9.

vii "Nova Scotia (1867)," *Canadian Confederation* (Ottawa: Library and Archives Canada), undated, http://www.bac-lac.gc.ca/eng/discover/politics-government/canadian-confederation/Pages/nova-scotia-1867.aspx.

viii Jack Stillborn, *Senate Reform: Issues and Recent Developments* (Ottawa: Library of Parliament, 2008).

ix See, for example, "Alberta and Saskatchewan join Confederation" www.clo-ocol.gc.ca/en, undated.

x Bill Waiser, "Teaching the West and Confederation: A Saskatchewan Perspective,"*The Canadian Historical Review*, vol. 98, no. 4 (December 2017), 760.

xi George F.G. Stanley, "Act or Pact: Another Look at Confederation," presidential address to the Canadian Historical Association, 1956, https://cha-shc.ca/_uploads/4zubg8jrd.pdf.

xii Donald Creighton, *John A. Macdonald: The Young Politician* (Toronto: Macmillan, 1952).

xiii Quoted in Joseph Pope, *Memoirs of the Right Honourable Sir John Alexander Macdonald, G.C.B., First Prime Minister of the Dominion of Canada*, volume I (London: Edward Arnold, 1894), 229.

xiv Claude Bélanger, "The Powers of Disallowance and Reservation in Canadian Federalism," (Montreal Marianopolis College), 19 February 2001, http://faculty.marianopolis.edu/c.belanger/quebechistory/ federal/disallow.htm.

xv Ibid.

xvi Ibid.

xvii Ibid.

xviii "Responsible Government," www.historicacanada.ca, undated.

xix See, for example, J.M.S. Careless, *Careless at Work: Selected Canadian Historical Studies* (Toronto: Dundurn Press, 1996), 67-77.

xx Howard Pawley, "Mulroney, Me and the CF-18," *Winnipeg Free Press*, 19 March 2011.

xxi Ernest R. Forbes, ed., *Challenging the Regional Stereotype: Essays on the 20th Century Maritimes* (Fredericton: Acadiensis Press, 1989), 180.

xxii "Atlantic Canada lawyers challenge Trudeau on changes to Supreme Court appointment," www.cbc.ca/news, 19 September 2016.

xxiii Supreme Court of Canada, *Reference Re: Senate Reform SSC32*, File no. 35203 (Ottawa: Supreme Court of Canada [2014]), par. 16, 13.

xxiv Brad Wall wrote this on 24 May 2013, on his Facebook account, www.facebook.com/PremierBrad Wall/posts/10161623726474267.

xxv Canadian Press, "Montreal-Area Mayors' Energy East Criticisms 'Short Sighted': Notley Says," *CTV News Atlantic*, 22 January 2016, http://atlantic.ctvnews.ca/montreal-area-mayors-energy-east-criticisms-short -sighted-notley-says-1.2748041.

xxvi Richard Gwyn, *Nation Builder: Sir John A. Macdonald – His Life, Our Times, Volume Two: 1867-1891* (Toronto: Vintage Canada, 2012), 43.

xxvii Donald J. Savoie, *Governing from the Centre: The Concentration of Power in Canadian Politics* (Toronto: University of Toronto Press, 1999).

xxviii Senator Lowell Murray, "Power, Responsibility and Agency in Canadian Government," in *Governing: Essays in Honour of Donald J. Savoie*, James Bickerton and B. Guy Peters, eds. (Montreal: McGill-Queen's University Press, 2013), 27; and Janice Gross Stein and Eugene Lang, *The Unexpected War: Canada in Kandahar* (Toronto: Viking Canada Press, 2007), 2.

xxix "PMO completes hiring chiefs of staff to 26 cabinet ministers, 10 ministers still waiting to recruit their top aides," *The Hill Times*, 9 December 2019.

xxx "Prime Minister Welcomes New Cabinet," www.pm.gc.ca, 20 November 2019.

xxxi Donald V. Smiley and Ronald L. Watts, Intrastate Federalism in Canada (Toronto: University of Toronto Press,1985).

xxxii See, among others, Donald V. Smiley and Ron Watts, *Intrastate Federalism in Canada* (Toronto: University of Toronto Press, 1985).

xxxiii See, Donald J. Savoie, *Democracy in Canada: The Disintegration of Our Institutions* (Montreal: McGill-Queen's University Press, 2019), 282-83.

xxxiv *Supplementary Estimates (2) 2014-15* (Ottawa: Parliamentary Budget Office, 26 February 2015).

xxxv See, among others, "Le programme fédéral de décentralisation : un réexamen," *Canadian Public Policy*, vol. XII, no. 3 (September 1986).

xxxvi I note, however, that McGuinty later apologized. See, Steven Chase, "Liberal MP McGuinty Apologizes for Comments; Resigns as Energy Critic," *Globe and Mail*, 21 November 2012, A3.

xxxvii Greg Keenan, "Canadian taxpayers lose $3.5-billion on 2009 bailout of auto sector," *Globe and Mail*, 7 April 2015, https://www.theglobeandmail.com/report-on-business/canadian-taxpayers-lose-35-billion -on-2009-bailout-of-auto-firms/article23828543/.

xxxviii Robert Fife and Steven Chase, "Davie shipyard suspected Scott Brison of favouring Irving in dispute: affidavits," *Globe and Mail*," 23 August 2017, https://www.theglobeandmail.com/news/politics/ davie-shipyard-suspected-scott-brison-of-favouring-irving-in-dispute-affidavits/article36076369/.

xxxix Jeffrey Simpson, "State of the nation," *Globe and Mail*, 1 July 2016, https://www.theglobeandmail.com/ news/politics/globe-politics-insider/jeffrey-simpson-state-of-the-nation/article30716505/.

xl Eric Andrew-Gee, "Is the West fed up with Canada? What a new survey shows about the federation's growing fault lines," *Globe and Mail*, 23 March 2019, https://www.theglobeandmail.com/canada/ article-is-the-west-fed-up-with-canada-what-a-new-survey-shows-about-the/.

xli Ralph Allen, "The unknown giant K.C. Irving," *Maclean's*, 18 April 1964, https://archive.macleans.ca/ article/1964/4/18/the-unknown-giant-k-c-irving.

xlii Stéphane Dion, "Institutional Reform: The Grass Isn't Always Greener on the Other Side," in Hans J. Michelmann, Donald C. Story, and Jeffrey S. Steeves eds., *Political Leadership and Representation in Canada: Essays in Honour of John C. Courtney* (Toronto: University of Toronto Press, 2007), 185.

xliii "New Senate group forms to push regional interests in a fractured Parliament," www.thecanadianpress. com, 4 November 2019.

xliv For a persuasive argument on the centralizing bias of the Supreme Court, see F. L. Morton and Dave Snow, *Law, Politics, and the Judicial Process in Canada*, 4th Edition (Calgary: University of Calgary Press, 2018), Section 11.

Chapter Six: Mansell

i Although, as noted by Whalley and Trela (1986, p.192), the interregional effects of energy policies tend to dominate the interregional impacts of all other non-fiscal policies.

ii Note that unlike the case of personal debt such as a mortgage where the interest and amortized principal are regularly and jointly paid, the principal of federal debt is typically rolled over from year to year and, as such, not repaid.

iii For example, the fiscal equalization program was introduced in 1961, the Canada Pension Plan was created in 1965 and the Medical Care Act was passed in 1966.

iv Also, see Ruggeri and Yu (2000) for a detailed description of the approaches used to estimate the regional distribution of federal fiscal balances.

v As noted in Mansell and Schlenker (1995, p.5), from 1961 to 1972 the National Oil Policy resulted in a net transfer to Alberta of $1.8 billion (1994 dollars). This situation was reversed after 1972 until the mid-1980s as a result of federal price controls and then implementation of the National Energy Program in the early 1980s. Not counting the substantial additional taxation of the oil and gas industry, this program alone resulted in a net transfer of $69.8 billion (in 1994 dollars) out of Alberta and primarily toward Ontario and Quebec.

vi See annual values in Appendix Table 1.

vii See annual values in Appendix Table 1.

viii See values in Appendix Table 2.

ix That is, for individuals the federal income tax payable on personal incomes rises as income levels increase.

There are two effects at play. A region with higher incomes contributes more per capita the higher are per capita incomes and the more progressive is the tax.

x Most individuals with taxable incomes in excess of $12,000 will pay federal personal income taxes. Such taxes are, at first, 15 per cent of each incremental dollar earned, and rise to 33 per cent for incomes in excess of roughly $214,368 (the top income tax bracket for 2020). This tax structure implies that the average share of total income paid in income taxes is increasing in one's income. Those in the bottom 5 per cent of Canada's income distribution, for example, paid only 0.2 per cent of their income in income taxes in 2017, while the top 5 per cent paid nearly 27 per cent of theirs. Since the distribution of income across provinces is not identical, average federal income taxes paid will differ. Of Canada's top decile earners, 475,000 live in Alberta (or 17 per cent of the total in Canada), although the province accounts for only 11.6 per cent of the country's population. Prince Edward Island, meanwhile, accounts for only 0.2 per cent of the top decile tax filers, but 0.4 per cent of the country's total population. These differences mean the aggregate personal income tax payments per capita in Alberta will be larger on account of more high-income-earning individuals residing there.

xi Recall that a 5 per cent federal GST applies to most consumer purchases in Canada.

xii For example the federal stabilization (insurance) payment to the Alberta government of $60 per capita (or $248 million in total) in 2015-16 is in comparison to the drop of $2114 per capita (or $8.8 billion in total) in Alberta government revenues that year. (Dahlby, 2019).

xiii For a detailed discussion of the components of personal income in the SNA (system of national accounts) used in this paper, see https://www23.statcan.gc.ca/imdb/p3Var.pl?Function=DEC&Id=100736. In summary, personal income consists of before-tax income from employment (primarily wages, salaries and commissions), net income from self-employment, (that is, net income from unincorporated enterprises), investment and retirement income (interest, dividends and private pension plan payments), other market income, and income in the form of government transfer payments (such as Canada and Quebec Pension Plan payments, Employment Insurance payments, child benefits, social assistance benefits, workers compensation benefits, working income tax benefits , GST and HST credits and other transfers).

xiv For example, between 2013 and 2018 the ratio of personal income to GDP in Ontario and Quebec was essentially unchanged whereas in Alberta it went from 66 per cent to 72 per cent and in Saskatchewan it went from 63 per cent to 79 per cent.

xv For example, non-residents may obtain a share of the profits or payments to capital and, to this extent, GDP for the region will be an over-estimate of income received by residents of the region. Personal income is what each resident actually receives, and this can include income derived from elsewhere.

xvi See Mansell, Khanal and Tombe (2020).

Chapter Seven: Emery & Fellows

i https://www.rom.on.ca/en/blog/canada-old-cow

ii Courchene (1999, 24) observes that "British Columbia is oriented towards the Pacific Rim and the U.S. Northwest; the energy-based Alberta economy competes with the oil and gas producing regions of the Texas Gulf; the breadbaskets of Saskatchewan and Manitoba keep a competitive watch on the U.S. Midwest; the Great Lakes economies of Ontario and Quebec are integrated with each other and with their counterparts south of the border; and the fortunes of Atlantic Canada likely will increasingly be linked to the Atlantic Rim and the Boston/New York".

iii Shortly after the election of Stephen Harper's Conservative government with an Ontario-Western Canada coalition, Courchene (2007) observed that Alberta's "economic and fiscal pre-eminence" arising from its energy economy since 2000 have not translated in a corresponding degree of political power and influence within Canada. While the Harper Conservatives led Canada for a decade, the West seems to have little power and influence under the Trudeau Liberal government elected in 2015.

iv Courchene (1999, 22-23, 29) argues that "if Ontario could not be the location of the next North America auto assembly plant, then the province would obviously prefer a Michigan location to a Vancouver location."

v Courchene (1999, 27) predicted that "As north-south integration intensifies further, both in terms of trade flows and even more importantly in terms of arrangements/ agreements covering trade, institutional and legal issues, it will become progressively more difficult for the provinces to tolerate abrupt shifts in the Canadian/US exchange rate... Over the last quarter century the Canadian dollar has moved from 104 US cents per dollar in the early 1970s to 71 cents in 1986 to 89 cents in 1981, to the low-to-mid 70 cent range for most of the 1990s, culminating with a plunge to just over 63 cents in August of 1998... increased attention is now being directed to the case for fixing the Canadian dollar to the US dollar".

vi Tammy Nemeth "Continental Drift: Canada—U.S. Oil and Gas Relations, 1958-1988" (PhD., diss, University of British Columbia, 2005), points out that this was done through the U.S. Mandatory Oil Import Program or MOIP, from which Canada was exempted.

vii MacFadyen and Watkins (2014, 118)

viii Description of Alberta and energy in the 1980s from Emery (2006).

ix James Laxer (1983, 118-119).

x Bunner (2003).

xi Mansell and Schlenker (1995).

xii Mansell (1997, 26).

xiii Doern and Toner *The Politics of Energy Appendix III*. The price for "old oil" conventionally produced from existing fields was to rise to 75 percent of the world price, and was expected to be $57.75 by mid-1986. The price for "new oil", produced from newly discovered fields, oil sands or in frontier regions, would fetch the world price expected to be $77.48 in 1986.

xiv Fellows and Mertin (1990); McRae (1982)

xv Fellows and Mertin (1990); Watkins (1984)

xvi Statistics Canada, Supply Use Tables, 2015 Catalogue 15-602-X

xvii This model is described in Fellows et al. (2018). The modelling of the trade shocks is based on the approach used in Fellows and Tombe (2018).

xviii Specifically, sensitivity analysis using increases in the modelled tariff well above 100 percent produce trade reductions that are only marginally higher than 75%.

xix The model doesn't account for any investment/capital-formation linkages. So, as interprovincial oil and gas exports are reduced with higher trade costs, there is no direct impact on investment demand to the rest of Canada in the model. There is an indirect impact, because the "representative agent" has less to spend on investment due to lower GDP so investment demand drops.

xx The calibration data comes from the Statistics Canada symmetric input-output tables and uses the North American Industry Classification System (NAICS) at roughly the 2-digit level. The small GDP reductions in other provinces relative to the GDP loss from restricted interprovincial trade generally reflects that exports of crude oil and natural gas in the model do not include the value of refined products like gasoline, diesel, petroleum chemicals etc. (as these are counted as "manufactured goods" in the underlying calibration data). Refined products are an important part of the values of overall interprovincial trade.

xxi http://www.ctvnews.ca/politics/mcguinty-resigns-critic-post-for-saying-mps-should-go-back-to-alberta-1.1047079#ixzz2OfxjN1G2 It seems that at least four MPs have taken his advice. Jim Prentice returned to Alberta to be Premier, as did Jason Kenney. Brian Jean returned to Alberta to lead the provincial Wildrose Party. Stephen Harper and Rona Ambrose have returned to Alberta and presumably lend their expertise to provincial MPs and MLAs with respect to selling the Alberta energy sector to the rest of Canada.

xxii Alberta Senator Doug Black said "[Morneau] went one step further yesterday which is to say we're hoping to find some kind of programs that are agnostic to the industry. By that I presume he meant that there could be one-size-fits-all. Well, there isn't one-size-fits-all for industries in this country. ... I am concerned." Sarah

Regier 'What's the hold-up?' Alberta senators want to know when help for the energy industry is coming Sarah Rieger · CBC News · Posted: Apr 13, 2020 6:56 PM MT https://www.cbc.ca/news/canada/calgary/oil-and-gas-federal-support-1.5531151

xxiii Laurie Adkin & Debra Davidson, "265 academics to Trudeau: No bail out for oil and gas in response to COVID-19" The National Observer, March 25, 2020. "A bailout for the oil and gas industry? Here's why experts say it's not a long-term solution", Sharon J. Riley Mar 24, 2020 *The Narwhal*. The experts consulted, several from Alberta, and the IEA, posit that the oil era is rapidly coming to an end and Alberta should only be given aid to transition to greener alternative economy. There is also a view that workers, not companies or a sector, should be the target for support.

xxiv John Ivison, "Grits couldn't resist anti-oil pandering on business backstop", *National Post*, May 11, 2020. https://nationalpost.com/opinion/john-ivison-liberals-couldnt-resist-anti-oil-pandering-with-their-badly-needed-business-backstop

xxv Tom Courchene, Policy Options, Jan-Feb 2000, page 102. Tom Courchene replies [Is Ontario a region-state?] Courchene, Thomas J.Policy Options; Montreal Vol. 21, Iss. 1, (Jan/Feb 2000): 100-105.

xxvi https://business.financialpost.com/news/economy/turns-out-theres-more-to-albertas-economic-story-than-pipelines

xxvii Ben Brunnen and Tom Kmiec, *Policy Options*, March 2013, page 44

xxviii Fellows (2018)

xxix "An imperializing Athens demands tribute from the autonomous island of Melos. The Melians prefer their independence. The Athenians reply that independence is no longer possible. When the Melians protest that such strong-arming is not fair, the Athenians respond that fairness can only exist among equals; this about power not fairness." (Heaman 2017.)

Chapter Eight: Burney & Hampson

i The authors would like to thank Philip Hampson and Glenn Mifflin for their observations and suggestions on an earlier draft of this paper and Christopher Anthony for his research assistance.

ii The Royal Commission on the Canadian Economy led by former Liberal finance minister Donald Macdonald preceded Canada's free trade negotiations with the United States by laying the analytical groundwork for the removal of longstanding barriers to trade as well as helping to build public and political support for free trade.

iii Government of Alberta, *Economic Dashboard*, Gross Domestic Product. Available at: https://economicdashboard.alberta.ca/GrossDomesticProduct.

iv Ibid.

v Simon Richards, *Economics*, Resources and International Affairs Division Parliamentary Information and Research Service, *Trade and Investment: Alberta*, Publication No. 2018-506-E (Ottawa: Library of Parliament, August 2018).

vi Government of Alberta, Economic Commentary: Inter-Provincial Exports, March 16, 2018.

vii Ibid.

viii Carl Meyer, "Guess Where Quebec Got Its Oil," *National Observer*, November 13, 2018.

ix Government of Alberta, Alberta's Imports from the other Provinces and Territories, April 19, 2018.

x Ibid.

xi Business Council of British Columbia, Ties that Bind: Economic Interdependence between B.C. and Alberta, May 2019.

xii Government of Alberta, Alberta's Imports from the other Provinces and Territories.

xiii Steve Lafleur, Ben Eisen and Milagros Palacios, *A Friend in Need: Recognizing Alberta's Outsized Contribution to Confederation* (Vancouver, B.C.: Fraser Institute, 2017).

xiv Nina Lakhani, "Major blow to Keystone XL pipeline as judge revokes key permit," *The Guardian*, April 16, 2020.

xv Fletcher, "Alberta face 'mild recession.'"

xvi Portions of this discussion about the recent history of pipelines are adapted from our forthcoming book, *Braver Canada: Shaping Our Destiny in a Precarious World* (Montreal and Kingston: McGill-Queen's Press).

xvii Shawn McCarthy and Jeff Lewis, "Court Overturns Ottawa's Approval of Northern Gateway Pipeline," *Globe and Mail*, 30 June 2016.

xviii National Energy Board, Government of Canada, "Energy East and Eastern Mainline Projects," 2019, https://www.cer-rec.gc.ca/pplctnflng/mjrpp/nrgyst/index-eng.html?=undefined&cwbdisable=true.

xix Kalina Lafromboise and Kamila Hickson, "Quebec Politicians, Environmentalists Hail Demise of Controversial Energy East Pipeline," *CBC News*, 5 October 2017.

xx Bruce Cheadle, "Justin Trudeau Halts Northern Gateway, Approves Kinder Morgan Expansion, Line 3," *Global News*, 29 November 2016.

xxi Cited in "'It's What's in the Pipeline': Green Party Outlines Plan to Only Use Canadian Crude," *CBC News*, 28 May 2019.

xxii Department of Finance Canada, "Agreement Reached to Create and Protect Jobs, Build Trans Mountain Expansion Project," 29 May 2018, https://www.fin.gc.ca/news-nouvelles/speeches-discours/2018/2018-05-29-eng.asp.

xxiii John Paul Tasker, "Trudeau cabinet approves Trans Mountain expansion project," *CBC News*, June 18, 2019.

xxiv Shawn McCarthy, Justine Hunter, and James Keller, "NEB Says Trans Mountain Pipeline Expansion in Public Interest Despite 'Adverse' Impact on Whale Population," *Globe and Mail*, 22 February 2019.

xxv House of Commons of Canada, 1st Session, 42nd Parliament, 21 June 2019, Bill C-48, An Act Respecting the Regulation of Vessels That Transport Crude Oil or Persistent Oil to or from Ports or Marine Installations Located along British Columbia's North Coast, https://www.parl.ca/LegisInfo/BillDetails.aspx?Language=E&billId=8936657&View=0.

xxvi House of Commons of Canada, 1st Session, 42nd Parliament, 21 June 2019, Bill C-69, An Act to Enact the Impact Assessment Act and the Canadian Energy Regulator Act, to Amend the Navigation Protection Act and to Make Consequential Amendments to Other Acts, https://www.parl.ca/legisinfo/BillDetails.aspx?Language=E&billId=9630600.

xxvii Cited in Nelson Bennett, "Canada Lost $100B in Energy Projects in Two Years: Report," *JWN: Trusted Energy Intelligence*, 13 March 2019, https://www.jwnenergy.com/article/2019/3/canada-just-lost-100b-can-celled-stalled-oil-and-gas-projects-report/. Cited in Geoff Zochodne, "'We're Squandering an Opportunity': CEOs of RBC and Enbridge Urge Action on Energy Strategy," Financial Post, 21 February 2019.

xxviii Geogg Zochodne, "'We're squandering an opportunity': CEOs of RBC and Enbridge urge action on energy strategy," *Financial Post*, February 21, 2019.

xxix Bryce Baschuk, "Trade Peace May Hurt Countries Left Out of the U.S.-China Deal," *Bloomberg*, January 14, 2020.

xxx Barrie McKenna, "The U.S.-China trade deal is bad for Canada – and we can't do a thing about it," *Globe & Mail*, January 12, 2020.

xxxi Jacob M. Schlesinger, "Will the U.S. Bring Down the WTO?" *The Wall Street Journal*, November 28, 2019.

xxxii Quoted in McKenna, "Trade Peace May Hurt Countries Left Out of the U.S.-China Deal."

xxxiii *Canadian Free Trade Agreement*, Consolidated Text and First Protocol of Amendment, December 10, 2019. Available at: https://www.cfta-alec.ca/canadian-free-trade-agreement/.

xxxiv Rita Trichur, "Jason Kenney and Brian Pallister are Ottawa's best hopes for fixing interprovincial trade," *The Globe and Mail*, December 19, 2019. Also see, Calgary Chamber of Commerce, "Government of Alberta Lifts More Internal Trade Restrictions," September 23, 2019.

xxxv *New West Partnership Agreement 2019*. Available at: http://www.newwestpartnershiptrade.ca/pdf/NWPTA_Jan_1_2019.pdf.

xxxvi International Monetary Fund, "Canada: Staff Concluding Statement of the 2019 Article IV Mission," May 21, 2019.

xxxvii Martha Hall Findlay, "Internal trade barriers make Canada less attractive for foreign investment," *The Globe and Mail*, October 2, 2019.

xxxviii Jessie Snyder, "'Not going to do anything:' Oil executives say federal abandoned well program comes too late," *National Post*, April 17, 2019.

xxxix See Geoffrey Morgan, "Shockproofing Canada: Why we need a Strategic Petroleum Reserve of our own," *Financial Post*, April 8, 2020.

xl Emma Foehringer Merchant, "With 43 Carbon-Capture Projects Lined Up Worldwide, Supporters Cheer Industry Momentum," *Greentechmedia.com*, 11 December 2018, https://www.greentechmedia.com/articles/read/carbon-capture-gains-momentum.

xli Charles Lammam and Taylor Jackson, *Examining the Revenue Neutrality of British Columbia's Carbon Tax* (Vancouver, B.C.: Fraser Institute, 2017). Also see, Nick Murray, "Nunavut Gov't Unveils the First Part of Carbon Taz Mitigation Measures," CBC News, May 30, 2019.

xlii Dan Healing, "Canadian petrochemical growth spurt expected despite rising desire for fewer plastics," The Canadian Press, January 17, 2017. Also see, Canadian Energy Research Institute, *Competitive Analysis of Canadian Petrochemical Sector*, Study No. 160 (CERI: Calgary, October 2016); and Canadian Energy Research Institute, *Examining the Expansion Potential of the Petrochemical Industry in Canada*, Study No. 153 (CERI: Calgary, August 2015).

xliii See, Emma Lui, "Suncor sneaks tar sands tankers into St. Lawrence and Great Lakes," *Rabble.ca*, October 9, 2014. There are also other ideas in circulation. See, for example, "Retired oil worker floats proposal to ship Alberta bitumen through Thunder Bay," *CBC News*, March 17, 2019.

xliv See Government of Canada, "Tanker Safety by the Numbers Infographic." Available at: https://www.tc.gc.ca/eng/marinesafety/tanker-safety-infographic-4382.html.

xlv Suncor, "Oil traffic no stranger to the St. Lawrence," Oil Sands Question and Response, February 4, 2014. Available at: https://osqar.suncor.com/2015/02/oil-traffic-no-stranger-to-the-st-lawrence--1.html.

xlvi Geoffrey Morgan, "Irving Oil finally gets approval to source Alberta oil — but through the Panama Canal," *Financial Post*, May 4, 2020.

xlvii See, for example, Bill Kaufman, "Albertans sympathetic with separatist feelings but wouldn't vote to leave: poll," *Calgary Herald*, October 18, 2019. But public opinion could shift in the other direction as economic conditions in the province worsen in a post-COVID19 world. It is also interesting to note the degree of affinity that Albertans have with Americans, which is also born out in public surveys. See, for example, "Britanny Burr, "Almost 50percent of Albertans Admit They're More Like Americans Than Other Canadians," *Narcity*, August 15, 2019.

xlviii In such a scenario, one also has to ask what would be in it for the US. Any kind of common market arrangement or customs union would probably include Alberta's adoption of the US dollar and the harmonization of most commercial laws. Alberta may also have to establish joint defense arrangements with the United States.

xlix This would be done, possibly with Saskatchewan, in conjunction with deliberate efforts at Options 1 and 2.

Chapter Nine: Ogle

i Alberta and Saskatchewan growth is three times more volatile that the average for all provinces, mainly due to higher dependence on resource sectors. Prior to the MRF, the Alberta Royalty Framework was created in 2007 and applies to oil and gas wells drilled before December 31, 2016. Wells drilled before this date are grandfathered to the end of 2026, at which point they move to the MRF. It also treats hydrocarbons differently from each other.

ii http://unohrlls.org/custom-content/uploads/2013/09/The-Rights-of-Land-Locked-States-in-the-International-Law-The-Role-of-Bilateral-and-Multilateral-Agreements.pdf. https://www.nasdaq.com/market-activity/commodities/ng%3anmx

iii S.Thomson, "Canada is broken" February 2020. https://nationalpost.com/news/one-thing-canadians-arent -divided-on-blaming-the-government-for-theblockades. https://www.policyschool.ca/wp-content/uploads/2016/03/mckenzie-mintz-fossil-fuel.pdf

iv This order-in-council was rescinded in 1910 and thereafter petroleum and natural gas rights were leased for defined periods. See David H. Breen, *Alberta's Petroleum Industry and the Conservation Board* (Edmonton Alberta: The University of Alberta Press, 1993), 6-7. Later in 1910, as the arms race in Europe accelerated and the strategic importance of oil from a naval perspective was amplified, the Canadian government reserved the right to expropriate all oil products for the use of "His Majesty's Canadian navy.", 7. https://business.financialpost.com/opinion/imfs-imagined-34-billion-silly-stats-are-behind-claims -that-canada-subsidizes-oil-industry

v Ibid, 52-3. https://www.taxpayer.com/media/CorporateWelfareCash.pdf

vi In 1930 the British Parliament approved the *Constitution Act* which entrenched the Natural Resource Transfer Agreements. http://www.solon.org/Constitutions/Canada/English/ca_1930.html. Vanessa Corkal, Julia Levin, Philip Gass, Canada's Federal Fossil Fuel Subsidies in 2020, The International Institute for Sustainable Development (February 2020) https://www.iisd.org/sites/default/files/publications/canada-fossil-fuel-subsidies-2020-en.pdf

vii Albertans own 81% of the province's mineral rights and the Alberta government manages those resources on their behalf. The remaining 19% is owned by the federal government, individuals, and corporations. https://www.capp.ca/resources/statistics/

viii Oil and Gas Taxation in Canada, Price Waterhouse Coopers (2016) https://www.pwc.com/ca/en/energy-utilities/publications/pwc-oil-gas-taxation-2016-09-en.pdf

and Guide to Oil and Gas Taxation in Canada, KPMG (May 2018) https://assets.kpmg/content/dam/kpmg/ca/pdf/2018/05/oil-gas-guide.pdf

Capital expenditures in the US increased consistently from 2008-2018, except for the severe 2009 recession and 2016. Capital expenditures in 2018 for Canada were around 19 percent higher than in 2008, whereas US capital expenditures in 2018 were about 40 percent higher than in 2008.
https://www.fraserinstitute.org/sites/default/files/investment-in-canadian-and-us-oil-and-gas-sector.pdf

ix https://ecofiscal.ca/reports/bridging-gap-real-options-meeting-canadas-2030-ghg-target/

x https://www.econlib.org/library/Enc/bios/Nordhaus.html

xi United Nations Special Report, "Global Warming of 1.5°C," Intergovernmental Panel on Climate Change (IPCC). https://www.ipcc.ch/sr15/

xii W. Nordhaus, (1992), 'The 'DICE' Model: Background and Structure of a Dynamic Integrated Climate-Economy Model of the Economics of Global Warming', Cowles Foundation Discussion Papers No. 1009, Cowles Foundation for Research in Economics, Yale University.

xiii World Bank. (2020). Data Bank. https://databank.worldbank.org/home.aspx

xiv Business Council of Canada. (2019, October 30). A Better Future for Canadians – Report and Recommendations. https://thebusinesscouncil.ca/publications/a-better-future-for-canadians-report-and -recommendations/

xv Business Council of Alberta. (2019, November 1). https://www.businesscouncilab.com/work/canadian -economy-doing-worse-than-we-think/

xvi Statistics Canada. (2020). Gross domestic product, expenditure-based, Canada, quarterly (x1,000,000). https://www150.statcan.gc.ca/t1/tbl1/en/cv.action?pid=3610010401

xvii United Nations Conference on Trade and Development. (2019). Country Facts Sheets 2019. https://unctad.org/en/Pages/DIAE/World%20Investment%20Report/Country-Fact-Sheets.aspx https://unctad.org/en/Pages/DIAE/World%20Investment%20Report/Country-Fact-Sheets.aspx

xviii The World Bank. (2018). International LPI: Global Rankings 2018. https://lpi.worldbank.org/international/global

xix B. P. W. Robson, (2019), "Thin Capitalization: Weak Business Investment Undermines Canadian Workers" C.D. HOWE Institute: Commentary.

xx Data: Statistics Canada; Analysis: Viewpoint Research, https://www.macvw.ca/

xxi Mac Van Wielingen, "Canada in Crisis: Neglect of Essential Fundamentals and the Failure of Governance" (2020) https://static1.squarespace.com/static/5b621c23f8370a2a9d28c0e9/t/5e9a8c160feebf4d4810c99d/1587186717821/Canada+in+Crisis+-+Mac+Van+Wielingen+-+CAPP+Speaking+Notes_April+8+2020.pdf

xxii Ibid.

xxiii Canadian Energy Research Institute, "Competitiveness of Canada's Regulatory Framework for the Oil and Gas Sector" (April 2020)
https://ceri.ca/studies/competitiveness-of-canadas-regulatory-framework-for-the-oil-and-gas-sector

xxiv Rohmer's grand plan was to settle a 'second Canada' below the Arctic. 'Mid-Canada' would have new highways, railways, and booming resource-based metropolises. R. Rohmer, *The Green North* (Toronto: Maclean-Hunter, 1970).

xxv https://nationalpost.com/news/canada/the-grandiose-but-failed-1960s-plan-by-an-ontario-war-hero-to-settle-a-second-canada-below-the-arctic

xxvi The construction of the original TransCanada mainline was such a time. In the mid-1950s, TransCanada was a fledgling corporation with no assets, not big enough to complete a project of that magnitude. Construction was to begin in the summer of 1956, two years behind schedule. When financial problems threatened construction, the Ontario and federal governments agreed to form a Crown corporation, Northern Ontario Pipeline, to pay for the portion of the line through the worst part of the Canadian Shield. Unfortunately, TransCanada needed help as well, and the corporation turned to the federal government for financial aid. In May of that year, Howe proposed a bill whereby the Crown corporation would loan TransCanada $80 million, repayable a year later or TransCanada would turn the whole project over to the government. For construction to begin by summer 1956, this proposed bill needed to move rapidly through Parliament. In June of 1956, the Liberal government of Louis St. Laurent invoked closure in the House of Commons so that construction of the pipeline could begin. This overt action was led by C.D. Howe, the federal minister of trade and commerce, and caused uproar in the House. The Opposition claimed patronage, secrecy, abuse of power and lack of due process. Nonetheless, the Liberals stifled debate at the committee level, rushed the bill through first and second readings, and used closure to force third reading and approval. Many believe that the imposition of closure contributed to the demise of the St. Laurent government in 1957. However, one could also argue that had the St. Laurent Liberals, led by How, not done this, the TransCanada mainline may never have been built.

xxvii In April 2020, the Keystone XL pipeline was dealt a major setback, after a judge revoked a key permit issued by the US army corps of engineers did not properly assessing the impact on endangered species. In a legal challenge brought by a coalition of environmental groups, a federal judge in Montana ordered the army corps to suspend all filling and dredging activities until it conducts formal consultations compliant with the Endangered Species Act. The ruling revokes the water-crossing permit needed to complete construction of the pipeline, and is expected to cause major delays to the project. https://www.eenews.net/stories/1062981533; https://www.eenews.net/stories/1062937033

xxviii Andrei Sulzenko and G. Kent Fellows, "Planning for Infrastructure to Realize Canada's Potential: The Corridor Concept," (Volume 9, Issue 22, May 2016)
file:///C:/Users/kjogl/Dropbox/Personal%20Documents/Current%20Writing/Resource%20Development/northern-corridor-sulzenko-fellows.pdf

xxix Manitoba recently completed a long transmission line of its own from northern dams to southern communities. It cost $5 billion to cover roughly 1,400 kilometres, less than the distance from Winnipeg to Toronto. Manitoba's Progressive Conservative government pushed the idea of cross-country grid at a national energy industry conference in 2017 but said federal money would be needed to get it built. https://www.thespec.com/news/canada/2019/09/24/singh-promises-cross-canada-clean-energy-corridor-electric-transit.html

xxx Standing Senate Committee on Banking, Trade and Commerce, "National Corridor Enhancing and Facilitating Commerce and Internal Trade," The Honourable David Tkachuk, Chair, the Honourable Joseph A. Day, Deputy Chair, (June 2017). file:///C:/Users/kjogl/Dropbox/Personal%20Documents/Current%20Writing/Resource%20Development/CorridorStudy(Final-Printing)_e.pdf

xxxi Ibid, p.14. Between 5 October 2016 and 2 April 2017, a multitude of experts were called upon to discuss the corridor concept. p.44.

xxxii P. Whitney Lackenbauer and Suzanne Lalonde, "Breaking the Ice Curtain? Russia, Canada, and Arctic Security in a Changing Circumpolar World", Canadian Global Affairs Institute (2019) https://d3n8a8pro7vhmx.cloudfront.net/cdfai/pages/4193/attachments/original/1558816637/Breaking_the_Ice_Curtain.pdf?1558816637 and Andrea Charron and Jim Fergusson, "NORAD: Beyond Modernization" Centre for Defence and Security Studies University of Manitoba (January 2019) https://umanitoba.ca/centres/cdss/media/NORAD_beyond_modernization_2019.pdf

xxxiii Conversation via email with Dr. Jennifer Winter, 8 June 2020. See also, www.canadiancorridor.ca.

xxxiv Deloitte Canada, "Canada's history of boldness: How business and government can learn from our past to achieve more in the future." https://www.canada175.ca/en/blog/canadas-history-boldness-how-business-and-government-can-learn-our-past-achieve-more-our

xxxv https://www.newswire.ca/news-releases/canada-infrastructure-bank-and-government-of-alberta-sign-a-memorandum-of-understanding-for-the-calgary-banff-rail-project-813557592.html

xxxvi Mary Janigan, *Let the Eastern Bastards Freeze in the Dark: The West versus the Rest since Confederation* (Toronto: Alfred A. Knopf Canada, 2012), 334

xxxvii Tammy Lynn Nemeth, "Canada-U.S. Oil and gas Relations 1958-1974" (PhD Thesis, University of British Columbia, May 2007), 32.

xxxviii https://www.nrcan.gc.ca/sites/www.nrcan.gc.ca/files/energy/pdf/Energy%20Fact%20Book_2019_2020_web-resolution.pdf

xxxix Canada's total refining capacity is 295 103m3/d (1.9 MMb/d) (Figure 3). Quebec and Atlantic Canada have the most refining capacity at 124 103m3/d (782 Mb/d), followed by Western Canada at 109 103m3/d (686 Mb/d) and Ontario at 62 103m3/d (390 Mb/d). https://www.cer-rec.gc.ca/nrg/sttstc/crdlndptrlmprdct/rprt/2018rfnryrprt/cndsrfnrs-eng.html

xl Aaron Hutchins, Buy Alberta? Prepare for a civil War? What Americans think in the age of Trump, Macleans (June 18, 2020) https://www.macleans.ca/news/world/buy-alberta-prepare-for-a-civil-war-what-americans-think-in-the-age-of-trump/?utm_source=OneSignal&utm_medium=WebNotifications&utm_campaign=MME_WN&utm_term=18-Jun-2020&utm_content=America_poll

xli Peter Zeihan, "The Accidental Superpower" Twelve Hatchett Book Group, New York NY, 2014, p.252-259.

xlii Ibid.

xliii https://ca.rbcwealthmanagement.com/harp.dhillon/blog/2250766-GDP-Per-Capita--Canadian-provinces-and-US-states Developed by Trevor Tombe, associate professor at the University of Calgary, incorporating data from Statistics Canada on 2018 provincial economic accounts, the map is a reflection of GDP per capita in each of the Canadian provinces and U.S. states, in U.S. dollar terms (adjusted for purchasing power parity).

Chapter Ten: Albert

i Reference re Secession of Quebec, [1998] 2 S.C.R. 217 (Canada). ["Secession Reference"]

ii Secession Reference, para. 83.

iii An Act to give effect to the requirement for clarity as set out in the opinion of the Supreme Court of Canada in the Quebec Secession Reference, S.C. 2000, c. 26. ["Clarity Act"] iv Ibid. para. 87.

v Ibid.

vi Clarity Act, s. 1(1).

vii Ibid. If the official release occurs during a federal general election, the House of Commons has an additional forty days to evaluate the question. Ibid. s. 1(2).

viii Ibid. s. 1(5).

ix Ibid. s. 1(3).

x Ibid. s. 1(4)(a).

xi Secession Reference, para. 87.

xii Ibid.

xiii Secession Reference, para. 88.

xiv Clarity Act, s. 2(1).

xv Ibid. s. 2(3).

xvi Ibid. ss. 1(6), 2(4).

xvii Secession Reference, para. 88.

xviii Ibid. para. 90.

xix Ibid.

xx Ibid. para. 92.

xxi Ibid. para. 97.

xxii See Constitution Act, 1867, 30 & 31 Victoria, c. 3, ss. 22, 37, 40 (U.K.).

xxiii See Supreme Court Act, R.S.C., 1985, c. S-26, s. 6. The Court has constitutionalized this statute, making it no longer amendable by ordinary law. See Reference re Supreme Court Act, ss. 5-6, [2014] 1 S.C.R. 433 (Can.).

xxiv Ibid. para. 96.

xxv See generally *The Secession of Quebec and the Future of Canada*, ed. Robert Young (Montreal: McGill-Queen's University Press 1998) (exploring the costs and consequences of secession in Canada).

xxvi Secession Reference, para. 96.

xxvii Ibid. para. 84.

xxviii Clarity Act, s. 3(2).

xxix Richard Albert, *Constitutional Amendments: Making, Breaking, and Changing Constitutions* (Oxford: Oxford University Press, 2019) 64.

xxx Constitution Act, 1982, s. 45, enacted as Schedule B to the Canada Act 1982, 1982, c. 11 (U.K.)

xxxi Ibid. s. 44.

xxxii Ian Greene, "Constitutional Amendment in Canada and the United States" in *Constitutional Politics in Canada and the United States*, ed. Stephen L. Newman (Albany: State University of New York Press 2004): 249 at 251.

xxxiii Constitution Act, 1982, s. 43.

xxxiv Ibid. s. 41.

xxxv Ibid. s. 38.

xxxvi Ibid. s. 42.

xxxvii Ibid. s. 35.

xxxviii For a discussion, see Richard Albert "The Conventions of Constitutional Amendment in Canada," *Osgoode Hall Law Journal* 53, no. 2 (2016): 399.

xxxix Accordance with International Law of the Unilateral Declaration of Independence in Respect of Kosovo, General List No. 141, International Court of Justice, July 22, 2010, para. 84.

xl Secession Reference, para. 155.

xli Constitution of Spain, s. 2.

xlii Texas v. White. 74 U.S. 700, 726 (1868).

xliii Treaty of the European Union, art. 50(1).

xliv Ibid. art. 50(2).

xlv Ibid. art. 50(3). The European Council and the member state may decide to extend this two-year period but unanimous agreement is required. Ibid.

xlvi What follows in this paragraph and the next is drawn from the platform of Wexit Canada, current as of January 30, 2020. See Wexit Alberta, Platform, available at: https://wexitalberta.com/platform.html.

xlvii Sarah Rieger, "Alberta addresses separatist sentiment by studying measures that would give province more autonomy," CBC News, Nov. 9, 2019.

xlviii Government of Alberta, "Members, mandate for Fair Deal Panel announced," Nov. 9, 2019.

xlix Lisa Johnson, "Alberta 'fair deal' panel report submitted to government, not to be released publicly yet,' *Edmonton Journal*, May 20, 2020.

l Fair Deal Panel, Report to Government, May 2020.

li Ibid. pp. 7-8.

lii Ibid. p. 7.

liii Ibid. p. 9.

liv Ted Morton, one of the co-editors of this volume, has suggested that Alberta needs a fiscal constitution. See F.L. Morton, "Why Alberta Needs a Fiscal Constitution," University of Calgary School of Public Policy Research Papers, v.11:25 (2018), online at: https://www.policyschool.ca/wp-content/uploads/2018/09/Fiscal-Constitution-Morton-final.pdf. I have also previously suggested that provinces should codify their own constitution. See e.g. Richard Albert, "A new Constitution for Ontario and new hope for Doug Ford," *Toronto Star*, August 25, 2019.

lv Jonathan L. Marshfield, "Models of Subnational Constitutionalism," *Pennsylvania State Law Review* 115, no. 4 (2011): 1151, 1158 n. 33.

lvi See Constitution Act, 1982, s. 45 (U.K.) ("[T]he legislature of each province may exclusively make laws amending the constitution of the province."); Constitution Act, 1867, s. 92.1 ("In each Province the Legislature may exclusively make Laws in relation to … The Amendment from Time to Time, notwithstanding anything in this Act, of the Constitution of the Province, except as regards the Office of Lieutenant Governor.") (repealed by Constitution Act, 1982, s. 45).

lvii For example, a provincial assembly must sit at least once every twelve months, Constitution Act, 1982, s. 5. In addition, a province may not deny minority language educational rights. Ibid. s. 23. A province moreover cannot abolish its connection to the monarchy without recourse to a federal-provincial amendment procedure. Ibid. Part V.

lviii For a discussion of the desuetude of the federal government's powers of disallowance and reservation, see Richard Albert, "Constitutional Amendment by Constitutional Desuetude," *American Journal of Comparative Law* 62, no. 3 (2014): 641, 656-69.

Chapter Eleven: Cooper

i https://globalnews.ca/news/4925521/western-canada-party-angus-reid-poll

ii https://theglobeandmail.com/business/commentary/article-how-alberta-will-pay-the-price-for-its-vote/

iii https://theglobeandmail.com/Canada/Toronto/article-get-used-to-it-toronto-is-the-key-to-winning

iv For the first time since records have been kept, 1949, the U.S. became a net exporter of petroleum in September, 2019. See Stephen Cunningham, "U.S. Posts First Full Month as a Petroleum Exporter," *Financial Post*, 30 November, 2019, FPB.

v https://www.nationalpost.com/news/politics/election2019/andrew-coyne-sorry-albertchewan-cabinet-ministers-are-supposed-to-be-elected-not-selected.

vi https://www.theglobeandmail.com/opinion/article-jason-kenneys-dangerous-power-play

vii Gary Mason, "Why Talk of Separatism is Hurting Alberta," *The Globe and Mail*, December 6, 2019, A15.

viii https://www.calgaryherald.com/opinion/columnists/morton-its-time-for-albertas-revolutionary-boston-tea-party-moment

ix See David. J. Bercuson & Barry Cooper, *Deconfederation: Canada without Quebec*, (Toronto, Key Porter, 1991).

x Maura Forrester, "Clash of Alberta and Quebec," *National Post*, (14 November 2019), p.1

xi Clark, "Kenney Should Not Attack Quebec for Blanchet's Remarks," *The Globe and Mail*, 15 November, 2019, A6. A few weeks later, the equally sophisticated Konrad Yakabuski chastised Manitoba premier Brian Pallister for his "unhelpful role in national affairs" for taking out ads in Quebec newspapers criticizing Bill 21. "Good Job, Brian Pallister: You've Only Make Bill 21 Even More Popular in Quebec," *The Globe and Mail*, 5 December, 2019, A15.

xii Braid, "Alberta Premier Shouldn't Take Bloc Quebecois Bait," *Calgary Herald*, 19 November, 2019, A1.

xiii David A. Smith, "A Comparison of Prairie Political Movements in Saskatchewan and Alberta," *Journal of Canadian Studies* 4:1 (1969) 17-25.

xiv See Sylvia van Kirk, *Many Tender Ties: Women in Fur-Trade Society, 1670-1870*, (Winnipeg, Watson and Dwyer, 1980) 2.

xv Cooper, *Alexander Kennedy Isbister: A Respectable Critic of the Honourable Company*, (Ottawa, Carleton University Press, 1988)

xvi Cooper, *Alexander Kennedy Isbister*, 270.

xvii Morton, "Introduction," to *Alexander Begg's Red River Journal*, (Toronto, Champlain Society, 1956), 12.

xviii Creighton, *The Commercial Empire of the St. Lawrence, 1760–1850*, (Toronto, The Ryerson Press, 1937), 1.

xix Creighton, The Commercial Empire, 6-7.

xx I have discussed the political evolution of the West and the parallels with the Thirteen Colonies during the eighteenth century in *It's the Regime, Stupid! A Report from the Cowboy West on Why Stephen Harper Matters* (Toronto, Key Porter, 2009), ch. 3.

xxi See David. E. Smith, "James R. Mallory: His Legacy," *Canadian Journal of Political Science*, 37 (2004) 715-29.

xxii Toronto, University of Toronto Press, 1954.

xxiii Allison Bench, "Hundreds Gather for Wexit Rally in Edmonton as Group's Leader Pens Letter to Jason Kenney," *Global News*, 2 November, 2019.

xxiv https://www.alberta.ca/fair-deal-panel.aspx

xxv Arthur White-Crummey, "Separatism Not the Answer, says Moe, While Refusing to Denounce Views [on independence]" *Regina Leader-Post*, 13 November, 2019. See also Brendan Ellis, "'No Opportunities for Any Benefits': Premier Moe Curbs Separatism Speculation," *CTV News*, 26 November, 2019. Available at: https://regina.ctvnews.ca/no-opportunities-for-any0benefits-premier-moe-curbs-separatism-speculation-/4703477

xxvi See Tom Flanagan, "The Return of the Alberta Agenda" *C2C*, 22 November 2019. See also Mark Milke, "Firewall Fantasies" available at markmilke.com. 1 December 2019.

xxvii See Niels Veldhuis and Jason Clemens, "How Alberta Can Make Ottawa Feel the Pain," *National Post*, 25 October, 2019, A8.

xxviii See Peter W. Hogg. *Constitutional Law of Canada*, 3rd Edition, (Toronto, Carswell, 1992) ch. 6.6; Dan Usher, *The Uneasy Case for Equalization Payments*, (Vancouver, The Fraser Institute, 1995).

xxix *Where the Money Goes: The Distribution of Taxes and Benefits in Canada*, (Toronto, C.D. Howe Institute, 1998) Commentary No. 105.

xxx See Cooper, *It's the Regime, Stupid!*, 177.

xxxi See: Dale Gibson, "The Canada Health Act and the Constitution," *Health Law Journal*, 4 (1996) 1-33; Hogg, Constitutional Law of Canada, ch. 6.6; Lorne Sossin, "Salvaging the Welfare State? The Prospects for Judicial Review of the Canada Health and Social Transfer," *Dalhousie Law Journal*, 21 (1998), 141-98.

xxxii See also the remarks of Pierre-Elliott Trudeau (of all people), *Federalism and the French-Canadians*, (Toronto, Macmillan, 1968), 81.

xxxiii See Cooper, *It's the Regime, Stupid!*, ch.5 and Burton H. Kellock and Sylvia Le Roy, *Questioning the Legality of Equalization*, (Vancouver, The Fraser Institute, 2006), 12-18.

xxxiv E.A. Driedeger, "The Spending Power," *Queen's Law Journal*, 7 (1981), 124.

xxxv Scott, "The Constitutional Background of Taxation Agreements," *McGill Law Journal*, 2 (1955) 1-10. I have discussed this opinion at length in *It's the Regime, Stupid!*, 186-9. See also Andrew Petter, "Federalism and the Myth of the Federal Spending Power," *Canadian Bar Review*, 68 (1989), 448-79.

Chapter Twelve: Bercuson

i Abraham Maslow, *Motivation and Personality*, New York: Harper, 1954.

ii ASSIST, "Security Intelligence Framework Discussion", nd.

iii For discussion of Crown prerogatives in relation to defence see "National Security and Intelligence Committee of Parliamentarians, Annual Report, 2018," p. 73

iv http://www.rcmp-grc.ca/fio-ofi/index-eng.htm

v Department of Homeland Security, National Cyber Awareness System, May 6, 2019.

vi Highlights of the Alberta Economy, 2019

vii *CNN Business*, July 28, 2017.

viii *National Post*, August 13, 2019

ix *Global News*, March 2, 2020.

Chapter Thirteen: Flanagan, Mintz, & Morton

i The Liberals won 147 of the 282 ridings. Eighty-six percent of their MPs came from Ontario (52) and Quebec (74). They did not elect a single MP in British Columbia, Alberta or Saskatchewan.

ii G.Bruce Doern and Glen Toner, *The Politics of Energy: The Development and Implementation of the NEP* (Toronto: Methuen, 1985).

iii In 2015, the Liberals won 184 seats and another majority government with only 4 seats from Alberta and one from Saskatchewan. Ontario (80) and Quebec (40) provided the foundation for the Liberal majority. In the 2109 election, the Liberals again did not win a single seat in Alberta or Saskatchewan, but were kept in power, albeit a minority government, by winning 72 percent (119) of their 157 seats in Ontario (79) and Quebec (40).

iv See "Italy's richest regions vote overwhelmingly for greater autonomy," Rachel Sanderson (October 23, 2017). https://www.ft.com/content/38f625f6-b7dc-11e7-8c12-5661783e5589

v See "Catalan Independence Movement." https://en.wikipedia.org/wiki/Catalan_independence_movement

vi J.R. Mallory, *Social Credit and the Federal Power in Canada*, (University of Toronto Press, 1954), 10, 176.

vii Emery makes the same point: that "Alberta's 'economic and fiscal pre-eminence' arising from its energy economy since 2000 have not translated in a corresponding degree of political power and influence within Canada." Courchene (2007).

viii Donald Savoie, "Politics killed the Energy East Pipeline, *The Globe and Mail*, October 16, 2017. https://www.theglobeandmail.com/opinion/politics-killed-the-energy-east-pipeline/article36606985/

ix Canada ranks 69th of 190 countries in time taken to award construction contracts and well below the OECD average. Next to Hungary, it is the slowest of all OECD countries in arranging electricity connections. World Bank, "Cost of Doing Business 2020", World Bank, Washington D.C. 2020.

x "To connect the pipeline, connect the dots." Tom Flanagan, *Globe and Mail*, August 4, 2012. https://www.theglobeandmail.com/opinion/to-connect-the-pipeline-connect-the-dots/article4461040/

xi See Peter Bowal, "The Supreme Court of Canada Changes Its Mind," *Viewpoint*, January, 2020. https://www.lawnow.org/viewpoint-the-supreme-court-of-canada-changes-its-mind/

xii https://pm.gc.ca/en/news/news-releases/2019/05/14/prime-minister-announces-advisory-board-select-next-supreme-court

xiii Thomas M.J. Bateman, "The Other Shoe to Drop: Mark Nadon and Judicial Appointments Politics in Post-Charter Canada," *Journal of Parliamentary and Political Law* 9:1 (2015), 169-187, at 186,187.

xiv Bateman, 186.

xv See Peter Hogg, *Constitution Act 1982 Annotated*, Toronto: Carswell (1982). 92-93.

xvi Reference re Supreme Court Act, [2014] 1 SCR 433.

xvii Cyr, Hugo. "The Bungling of Justice Nadon's Appointment to the Supreme Court of Canada." *The Supreme Court Law Review: Osgoode's Annual Constitutional Cases Conference* 67. (2014). https://digitalcommons.osgoode.yorku.ca/sclr/vol67/iss1/3/

xviii Cyr, "The Bungling of Justice Nadon's Appointment," 104.

xix Harvey Feigenbaum, Richard Samuels, and R. Kent Weaver. "Innovation, Coordination, and Implementation in Energy Policy." R. Kent Weaver and Bert A. Rockman, editors. *Do Institutions Matter? Government Capabilities in the United States and Abroad.* The Brookings Institution (Washington, D.C.) 1993. 42-110. P.69.

xx Feigenbaum et al, "Institutions Matter," Pp. 67, 68.

xxi Feigenbaum et al, "Institutions Matter," Pp. 54, 55.

xxii The Senate Committee on Energy and Natural Resources is currently chaired by Lisa Murkowski of Alaska. Eight of the 11 Republicans on the committee are from the West, and 3 from the South. None are from the East or West Coast. Of the 9 Democrats on the committee, 4 are from the West and none from the East coast.

xxiii Feigenbaum et al, "Institutions Matter," 70. Also, William Thorsell, "How Trudeau's Energy Policy Sowed the Seeds of Senate Reform," *Globe and Mail* (Toronto), May 30, 1992, D1

xxiv Bateman, 187. Bateman describes this as "constitutionalization of politics."

xxv To win the approval of Quebec (and Ontario), the other provinces agreed to a rule that any deadlock between the Senate and the House of Commons was to be resolved by a joint sitting in which presumably the 337 MPs in Commons could outvote the 62 senators. This is why in the end the Reform Party and most Western Canadians opposed the Charlottetown Accord.

xxvi Jason Kenney, mandate letter, November 9, 2010, https://www.alberta.ca/external/news/letter-from-premier-to-panel.pdf.

xxvii Jason Kenney, mandate letter, November 9, 2010, https://www.alberta.ca/external/news/letter-from-premier-to-panel.pdf.

xxviii https://open.alberta.ca/dataset/d8933f27-5f81-4cbb-97c1-f56b45b09a74/resource/d5836820-d81f-4042-b24e-b04e012f4cde/download/fair-deal-panel-report-to-government-may-2020.pdf.

xxix https://www.alberta.ca/fair-deal-panel.aspx#response.

xxx See F.L. Morton, "Why Alberta needs a Fiscal Constitution," University of Calgary School of Public Policy Research Papers, v.11:25 (2018). https://www.policyschool.ca/wp-content/uploads/2018/09/Fiscal-Constitution-Morton-final.pdf.

xxxi Woods, *Lougheed Legacy*, p. 166.

About the Authors

Richard Albert, born and raised in Canada, is the William Stamps Farish Professor of Law and professor of government at The University of Texas at Austin, a former law clerk to the Chief Justice of Canada, and a graduate of Yale, Oxford, and Harvard.

David Bercuson has written on Canadian labour history and more recently on Canadian foreign and defence policy and Canadian military history. He holds two honourary doctorates, is a fellow of the Royal Society of Canada, and is an officer of the Order of Canada. His most recent book is *Our Finest Hour: Canada Fights the Second World War* (2015).

Michael Binnion, FCA, was born and raised in Alberta. He has been a serial entrepreneur in both the profit and not-for-profit sectors throughout his career. He has published a peer reviewed paper in an international geology periodical as well as papers on economic and tax policy.

Derek H. Burney, O.C., is a career diplomat who served as chief of staff to Prime Minister Brian Mulroney, and ambassador to the United States. He was subsequently CEO of CAE Inc. He is Chairman of GardaWorld's International Advisory Board, a member of Paradigm Capital's Advisory Board, and a ranch hand on ranches operated by two of his sons in Colorado.

Barry Cooper is a fourth-generation Albertan. He has been a professor of political science at the University of Calgary since 1981.

Herb Emery is the Vaughan Chair in Regional Economics at the University of New Brunswick and holds a PhD in Economics from the University of British Columbia.

G. Kent Fellows is an economist at the School of Public Policy (University of Calgary) and the associate director of the Canadian Northern Corridor Research Program. He holds a PhD in economics from the University of Calgary.

Tom Flanagan is professor emeritus of political science at the University of Calgary and the author of numerous books on Canadian politics and history. He has also been a campaign manager for conservative leaders and political parties.

Fen Osler Hampson is Chancellor's Professor at Carleton University. He is a fellow of the Royal Society of Canada and former director of the Norman Paterson School of International Affairs, as well as the author/co-author of numerous books and articles on international affairs.

Robert Mansell has a Ph.D in economics with specialization in resource and regional economics. He is a research fellow at the School of Public Policy and a professor emeritus of economics at the University of Calgary.

Preston Manning is the founder of the Reform Party of Canada and the Canadian Reform Conservative Alliance, both of which became the official opposition in the Canadian Parliament and laid the foundation for the Conservative Party of Canada. He served in Parliament from 1993 to 2001 and as leader of the opposition from 1997 to 2000 with a strong commitment to strengthening the position of Western Canada within confederation.

Jack Mintz is the founding director and President's Fellow at the School of Public Policy (University of Calgary) with a specialty in public economics. Widely published, he has consulted in Canada and internationally on fiscal reforms. He was made a member of the Order of Canada in 2015.

Ted Morton is an executive fellow at the School of Public Policy and professor emeritus of political science at the University of Calgary where he taught for thirty-six years. He also served as a minister of finance, minister of energy, and minister of sustainable resource development in the Alberta government.

Kelly J. Ogle ICD.D, is the president and CEO of the Canadian Global Affairs Institute. For several decades, Mr. Ogle was an energy executive. He has a master of strategic studies degree from the University of Calgary.

Donald J. Savoie holds the Canada Research Chair in Public Administration and Governance at l'Université de Moncton (Tier 1). He has been awarded numerous prizes including eight honorary degrees from Canadian universities. He was elected a fellow of the Royal Society of Canada in 1992 and made an officer of the Order of Canada in 1993.